THE RESURGENCE
OF THE REAL

OTHER BOOKS
BY CHARLENE SPRETNAK

Lost Goddesses of Early Greece

The Politics of Women's Spirituality
(editor)

Green Politics: The Global Promise
(with Fritjof Capra)

The Spiritual Dimension of Green Politics

States of Grace:
The Recovery of Meaning in the Postmodern Age

THE RESURGENCE OF THE REAL

*Body, Nature, and Place
in a Hypermodern World*

CHARLENE SPRETNAK

ADDISON-WESLEY PUBLISHING COMPANY, INC.

READING, MASSACHUSETTS • MENLO PARK, CALIFORNIA • NEW YORK
DON MILLS, ONTARIO • HARLOW, ENGLAND • AMSTERDAM • BONN
SYDNEY • SINGAPORE • TOKYO • MADRID • SAN JUAN
PARIS • SEOUL • MILAN • MEXICO CITY • TAIPEI

Library of Congress Cataloging-in-Publication Data

Spretnak, Charlene
     The resurgence of the real : body, nature, and place in hypermodern world /
  Charlene Spretnak.
        p.   cm.
     Includes bibliographical references and index.
     ISBN 0-201-53419-3 (alk. paper)
     1. Ecology—Social aspects. 2. Civilization. Modern. 3. Postmodernism.
  I. Title.
GE195.S67   1997
303.4—dc21
                                   96-52140
                                    CIP

Jacket design by Suzanne Heiser
Text design by Eugenie Seidenberg Delaney
Set in Galliard 10.5/14.5 point

123456789-MA-0100999897
First printing, May 1997

for Maggie, *in memoriam*

and for the far-flung Portrackers

CONTENTS

THE RESURGENCE
OF THE REAL

INTRODUCTION

❧

T HE DISINTEGRATION IN RECENT YEARS of so much that
previously seemed stable is disconcerting to anyone who has
been paying attention. Every night the national news docu-
ments breakdown and upheaval, interspersed with "in-depth" analysis
(two minutes instead of twenty seconds) of radically shifting conditions
in the economy, world order, healthcare, and the social fabric. Independence wars in Bosnia, Chechnya, and Kashmir reflect the pressures of disintegration on the modern nation-state. The uprising in Chiapas on the
day the North American Free Trade Agreement (NAFTA) went into effect, as well as the high rate of failure for projects financed by the World
Bank, both reflect critical flaws in the modern model of development.
At home, the fragmentation of American society into agonistic ethnic and
racial groups is troubling and unexpected in its intensity. Internationally, the instability issuing from new geopolitical alignments in the post-
Cold War period was widely predicted, but the much broader emergence
of intranational fissures and resistance was not. Apart from overt struggles, there is a common mood of disaffection around the world with the
United Nations, national governments in general, and various other institutions of modern life. Perceptions and conclusions that seemed self-
evident for decades no longer feel convincing.

In this unsettling historical moment, I suggest, much of the breakdown is actually part of a larger dynamic that has the potential to effect a
profound correction of the assumptions and conditions that have led to the
crises of the modern era. Numerous events and developments in nearly
all fields are challenging the problematic elements of the modern worldview in the 1990s as never before. They do so not merely with complaints
about what is wrong but, for the most part, with fresh perceptions and creative alternatives. Suddenly new possibilities are springing to life where previously deadlock and despair held sway. Yet most of these developments fall
outside the scope of our expectations and often appear to be puzzling
anomalies. This book presents a lens through which to view the emergent corrective efforts so that their coherence might become more clear.

Although modern life is shaped by interlocking ideologies, that is,

1

normative belief systems, we generally give them little thought because they seem to be merely the natural result of social evolution. The fact that they are, in many respects, quite *un*natural is wrenchingly apparent to people who have had to move directly into a modern, industrialized society from a traditional agrarian community, as immigrants or refugees, or from an indigenous society. To such newcomers, it is painfully obvious that modern thinking emphasizes certain things but forcibly ignores or devalues others, including quite basic elements of life. After two or three generations, the sense of loss is diluted and felt only as a deep pool of unease that occasionally rises in the mind.

In the modern worldview, a salvational sense of progress places economic expansion and technological innovation at the center of importance. Modern government, whether socialist or capitalist, is charged with safeguarding and furthering that expansion because social and cultural development is believed to follow in its wake. Thanks to modern advances, traditional concerns stemming from the human condition have been largely conquered, managed, or replaced altogether: Modern life promised freedom from the vagaries of the body, the limits of nature, and the provincial ties to place. The body came to be seen as a biological machine, the natural world as a mere externality in modern economies, and the sense of place as a primitive precursor to cosmopolitan sophistication. All three were pushed into the background, as the more compelling issues of the day—principally the modern political economy—were debated.

Today corrective challenges to some of the most destructive dynamics of "progress" are coming from entirely unexpected directions, the very areas that were marginalized by the modern age: the knowing body, the creative cosmos, and the complex sense of place. During the past decade, many of the abstract concepts shaping the modern worldview have been ruptured by elements of "the real" that are breaking through false projections. The mechanistic sense of life, for instance, yielded a perception of the body as a biomachine operating on simple cause-and-effect principles. Modern medicine evolved to fit that model, banishing as anomalies any evidence that the human body has complex capabilities for creative and corrective responses to illness. Recent discoveries in psychoneuroimmunology, physiology, biology, and the paradoxes of infectious diseases, however, have challenged the modern, mechanistic model of the body by revealing unpredictable and often wise responses to perturbations and crises. The self-healing capacities of the body are the basis of "complementary," or "alternative," therapies, which have been found so effective for various ailments that the entire field of medicine is now undergoing radical change, albeit with a good deal of resistance from the "pill and knife brigade."

The modern, mechanistic ideology also shaped our perception of the physical world: dead—or at least dumb—matter acted upon by mechanistic laws. Our understanding of nature is now radically shifting, however, because of recent discoveries in the new sciences. In the new biology, a postmechanistic, expanded-Darwinian sense of evolution is emerging, as is a correction of the reductionism that has declared *everything* to be a result of DNA. Studies known as "complexity science" have revealed that properties *emerge* creatively within systems, while chaos theory has shown that nature moves in and out of patterns of self-organization. Nature at large—from the turbulence of streams in an ecosystem to the self-organizing abilities of galaxies throughout the universe—is now understood to function much more like a creative unfolding than a mechanistic play of stimulus and response. In addition, postmodern physics has discovered evidence of distant yet profound interrelationship as the nature of the real. All of this contributes to a new understanding of our context as a dynamic community.

In the modern worldview, the sense of *place* was no longer to be important. After all, modern society lives on top of nature. Modern furniture and modern architecture (the International style) are liberated from any "constraining" references to community, tradition, or place. Yet the importance of place, both for its subtle influences on the human and for its relevance as an ecosocial frame of reference, is now making itself felt. The resurgence of place is also behind hundreds of thousands of community-based alternatives to the dominance of the global economy.

Politically, the reassertion of place (love of one's ecosocial community) is behind scores of independence efforts in recent years, although one would never guess it from the media coverage or the expressions of disgust from modern statesmen. Only the ideology of the modern nation-state has validity for them, so any efforts to challenge it are considered "unfathomable separatist squabbles." They deem it of little consequence that the borders of the nation-states cut through or surround the land of ancient nations, whose inhabitants were simply expected to accept being absorbed by the powerful abstraction of the sovereign modern state. Refusing to be erased, yet not *seeking* military confrontation, many of the

five thousand unrepresented nations (a total that includes all the indigenous peoples) are currently forcing the devolution of the modern nation-
state. If international law would recognize the legitimacy of their claims
to sovereignty, an enormous amount of carnage could be avoided.

The contemporary resurgence of all three of these aspects of the
real—the knowing body, the creative cosmos, and the complex sense of
place—is presented in Chapter 1, Epochal Rumblings in the 1990s. My
main assertion is not that it would be a good idea if we were to pay more
attention to body, nature, and place but, rather, that the actual presence
and power of body, nature, and place *are* now asserting themselves and
poking large holes through the modern ideologies of denial. In doing so,
they challenge the assumptions of the modern worldview as never before. It is because that worldview is so abstract—favoring the projections
of mind over the "constraints" of the body, technological "progress"
over dumb nature, and cosmopolitan sophistication over "backward" attachment to place—that I have emphasized the concrete. By "body" I
mean the unified bodymind; by "nature" I mean not a scientifically theorized system or a culturally perceived looming threat, but our physical context, from which our bodies are not separate; by "place" I mean the
bioregion, the physical site of community and personal unfolding. When
I speak of the "Earth community," a term used by the "geologian" Father Thomas Berry, I refer to our physical connections: All species participate in the metabolic exchange of the biosphere and are molecularly
linked with one another from their earliest origins in the birth of the universe. Human culture can either enrich and build upon that physical level
of community, and thus enjoy a rich ecosocial experience, or deny and
ignore it, as the modern worldview tends to do.

In addition, I focus on the physicality of the human experience and
the Earth community because the influence of relativism in the air today
has further confused our relationship to the real. One hears all too often,
especially from young people, that everything in life is "just made up," a
social convention, a discourse, a mere "narrative." Yet our narratives, or
ways of thinking, are *grounded* in our bodily experiences in nature and
society. The current attention in intellectual circles to the ways in which
our collective "narratives" and perspectives are situated in particular cultural constructions should be expanded: All human thought, social or individual, is also situated in the processes of body, nature, and place. (The
very use of the label "narratives" in those circles to refer to social devel-

opment, or "social construction," emphasizes the role of human invention while deemphasizing the role of our physical grounding.)

Today cracks and crevices in the modern worldview are widening, yet the complex web of assumptions and conditions in which modern society's predicaments are embedded is not widely recognized. In considering the cause of various problems, people tend to cite corporate capitalism or resurgent communism, profit-driven technology or industrialism, materialism or consumerism, or the lack of respect for spiritual concerns. All of these are indeed worrisome realities of our time, but they are all aspects of an encompassing phenomenon called "modernity." The deep structure of our age is not economism or technocracy; these are merely facets. The deep structure is modernity. I discovered how little understood this phenomenon is after I had written a book about comparative religion titled *States of Grace: The Recovery of Meaning in the Postmodern Age* (1991) and heard from a surprisingly wide range of people that "all that stuff about modernity" was new to them. Once the conceptual framework of modernity is recognized, however, a relationship becomes evident among many of the seemingly disparate events and developments of our time: They each challenge a failed aspect of modernity. An overview of this phenomenon illuminates the significance of each of the corrective actions.

The general lack of a clear grasp of the conceptual structure of modernity has left American society vulnerable, to two exceedingly tiresome developments recently. First, the "culture wars" of the past ten years continue to be waged with proposed solutions to our social problems that are all situated within the ideological assumptions of the modern worldview. Neither the conservative nor liberal side seems to realize that we cannot get out of our modern crises with the same kind of reductionist thought that created them. Seizing on one cause and inflating its opposite *within* a problematic framework of assumptions is not the answer. Second, the rippling effects of the fifteen-year grip of deconstructionist postmodernism on academia has framed an attack on modernity that has been oblivious to the core problem: the repression of the real. The modern worldview has imposed devastating discontinuities between humans and the rest of the natural world, between self and others, and between body and mind. (In the deconstructionist analysis, there is no "real"—only "social construction" of language and concepts that structure all aspects of human experience.)

Intellectual fads aside, however, why do we give so little attention to the dynamics of modernity when the very shape of our lives is enmeshed in the assumptions and conditions of a way of being we call "modern"? Good moderns that we are, we tend to see only fragmentation, disparate events, and distinct spheres of activity in the world. We seem to be living in the midst of some sort of inertial force but cannot quite grasp what it might be or where it came from. Since the informing constellation of values and consequences called "modernity" is future-oriented, a sense of historical context has withered by neglect. Consequently, the modern condition seems inevitable rather than the result of certain choices. Very different choices can and are being made today. Chapter 2, The Rise and Fall of Modern Ideologies of Denial, presents an interpretation of the emergence of modernity, its failed aspects, and its eclipse in several areas by corrective efforts. Those efforts are part of an emergent worldview I call "ecological postmodernism."

Ideas and initiatives must succeed or fail, of course, through engagement with the *realpolitik* of their day, which is the subject of Chapter 3, Prometheus on the Rebound. In the 1990s, the emergent frame of reference for much of life on earth is the new globalized political economy, which is furthered by all major institutions, including nearly all liberal and conservative parties in all modern nation-states. This new situation has caused a new alignment of political forces: "globalists" versus "localists" (community-based activists worldwide). (Nationalists can be seen as a middle level of opposition, challenged by the rising power of localists as well as by the globalists.) While macroeconomic so-called "free trade" under the Global Agreement on Tariffs and Trade (GATT) is still the dominant policy, community-based economics and "the politics of place" are making inroads, even at the World Bank. Similarly, the growing concerns about "techno-topia" and the "technological trance" of modern life challenges an ideology that infuses both left and right. Even the Unabomber's rather uninspired regurgitation of the critique of the spreading technosphere resonated with a large audience of readers. This debate is trivialized, however, by the media's simplistic framing of oppositional positions on technology and the globalized economy as "Cornucopians" ("Boomsters") versus "Catastrophists" ("Doomsters").

In these closing years of the twentieth century, modern institutions are displaying wildly contradictory reactions to initiatives that create alternatives to modern ideologies. For instance, after much prodding the World Bank is finally extending some loans to small-scale, community-based development projects (rather than their favorite customers: large-scale, capital-intensive, centralized modern projects), all of which will most likely be put out of business as the new global trade laws (GATT) force community-level enterprises to compete economically with the transnationals. Beyond economics, there is a resurgence of "relocalization," nurturing a sense of place (community, bioregion, and region) as a defense against the homogenizing effects of globalized mass culture. Countless examples of community-based development are rejecting the modern models and are truly making history—but they are not making the evening news. Both the current state of modernity's Promethean dreams and the emerging alternatives to them are considered in three areas—economics, politics, and education—in Chapter 3.

Although "modern" is almost universally considered to be synonymous with "Western," a counter-modern tradition of resistance has played a significant role in European cultural history. An impressive heritage of people and movements was not willing to live with the denials and diminutions inherent in the destructive aspects of modernity. Most people know little of this historical resistance, however, since modern schooling gives short shrift to critics of the worldview it inculcates. The insightful critiques and sound alternatives of the resistance movements made them widely influential for a few decades in various countries, but in the end they proved insufficient to withstand the forces they opposed. The resurgence of the real, in opposition to the mechanistic worldview, may be more potent now than in the past because several current developments in science are, for the first time, on its side, but knowledge of the previous efforts remains critical for several reasons. In Chapter 4, Don't Call It Romanticism!, I suggest a new framing of that history, in which the full stream of ecospiritual movements, with all their differences, is seen to embed each of the particular forms. The Romantic movement is merely one of those versions, and I cite several reasons why it is inaccurate to consider the entire ecospiritual stream of resistance to be mere recurrences of Romanticism. I also challenge twentieth-century modernity's appropriation of some of its most outstanding critics, notably John Ruskin and William Morris. Today, despite their brilliant and lifelong opposition to the mechanistic, economistic modern worldview, they are often called "precursors of modernity"! In addition, Chapter 4 attempts to clarify some of the confusion about the Modernist movement in the arts, which spanned the first three decades of this century. I identify two distinct streams within Modernism, one that embraced the mechanistic, minimalist Machine Age (pro-modern Modernism) and one that challenged that worldview (counter-modern Modernism).

Reincorporating the knowing body, the creative cosmos, and the complex sense of place into the ways in which we think about life would reconstitute our sense of nearly every public debate and crisis. That process is already well underway because a deep sadness and haunting intimation of loss have now surpassed faith in the modern ideologies of denial. Although our inner lives have been relentlessly diminished by ecosocial isolation, the antidote lies in recovering awareness of our context. We are embodied and embedded in a dynamic sphere of physical relationships and processes that create *real* commonalities, which have been denied by ideologies of both the rugged individual and the fragmenting "politics of identity."

The mechanistic denial of relationship and process as *constitutive* to our being, not merely incidental to it, has delivered us to a point in the modern era at which only separateness seems real. Differences are real, of course, but so are various kinds of commonality and interrelatedness. Because a false uniformity has often been imposed by modern governments and societies, the denied uniqueness of self, ethnic group, and nation is now asserting itself. Once again the pendulum has swung from oppression to freedom; once again the freedom is narcissistic and oblivious to realities of context—especially our larger context, the sacred whole. Failure to perceive real connectedness, the curse of modernity, has led us to *inter-* and *intra-*species disasters. The final chapter, Embracing the Real, contains a visionary story about "getting there from here." That goal is a deeply pragmatic alternative to the drift into more intensified modernity, or *hyper*modernity, for freedom that flourishes *within* the web of life, not against it, will no longer be a flight from wisdom.

An appendix, Modernity Is to Us as Water to a Fish, contains a delineation of the modern worldview and condition as well as a brief tour through the confusing maze of labels, terms, and "isms." It closes with a remembrance of all those who have suffered deep loss from the destructive aspects of the modern shaping of life.

The growing crises of modernity are being met with corrective actions from a great many quarters. Whether such efforts will succeed constitutes the worldwide drama that is unfolding largely outside the spotlight but will shape the next century. I hope this book will encourage readers to recognize the resurgence of the real in all its manifestations. It already shapes events. In fact, it is impossible to fully understand the news of the day unless one comprehends that the seeming anomalies challenging various failed ideologies share common ground. They seek to preserve the constructive achievements of the modern age, such as the concept of universal human rights, but to dislodge and correct the harsh constrictions that have shrunk the fullness of our being.

In proposing a framework for understanding various events and developments in the 1990s that baffle modern expectations, I suggest not only a coherence among contemporary developments but also a historical coherence with earlier efforts to correct modernity. This particular line of work—perceiving an overarching framework of relationships and resonance—has attracted me before. In the late 1970s, I began work on a framing of the historical, philosophical, and political dimensions of the emerging women's spirituality movement, an anthology published as *The Politics of Women's Spirituality* (1982). In 1984 *Green Politics: The Global Promise* suggested a framework for understanding the new political movement in Europe and elsewhere, plus the possibility of Green parties in the United States. With *States of Grace* (1991), I proposed a new framework for comparative religion based on the revival of interest in cosmology. None of these was a case of finding myself drawn to those budding phenomena and then daring to impose a coherent conceptual framework onto the hapless movements. Rather, I have been drawn to such developments, I have come to realize, because of their *inherent* coherence, their wisdom, and their potential to heal all that has gone wrong. This coherence may also have been obvious to everyone else working in the formative stages of those movements, but people often get caught up with their own contribution to the expanding waves of new thinking and doing. In that event, they do not have a sense of all the other elements and their potential. Moreover, people outside the new movements often saw no coherence or relevance in them. This was not only frustrating but a hindrance to the spread of the new ideas. For those reasons, I jumped in and theorized, combining the organizing mentality of a camp counselor (I was one) with a passion for conceptualizations that just might help change the world. Still in print, these conceptual framings have never seemed to me to be syntheses—neither the Hegelian variety with smashing opposites, nor the blended variety. Rather, they are a fitting together of parts, each with its integrity intact.

It must be emphasized, however, that the framing to which this book contributes has been in progress, as I explain in Chapter 4, since the seventeenth century. Nonetheless, the fact that nearly all the books in this volume's bibliography happen to have been published within the last five years indicates that the 1990s are indeed a time of resurgence. Those books, as well as several other means of expressing the vision within them, often seem to be speaking in a language—one with spiritual resonance—that cannot be heard by modern sensibilities. The guardians of the status quo usually judge them to be beyond the pale. Perhaps that will change as the assertions of body, nature, and place grow stronger.

In my attempt to make sense of various developments of this decade, I have recently come to regard this particular framing in a different way. Besides writing and lecturing, I teach a couple of graduate courses per year in a philosophy program that is favorably disposed toward the ideas in this book. At the completion of a course called "Ecological Postmodernism," one of my students—a newly minted engineer from Duke on a quest to fill the holes in his education—wrote me a note explaining why his final paper was late. He added, "Thanks a lot for the course—for piecing it together and all." "Piecing it together"—so that's what I have been doing all this time, more like a quilt than a scaffold. "And all"—that would be my interpretations, I suppose.

That image feels particularly right because the nature of quilts has changed over the past twenty-five years. Traditional quilts combine the discipline of pattern with the artistic freedom to choose color and scale. As the art form spread to grassroots usage, however, the surface of community-made quilts became sculptural, three-dimensional, highly textured, and extremely eclectic. Quilts in which each square is created by a different individual—such as quilts for school or church raffles, celebratory quilts that tell stories or local history, or commemorative quilts such as the AIDS Memorial Quilt—have a remarkable vitality born of the jumble of quirky creativity that is harmonized into a pattern of coherence.

With that in mind, the "piecing together" in the following chapters seeks to identify significant developments of our time, to set them in conceptual relationship to one another, to draw inspiration from their vitality, their courage, and their historical depth, and then to unfurl, in the final chapter, the entire gestalt. This is a quilt made of complexity curves, native plants, ancient nations, farmers' markets, regional trade, and children with a future.

May it be of use.

1

EPOCHAL RUMBLINGS
IN THE 1990s

W E ARE TOLD THAT THE WORLD IS SHRINKING, that vast distance has been conquered by computer and fax, and that the Earth is now a "global village" in which all of us are connected as never before. It feels, however, quite the opposite. It feels as if distancing and disconnection are shaping modern life.

If anything is shrinking, it is the fullness of being that is experienced by the modern self. In spite of the unbounded "empowerment" promised by companies trying to sell us electronic hardware and software, the buoyant optimism so aggressively peddled in their commercials is hard to come by offscreen. Psychologists report record levels of depression and anxiety. Pollsters repeatedly detect deepening fears regarding economic insecurity as jobs continue to be eliminated or exported. Democratic rule by the people, once considered a sacred trust, has become so irrelevant to the majority of our countrymen that they do not even vote. For most people today, the web of friends, nearby family members, and community relationships is a shrunken fragment of what previous generations experienced. Far less time and energy are volunteered for community work and good causes because it is increasingly difficult just to cope, just to get by from day to day. "Leisure time" is now spent at a second, often low-paying, job or in a numbed state of recuperation, usually alone, in front of a television that urges viewers to escape discontent by purchasing the accoutrements of a "better" life.

The widespread collapse into an enervated self cannot be attributed solely to the economic and social problems of our day. Problems, even severe ones, can be addressed and usually solved—unless a society's general sense of ends and means no longer instills confidence. If the prevailing philosophical framework rings hollow and inadequate, even its most triumphalist plan for the future makes the political arena seem only more depressing and irrelevant.

Is a new century of prosperity and economic security really going to be ushered in by globalized "free trade"? The ideology of the global market is built on the assumption that every country will earn most of its income from exports. It is increasingly clear to nearly everyone, other than the corporate-and-governmental coalition, that this new orientation is a colossally bad idea. What could be more insecure than betting our future almost entirely on the sale of exports to distant markets with fluctuating circumstances, as more and more American-owned corporations move production (jobs) closer to those new markets? We are pulled by inertia—and corporate lobbying—in that very direction, yet how many of us believe the salvational spin put on this risky scheme? The ideal of ever-increasing levels of consumption in the export markets, besides its ecological unfeasibility, does not take into account the chaos of currency speculation or possible disruptions in those countries, such as social upheaval, political instability, epidemic disease, and natural disasters.

A new ideology—the globalized economy—has been put into place, but it is merely an intensification of a very old one. An ideology is simply the elevation of a particular set of perceptions, assumptions, and analyses to a normative belief system. It provides a framework by which adherents respond to events and developments. An idealogy also makes it difficult to see beyond the framework, however, so events reflecting other perspectives may seem nonsensical.

Modern life is structured by numerous ideologies that interlock and support each other. As modernization has spread throughout the world, modern attitudes have displaced traditional ways of thinking about what is important in life. In essence, that which can be measured, counted, and quantified is made central. It might seem that adopting such an orientation would yield concrete, reliable knowledge about the world, but certain ideological assumptions underlie the seemingly obvious decisions about how, what, and why to quantify. Modern science constructed mechanistic models of how the world works and then perceived only the sort of data that would fit the model. Modern political philosophy locates all legitimacy in the modern nation-state. Modern economic theory asserts that the market is guided by a "hidden hand" that benefits society as a whole. Modern aesthetics values design that is free of "constricting" references to tradition or place.

Like any cultural orientation, the modern worldview has accrued a complex record of successes and failures. Those two categories have something in common, however: The worst aspects of the failures and the nagging doubts about the successes both have roots in the modern denial of the powers of body, nature, and place.

The enormous outpouring of literature during the past two hundred years about "alienation" in modern times is, at base, an exploration of the conditions and situations that arise when a rich, full sense of body, nature, and place is shrunken and demoted to being the dumb matter on top of which modern culture is constructed. Poetic and literary protests, as we know, have not succeeded in correcting the denial inherent in modern ideologies, although they have certainly helped to identify it. Nor have corrective political and philosophical analyses carried the day. This is so because the modern belief system and its conceptualizations were able to filter, shape, or deflect all efforts to challenge it.

That effective lock on perception is yielding in the 1990s, not to opposing ideologies but to the assertion of the long-suppressed characteristics of body, nature, and place themselves. *The real* is poking its true nature through the modern abstractions that have denied it for several centuries. Many of the events reported in the news today that seem utterly baffling to the modern media are expressions of these epochal rumblings. For example, the attention to epidemics of infectious diseases has revealed that millions of people carry the virus or bacteria for a disease without ever developing any symptoms. This response belies a mechanistic model of the body, wherein the presence of dangerous microbes results in a simple, causal manifestation of the disease; clearly, other dynamics of the body are involved. Regarding nature, Darwin's mechanistic perceptions of the process of "natural selection" in evolution are currently being subsumed within a much richer, complex understanding of the natural world that is emerging from the new sciences. Finally, the scores of "separatist conflicts" disturbing *pax moderna* are unfathomable in the context of modern political theory, by which governance for the common good was stream-lined and centralized within and under the modern state. Recognition of cultures with deep bonds to place (that is, ancient nations whose territory was absorbed and erased) has no legal standing, so independence efforts tragically descend into armed conflict and, often, the utter devastation of the ancient nation.

All this is quite unexpected in the modern frame of reference. Significant challenges are anticipated in "significant" sectors, not from those elements of life so thoroughly deemphasized and marginalized that they have barely been given a second thought. Even more unexpectedly for the modern worldview, the reassertion of the powers of body, nature, and place is infused with a rekindled spiritual awareness, also long exiled to the margins of what matters. As ideological skirmishes rage on in small circles, our apprehension of the real is being revised on a far larger scale by the knowing body, the creative cosmos, and the complex sense of place.

THE KNOWING BODY

IN MODERN INDUSTRIALIZED CULTURE, a child learns all too soon to regard the body as a fleshy vehicle that carries around the important part: the brain/mind. The body is dumb matter that can be molded, toned, and groomed through an endless array of practices in order to create a desirable physicality. Occasionally the body "betrays" its owner, causing one to seek repair from modern medicine. Sometimes this works brilliantly, but many other times it does not. The concept of a split between the body and the mind, which has shaped modern thought for four hundred years, is so deeply ingrained in the realm of medicine that no matter how many thousands of times physicians have heard patients ask (actually *tell*) about possible linkage between their ailment and their emotional state, most doctors have dismissed such unscientific babble with a shrug, a raised eyebrow, or an authoritative rebuke. Efforts over the past thirty years by holistic physicians or practitioners of "alternative" or "complementary" therapies were successfully held at arm's length by the medical establishment—and its influence on medical insurance companies.

In the 1990s, however, events converged to provide an opening for an assertion of the real in the lives of millions of people, a refutation of the mechanistic ideology and its body-mind split that has introduced a very different *experiential* sense of being. It emerged as a silver lining in the otherwise onerous financial crisis in American healthcare, in which 41 million Americans are without medical coverage. The alarming inflation of healthcare costs during the 1980s placed a dangerous and growing burden on the public sector, from whence reimbursements are paid through Medicare and other programs. It also rattled the for-profit health maintenance organizations (HMOs), which are committed to channeling as much money as possible from the fees paid by subscribers into profit for the owners and shareholders. After the Clinton administration's failed attempt to reform the healthcare industry, the major responsive "reform" from within the industry was a range of cost-cutting innovations. Many of these are quite deleterious for the patient, as they link doctors' pay to keeping tests and treatments to a minimum. One extraordinary benefit of the financial crunch in healthcare, however, has been the new willingness of companies and government agencies who pay for medical treatment to sidestep the modern medical establishment and pay attention to the success rates of alternative and complementary therapies. This new acceptance has been facilitated by the accumulation of studies showing that for many ailments and illnesses, the symptoms clear up just as quickly, or faster, with alternative, holistic therapies, which cost the same or less and rarely cause the unwanted "side-effects" of mechanistic medical therapies. "Patient satisfaction" with alternative therapies is usually measurably greater, so the rates of follow-through (completion of treatment) and healing are often higher.

Before long, millions of Americans were informed by their medical insurance companies that they would not only be covered for various alternative treatments but were strongly urged to try them. In 1995, Blue Shield enclosed a newsletter with subscribers' billing statements that urged them to learn meditation, which is referred to simply as "mindfulness" or a technique for "breathing and muscular relaxation." A short article by a Harvard professor of medicine in one of the newsletters deftly framed the 180-degree turnabout on the part of the modern medical establishment: Their finally recognizing a link between emotional states and various illnesses was merely "recovering the common sense of an earlier day," such as the astute diagnoses made by his grandmother.[1] No *mea culpa* there! No admission of denying for so long the holistic insights of millions of patients and, consequently, serving them poorly, sometimes with dire results. Instead, the emergent attitude among those doctors who have been converted is usually, "We knew it all along."

A new field called "behavioral medicine" has been widely accepted only recently but has been growing on the margins of the medical establishment for twenty years, documenting the healing effects of non-physical therapies such as meditation, prayer, and relaxation techniques on depression, anxiety, high blood pressure, cardiac pain, insomnia, diabetes, ulcers, colds, fever, asthma, arthritis, and alcoholism. In fact, studies have found that prayer—which scientists prefer to call "intentionality"—has yielded beneficial results with postoperative heart patients and with patients in advanced stages of AIDS, even when offered from a great distance by persons not acquainted with the recipients.[2] One of the pioneers in behavioral medicine has come to understand it as "the biology of hope."[3]

In addition to the financial incentives for interest in "mindbody medicine," popular knowledge of its possibilities was spread by a Bill Moyers series on PBS in 1993 called "Healing and the Mind," and by several best-sellers written by doctors to share their experiences with an integral approach to healing. *Spontaneous Healing* by Andrew Weil, *Women's Bodies, Women's Wisdom* by Christiane Northrup, and *Love, Medicine, and Miracles* by Bernie Siegal are only a few examples of this growing field.[4] Teaching hospitals attached to several universities around the country have recently instituted programs in "integrated medicine," and, in January 1993, the staid *New England Journal of Medicine* published an overview article on alternative, or "unconventional," therapies.[5] Even the prestigious National Institutes of Health finally loosened its embrace of the mechanistic model and the body-mind split when, in 1993, its newly established Office of Alternative Medicine issued its first research grants. It funded thirty projects, directed jointly by a clinical investigator and an alternative practitioner, to study, for example, the effect of acupuncture on depression, biofeedback on diabetes, and massage on bone marrow transplants. It should be noted, however, that there is still a great deal of resistance among many physicians to holistic treatments, which they categorically dismiss as "spoon-bending" quackery.[6]

Still, the skirmishes between dueling doctors have not interrupted the phenomenal *experiential* displacement at the grassroots level of the mechanistic ideology about our bodily reality. Many people have experienced the successful controlling of disease or pain through modalities of behavioral medicine such as biofeedback, meditation, imagery, or visualization. Many others have seen positive results from "somatic" techniques that subtly "listen" to the bodymind to perceive problems such as energy blocks or emotional strain held in the musculature; these modalities include Therapeutic Touch, many types of massage, and several "bodywork" techniques. Yoga, tai chi, and other movement practices also heal certain chronic ailments by restoring tone and balance to the entire organism. Finally, millions of people have discovered that ingesting herbs—usually European, North American, or Chinese—is extremely efficacious for various illnesses without the harsh overkill delivered by many pharmaceutical drugs, whose unwanted "side" effects are often as strong as the desired ones. Homeopathic formulas and acupuncture are also becoming widely used.

The combination of Chinese herbs and acupuncture, the fruits of a two-thousand-year-old system born of great subtlety and wisdom, has been found highly effective in treating a wide range of problems, including arthritis, whole-body trauma such as that occurring after an automobile accident, infertility, bacterial infections, and many others. In March 1996, the U.S. Food and Drug Administration (FDA) finally reclassified acupuncture needles from the category "experimental devices" to acceptance for "general acupuncture use" by "qualified practitioners," clearing the way for much broader reimbursement of that therapy by HMOs and other medical insurance companies, many of which began covering acupuncture treatments almost immediately. The FDA's decision was based on clinical research indicating high levels of success in the use of acupuncture for treating asthma and other respiratory conditions, pain, nausea and vomiting, substance abuse, and stroke and paralysis. The FDA did not comment on the perception of an energy system (*chi*), which is the basis of acupuncture, and pointedly called the procedure "a healing art" (but an effective one, nonetheless).[7]

What have people learned about their own being from experiencing the results of such practices? At very least, it becomes evident that the body is something other than a biomachine whose parts occasionally break, requiring repair work by a medical mechanic. Millions of people who have received successful alternative therapies have concluded *experientially* that the body must indeed be some sort of self-correcting energy system, even if they remain unconvinced about the holistic theory underlying such practices. Again and again, people have found that the bodymind, if assisted instead of assaulted, demonstrates remarkable capabilities of self-healing. It can correct a problem in several different ways, drawing on a creative array of possibilities for returning to balance, or homeostasis, after a disturbance or injury. It can often grow new synapses around damaged parts of the brain, for instance, and it can heal the tissue involved in a bone fracture so well that a radiologist may not be able to tell where the bone was broken. The bodymind's healing abilities can sometimes reconstruct the fallopian tubes even after they have been surgically seared—causing 18.5 unexpected pregnancies per every 1000 tubal ligations, as a study surprisingly revealed in 1996.[8]

Our healing system extends even to the level of macromolecules in cells, where it makes diagnoses (identifies damage), removes damaged tissue structure, replaces it, and neutralizes the effects of serious injury (such as mounting an SOS response to the presence of *E. coli* bacteria). Our DNA also has the information necessary to repair itself and often does. At the cellular level, the same dynamics of recognizing, removing, and replacing a damaged structure, such as a cell membrane, work as a continual healing process. At the level of tissues, organs, and systems, the same healing capabilities are at work. Regeneration of lost tissue is constantly achieved by the skin and the lining of the intestines; in fact, the liver can regenerate a lost portion within hours. The key to all of it is the balance of a self-organizing, self-healing system, such as the coordinated interaction of stimulating and inhibiting factors affecting the growth and proliferation of cells.

The various techniques within the holistic orientation bear witness that the bodymind is a balanced system of energy. Moreover, that energy does not seem to end at the encasement of our skin. Therapeutic Touch and other forms of bodywork engage with the "energy field" that pervades and surrounds each person. Patients find that their own recuperative processes are accelerated by the application of subtle, attuning touch along with the intentionality of the practitioner's meditative state, which aids in repatterning and redirecting accumulated tension. Balance and harmony are sought and desired by the bodymind. In fact, many clinical investigators and practitioners have concluded that the various holistic therapies serve merely to halt whatever interference is interrupting the bodymind's self-healing capabilities. Once the problem is cleared, nature does the healing. It is assisted by conscious intention on our part to recover balance and vibrant health.

The long-standing folk wisdom that links negative emotional states to susceptibility to illness has been demonstrated both at the grassroots and in the laboratory. Not only have large numbers of people noticed alleviation of various health problems once they became established in a practice of meditation, prayer, or similar calming and "centering" exercises, but an entire field of research in biopsychology—psychoneuroimmunology—has emerged to explore the connection between consciousness and immune capabilities. By measuring the level of T cells, and through other monitoring, psychoneuroimmunology research has found repeatedly that mental states of anxiety or negativity suppress the immune system, which is our cellular defense against external infection and aberrant cell division. The mechanistic notion that the autonomic nervous system, the endocrine glands, and the immune system are discrete entities has given way in the face of evidence of systemic integration. Nerve fibers connect the brain with the thymus gland, lymph nodes, spleen, bone marrow, and gut-associated lymph tissue, for instance, establishing an inherent relationship that facilitates communication and response. In addition, it is now known that the brain produces over fifty hormones that stimulate various organs to function. Cells in the immune system react to chemical signals from the central nervous system that are relayed by neuropeptides (messenger molecules), neuroendocrines, neurohormones, and neurotransmitters. Neuropeptide receptors are found in high levels in the emotionally modulated parts of the brain: the amygdala and the hypothalamus. They are also found throughout the immune system, where cells have receptors that can learn, recall, and produce neuropeptides themselves.[9] In short, there is a mutuality, at very least, rather than a one-way cause-and-effect. Moreover, the cellular responses are involved with the cumulative memory of the knowing body: The immune system can remember a molecule encountered twenty years ago! Entire organs apparently have some sort of memory as well, especially when trauma is involved. For instance, women who were sexually assaulted as girls often experience problems with one or more of their reproductive organs in adult life even though there was no physical damage to the organ during the assault.

The complexity of our self-healing and rebalancing defenses has finally displaced the mechanistic principle that disease is simply the result of the presence of a destructive virus or bacteria. After all, over half the world's population is infected with the tuberculosis bacterium at any time, but only 10 percent of those infected develop the disease.[10] Streptococcus is also recognized as ubiquitous, yet only a small percentage of the population develop symptoms of streptococcal infection. Even leprosy is apparently fended off by almost everyone: A study conducted in 1980 found that many people in the world had antibodies to it, indicating that they had been exposed without developing the disease. Poverty and unsanitary living and working conditions, of course, add physical and emotional stress to the bodymind that often overwhelm its abilities to expel foreign substances and control destructive processes.

Just as our cells, our organs, and our entire organism are finely attuned to subtle internal perturbations, so too are they engaged with the physical dynamics of the world around them. This very embeddedness of our bodymind in the natural world is also asserting itself in the 1990s, displacing the smug assertion that a modern, industrial society lives on top of nature. Increasing use of natural light in buildings, for instance, began with concern for energy efficiency but has yielded unexpected responses from the people affected. A study in 1995 found that businesses in largely "daylighted" buildings experienced fewer days lost to absenteeism and fewer work errors and defects—and, alas, that shoppers under special skylights buy more than their counterparts shopping in the artificially lit half of a huge store.[11]

The amount and kind of light received by the bodymind also influences sleep patterns, moods, degrees of hunger, and resistance to disease. The seasonal passage of the Earth around the sun affects moods (including the type of depression called "seasonal affective disorder"), metabolism, need for sleep, and sex drive. The phases of the moon influence the tides of oceans and women's menstrual cycles, of course, but they also influence libido in both sexes, sleep patterns, and behavior. Police departments are accustomed to an increase in violent acts when the moon is full.

Sound also influences us profoundly, which is not surprising since vibrations suffuse not only the bodymind but the entire cosmos. Whether it is noise or music, sound affects our psychological and physiological processes. Noise can create a level of stress so unnerving that it can suppress intelligence and creativity. Not only does noise pollution cause loss of hearing and impair concentration and cognition, it can also affect vascular, glandular, and digestive functions and provoke aggressive behavior. Conversely, certain tones and rhythms can induce relaxation and increase learning ability. Classical music has been used successfully to stimulate the immune system, especially the thymus gland, and to accelerate healing processes.[12]

The bodymind is indeed *knowing*, for it creates meaning. It is sensitive to an enormous range of subtle dynamics in and around it and from which it perceives, selects, and organizes information. It makes sense of this information—its own sense. It creates an informing history grown organically from past relations and interactions. It can care and repair. It can flourish or struggle cannily to survive. Each bodymind is unique and unpredictable. Each is attuned to the surrounding whole.

THE CREATIVE COSMOS

FROM THE VANTAGE POINT OF THE NEW SCIENCES in the 1990s, one looks back in amazement at all that modern society did not allow itself to see about the natural world for the past four hundred years. Once the mechanistic worldview came into ascendency with the Scientific Revolution in the sixteenth and seventeenth centuries, nature was perceived by the modern Western mind to be predictable within inertial frames of reference that could be determined by mathematical calculation. The entire universe was seen to be a play of dead, or at least dumb, matter: objects situated in empty space, acted upon by fixed laws of mechanical behavior and moving in a uniform flow of time. Viewed through this ideological lens, all of nature appeared to yield to the triumphant structure of knowledge that was modern science.

Whenever observations emerged that did not fit the mechanistic model, they were dismissed as insignificant anomalies. Moreover, the perceptions of ordinary people who were intimately familiar with the creative strategies of nature were uniformly ignored as childlike and unscientific. The same judgment dismissed the knowledge of the natural world held by Asian and indigenous societies, who saw, in various ways, all events as connected. It was considered rather pathetic, but irrefutable, that in all the world only the modern Western scientific tradition was sufficiently tough-minded to comprehend the true nature of reality.

Western science got it wrong in many crucial respects, as a few prophetic members of that tradition tried to establish. In the eighteenth century, Goethe railed against the reductionism of Newtonian physics, urging a "science of qualities" that would include the scientific experiential knowledge of seeing, for instance, rather than the mere objectification of light refracted through a prism. In the early nineteenth century,

Baron von Humboldt achieved international renown for discoveries in natural history, but his sense that a "chain of connection" linked all elements of earthly life and that knowledge of that interdependence was the "noblest and most important result" of all scientific inquiry was not widely embraced.[13] In the 1920s an Austrian biologist, inspired by Nicholas of Cusa's holistic perception of the creation, noticed that similar problems had arisen in several of the disciplines and subdisciplines of science: The mechanistic, statistical model was unable to account for wholeness, dynamic interaction, and organization. Ludwig von Bertalanffy proposed an "organismic conception" that would correct the modern overemphasis on individual parts—both in the physical sciences and the social sciences, in which the Lockean atomistic view of society still held sway.

From the work of organismic biologists, gestalt psychologists, and theoretical ecologists, a new discipline simultaneously emerged in the 1920s called "general systems theory." It sought to study "organized complexity," particularly such capabilities of systems as self-organization, self-regulation, directiveness, teleology, and differentiation—all of which were alien to conventional physics. General Systems Theory continued to develop through the 1930s and 1940s, especially the branch called "cybernetics," in which self-regulating capabilities were mapped as feedback loops and were used, for instance, in guidance systems for weapons. Eventually, in the postwar period, scientists withdrew interest from systems theory because its concepts could not be expressed mathematically, which relegated it to the scrap heap of "soft" theories.[14]

In recent years, however, a wide range of work in chaos theory and complexity science has revealed self-organizing capacities of nature that yield not only coherent systems but endlessly emergent creativity. The modern perception of determinism has yielded to a postmodern recognition of dynamic, unstable systems in which order and disorder arise in intimate relation. Ilya Prigogine, a pioneer in chaos studies and a Nobel Laureate, has concluded that the universe is essentially "formed by disorder, in which order floats."[15] States of nonequilibrium, which seem chaotic, move farther and farther from equilibrium and, finally, arrive in new patterns of coherence: events, order, and new equilibrium. One branch of chaos studies focuses on the deep structures of order hidden within chaotic systems, while another focuses on the order that arises out of chaotic systems.

As soon as the real was seen to include not-order as a state different from both order and anti-order—as Taoism has long held in the East—examples were identified seemingly everywhere: in air currents, fast-flowing rivers, volcanic lava flows, and tidal waves. The term "chaos theory" has fallen into disuse among most scientists, but the studies have been subsumed as a delimited area of the new field called "complexity science." Both flourished once extremely fast computers allowed researchers to display graphically the highly complex results of nonlinear equations used to model turbulence and other stochastic dynamics. Until recent years, math courses and, indeed, most of Western science focused on linear equations, even though the real-world dynamics explained by such equations are comparatively rare! The universe is far more nonlinear than the mechanistic worldview has allowed us to see.

One of the central findings of complexity science is that various properties of a system *emerge* through its dynamic behavior and interactions. Such properties cannot be predicted mechanistically at the outset from knowledge of the component parts. Order, or global properties, arise from the complex dynamic behavior of the system's aggregate parts. That is, the wide variety of components interact in a great many ways, and the components are then influenced by the new order or property that has emerged from their interactions. It is now increasingly apparent that the entire universe—from vast galaxies to microscopic cells—unfolds through systems of spontaneous self-organization.

In terms of biological evolution, complex adaptive systems seek patterns and learn from their interactions with the environment. They carry within their range of possibilities, which includes their genetic coding, information about adjacent and surrounding systems. The capabilities of biological organisms to generate form are now understood with the help of complexity science to involve far more than DNA, contrary to the smug reductionism of molecular biology. A leading theoretical biologist, Brian Goodwin, has presented the case for an expanded sense of evolution in *How the Leopard Changed Its Spots: The Evolution of Complexity* (1994). His work demonstrates that evolutionary properties emerge not only through totally random genetic mutation and "natural selection" but also through the complex dynamic qualities of the organism. "Natural selection" can be better understood as *dynamic stabilization*, the emergence of stable states in a dynamic system. The new view shifts the focus to the entire organism as a center of creativity dependent on the relational order among components. That is, emergent qualities predominate over quantities (the given components). The underlying degree of order and regularity among plant and animal life forms are a result of generic themes in the domain of an organism's morphogenesis. Genes cooperate with, and add variety to, the themes in the generative field of each organism.

Another systemic perception of nature's creativity that has been accumulating supporting evidence in recent years is the Gaia hypothesis, proposed by James Lovelock and Lynn Margulis. It asserts that the Earth behaves like a living organism, actively maintaining the life-supporting chemical composition of its atmosphere by self-regulating the quantity of marine algae and other living organisms in its biomass. Amid the disequilibrium of the Earth's atmosphere, the Earth maintains an improbable constancy of life-support conditions in the biosphere. The dynamics of this self-regulation can be understood as cybernetic feedback: The temperature, oxidation state, acidity, and other characteristics of the rocks and water are kept constant by the responding levels of biota (living organisms). Recent atmospheric research, for instance, has revealed that marine algae in remote regions of the oceans are the sole source of cloud condensation nuclei over those regions. The gist of all this is that life is an interactive phenomenon of planetary and biospheric scale. Living organisms, nested in communities within their ecosystems all over the world, regulate the planet's atmosphere. That is, Gaian homeostasis originates in the local activity of individual organisms. Contrary to the mechanistic sense of one-way causality, species and their immediate environment should be understood as a single, interactive system in which each adapts to and affects the other.

In physics, discoveries about the real have been getting "curiouser and curiouser," as Alice said of Wonderland. Ever since publication of Einstein's first paper on relativity in 1905, the description of the universe according to modern Newtonian physics has been relegated to a limited role, applying only within a particular range of observation. At the subatomic and astrophysical levels, postmodern physics has perceived the cosmos as a vast energy field of events, the arising and passing away of waves and particles interacting in ways that are decidedly non-Newtonian. For example, the discovery of nonlocal causality through the experimental work supporting Bell's Theorem overturned the long-standing belief that the mechanism of the universe is moved solely by a variety of local pushes and pulls. In 1964, John Bell devised a series of experiments by which the universe revealed yet another facet of its nature: When two particles whose spin is correlated in direction and velocity are shot off in different directions, any change in the spin of either particle is instantaneously matched in the other. The nonlocal implication is that occurrences in one region of space are inherently correlated with other distant regions. In short, the universe has a quantum wholeness.

Even today, some thirty-three years after Bell's extraordinary discovery, its implications in and beyond science are still rippling through the emergent postmodern apprehension of the real. The same can be said of the postmodern discovery that the universe is expanding. The physicist and cosmologist Brian Swimme sees in the nature of this expansion the antidote to the jarring effect on humans caused by the Copernican Revolution. Previously, medieval Europe had believed that the sun orbited around the Earth. When Copernicus and Kepler demonstrated that the opposite was the case, the shock of being displaced as the center of the universe was deeply unnerving to many. From this demotion, the modern age came to feel severed from cosmology as no other culture had ever felt before. In *The Hidden Heart of the Cosmos* (1996), however, Swimme has proposed that the current astrophysical understanding of our place in the cosmological unfolding is far more profound than either of the earlier two systems imagined: Since the universe is expanding away from every point within it, each one of us is the center of the universe!

The systemic point of view has also yielded new understandings of human social structures, such as economics, politics, and historical developments. For instance, the economist Brian Arthur, inspired by discoveries of complex dynamics in biology, has proposed that a principle he calls "increasing returns"—positive feedback that magnifies a particular pattern or condition, allowing it to grow and become a dominant characteristic of a system—explains the way market forces "pick winners." Examples include the dominance of the VHS videotape format over the technologically superior Beta format, the universal adoption of the inefficient QWERTY keyboard, and the acceptance of the early gasoline-driven internal combustion engine over the more fuel-efficient steam-driven models. In Arthur's dynamic analysis of economics, "The economy is constantly on the edge of time. It rushes forward, structures constantly coalescing, decaying, changing."[16]

In uncovering new knowledge about the creativity of the cosmos, complexity science has also sparked creativity in the arts. A number of the world's most famous architects, who had previously subjected the public to macho late-modern, high-tech, or deconstructionist buildings, have become intrigued in the 1990s with both the concepts and the graphic representations of chaos studies and complexity science: the undulating waves and twists of nonlinearity, the self-similarity of fractals, the organizing pull of "strange attractors," the organizational depth in systemic emergence, the folds and pleats representing phase transitions, and the recognition that creative order emerges from the edge of chaos. Many examples of this new mood in design, called "organi-tech" by the architectural historian Charles Jencks, are gathered in his book *The Architecture of the Jumping Universe: How Complexity Science Is Changing Architecture and Culture* (1997). The influence of "chaotics," that is, the awareness of the play of chaos and order, has been traced in the literary arts by N. Katherine Hayles in *Chaos Bound: Orderly Disorder in Contemporary Literature and Science* (1990) and *Chaos and Order: Complex Dynamics in Literature and Science* (1991). She is particularly interested in understanding the cultural constructions that authorize changing views of chaos and order in both the disciplines of science and the culture at large.

Clearly all this attention to process and change rather than structure and stasis might well be the beginning of a sea change in Western thought. It overturns various core assumptions of the modern worldview, yet the new sciences already seem to have been absorbed into the consuming quest for the modern grail: prediction and control. Other uses, of course, are also emerging, solely with the goal of enhancing creativity and designing wiser forms of organization than the rigid, hierarchical model. In fact, one of the pioneering books on rethinking organizational development, *Leadership and the New Science: Learning about Organization from an Orderly Universe* by Margaret Wheatley (1992), emphasizes the difference between order and control; the relationships among change, stability, and renewal; and the challenge of becoming comfortable with uncertainty.[17] Moving even further from the realm of nonlinear equations and high-speed computers, I wonder if a central insight from chaotics will ever result in new respect for the ways in which women have traditionally organized their group interactions: Systems appearing to be deficient in order are often fecund with information, the source of new possibilities.

THE COMPLEX SENSE OF PLACE

IN THE MODERN WORLDVIEW, place is not important except as a springboard from which the salvific ideology of progress would launch its grand trajectory. Place was associated with constraint: the binding ties of community, extended family, and tradition, as well as the local demands of nature. The heroic figures of modern literature boldly escape their place of origin and head for the new promised land: the city, with its sprawling urban *potential* rising from flattened hills and filled-in stream beds, offering anonymity and a heady autonomy in exchange for nearly everything else. Modernist architecture and design liberated itself from the local and the vernacular by a fierce reduction to sterile minimalism that is truly cosmopolitan, reflecting no place and no culture, only an ideology of freedom through denial. Examples of the International style of skyscrapers and kindred versions of the "dumb box" are nearly interchangeable, having gone forcefully beyond the constraints of place. With a similar sophistication, modern political boundaries have often been drawn with disdain for the integrity of place—with disastrous consequences that are now intensifying.

In recent years a different sort of disengagement from place has emerged alongside the modern: The deconstructionist postmodern analysis asserts that we never actually know anything about our local patch of the biosphere because we can know only the concepts our particular society has invented (including language and science) to refer to the natural world. While the more dogmatic forms of this orientation have finally faded, a softer "constructionist" version remains influential among many intellectuals today. It spawns books and articles that perceive only a one-way creative power: the projection by humans of their "social constructions" onto nature.[18] All this seems exceedingly odd—and more than a little pathological—to traditional native peoples, for instance. From an early age, they pay a great deal of attention to the dynamics of the natural world, both individually and collectively. They observe with great sensitivity the dramas, rhythms, and *presence* of place.

Even children who have been schooled in modernity's radical discontinuity between humans and nature often have a profound engagement with a natural place—a summer camp, a grandparent's farm, or a hideaway spot near home. Throughout their lives they carry in their minds that sense of place, a place they came to know with a child's deep capacity for personal response. The presence of a place evoked their interiority and shaped their unfolding, offering over the years refuge and sustenance, stability and grace.

A two-way process of communication, then, situates a people in place over hundreds or thousands of years. In fact, premodern and nonmodern cultures have no meaning or definition if their essential connection with place is denied. Yet their freedom to interact with place has most often been usurped and directed by conceptual inventions such as the modern nation-state. Even worse, their identity as a people-of-place has often been deliberately suppressed by the modern state in order to create a new cosmopolitan, modern society.

Viewed through the lens of the modern worldview, the contemporary crises and revolts that threaten the political status quo in many nation-states appear to be sporadic, unrelated occurrences that simply need to be brought under order and control. Modern institutions—nation-states, the media, corporations, the social sciences—cannot hear the "noise" of these rebellions as anything other than bothersome aberrations, lacking common ground or deep cause. Nonetheless, challenges to both the ideological assumptions and conditions of modern statehood are driving many of the crucial events of our time. If awareness of that dynamic eludes most people, it is because the news of the day is perceived, shaped, and presented to us through the filter of the modern worldview. One could hardly expect the modern media to do otherwise. Yet another perspective is possible, one that makes sense of seemingly baffling events by bringing attention to a broader and deeper context than the ideology of modernity allows.

The independence efforts of such peoples as the Kurds, Basques, Tibetans, Chechnyans, Slovenians, and Croatians can best be understood in the context of the thousands of *nations* (long-standing or indigenous cultural entities) whose ancient territory has been surrounded or divided by the boundaries of modern *nation-states*, either capitalist or communist. Since no level of autonomy below the state is recognized by the modern political system, these nations have no legal forum in which to present their case for sovereignty. The United Nations, the European Union, the North Atlantic Treaty Organization (NATO), and so forth are all clubs whose membership is open only to sovereign states. Consequently, 72 percent of the wars fought since World War II have been wars of independence initiated by ancient nations that have been gobbled up by modern states.[19] These independence efforts are invariably called "insurgencies," "ethnic uprisings," or regressive "tribalism" by diplomats and the media. They are usually viewed as disruptions of peace and stability that rightfully should be crushed by the state. That policy has created 23 million refugees worldwide, plus another 26 million displaced persons who have remained within the borders of their nation-state. A network called Unrepresented Nations and Peoples Organization (UNPO), headquartered in The Hague, estimates that there are some five thousand unrepresented nations, many of which are indigenous. Not all of them are pressing for total independence; some would prefer to be a largely autonomous unit within the surrounding state.

The yearning for freedom is not going to disappear among the "captive nations," as they have been dubbed by Richard Falk, a scholar of international law. Their deep love of place and tradition has not been replaced with the standardized culture imposed by a centralized modern state. The modern drive to homogenize cultural differences eventually overpowered the principle of tolerance that was foundational in the secular state. In hindsight, a confederal model would have been a wiser choice than the federal model whenever modern states were formed by the merging of ancient nations. In that way, ethnic and regional identity could have been formally honored at the same time the Enlightenment values of human rights and tolerance were adopted. Instead, the domination and elimination of difference has resulted in patterns of persecution and loss played out over generations.

The moral impulse propelling attempts to achieve self-determination has exposed a critical flaw in the very meaning of the modern state. That meaning is understood to derive from a mandate, or social contract, to defend territorial borders, exercise sovereignty, maintain domestic order, support the economic system of choice (capitalist or socialist), further prosperity, and, as Max Weber noted, legitimize all violence conducted by the state. Only recently has a full sense of state-sponsored violence come to wide attention through the voices of captive nations. Those whose geopolitical situations are sufficiently strategic to make "the news" tell of enforced suppression of their language, traditional culture, and religion. It has seemed perfectly correct, and indeed progressive, for the modern state to "phase out" such "backward" vestiges because its own origins are rooted in that very dynamic, that is, liberation from tradition. Leaping beyond the despotic rule of kings and cardinals, however, need not have included a sweeping contempt for all deeply rooted cultures of spirit and place. In the name of efficiency (and control), a standardized dominant culture was enforced. Modern France, for example, insisted until quite recently that all children be named after figures in French history or the Judeo-Christian tradition, thereby rendering illegal the ancient Celtic names traditionally given to children in Brittany. The U.S. federal government forced several generations of Native American children to attend boarding schools where they were beaten if they spoke their own language, even privately. The communist attitude was similar: Forced assimilation into the modern mold, with no respect for traditional culture, was the rule for dozens of ancient nations within the borders of the Soviet Union and the People's Republic of China. Now that the flattening of diversity has assumed global proportions through mass media and ubiquitous marketing, the protection of particularity has taken on a poignant urgency—at least for all those cultural nations struggling to survive.

It is rarely made clear in news coverage of those struggles, however, that the outbreak of war is not *caused* by the captive nations seeking freedom. A violent, military response is chosen by the state in response to an independence vote or declaration. The captive nations merely want to leave, not engage in warfare, especially not with the comparatively huge military capabilities of the state's armed forces. The modern states *could* choose to bid the newly independent nations a fond farewell and begin negotiating regional compacts with them for trade, transportation, and so forth. However, modern states are under no pressure to do so because the dominant interpretation of the principle of self-determination in international law since World War II considers secessionist efforts to be legitimate only in situations of colonized nations seeking to break free from an empire. Ancient nations who have been "colonized" at closer range have no standing. For that reason, modern nation-states are free to unleash devastating reprisals against their captive nations who attempt liberation.

In recent years an argument has been put forth by several legal scholars for expanding the category of legal independence efforts to include ancient nations surrounded or divided by modern states. A strong interpretation of this extension would make military or other reprisals by states clearly illegal, once a bona fide independence vote had been taken in the seceding nation. Had that been the case when the three independence votes were taken in the former Yugoslavia (first in Slovenia, then in Croatia, then in Bosnia), the federal government (by then mostly Serbian) would

not have been permitted to call out its armed forces and retaliate with impunity—first by bombing the capital of Slovenia and later by bombing
scores of villages, towns, and cities in Croatia and, still later, in Bosnia. Neither would the federal government have been permitted to incite and
supply surrogate groups (Bosnian Serbs in Bosnia, Krajina Serbs in Croatia) with weapons and other material support. In the absence of international law that would recognize captive nations, the international
community felt from the beginning that it could not intervene in a conflict
taking place within the borders of a modern state. Consequently, federal
and surrogate-federal bombings of civilian targets (including irreplace-
able medieval churches and museums), plus the establishment of rape
camps and concentration camps with starvation rations, were allowed to
continue *for four years.*

There are scores of Slovenias, Croatias, and Bosnias all over the world,
risking devastating retribution by their quest for freedom. The fact that
these three independence wars took place in south-central Europe made
them more newsworthy than the others, thereby focusing attention on the
shocking paralysis, for a very long while, of the United Nations, NATO,
the European Union, and the international community at large. It is possible that the wrong lesson will be learned from the protracted carnage
in the former Yugoslavia—that the international community should
quickly supply all means of military aid to states facing secessionist efforts
so that the "illegal" freedom-fighters will be crushed as soon as possible,
resulting in minimum loss of life to all parties. This, after all, was the attitude expressed by the U.S. ambassador to Yugoslavia when it became clear
that Belgrade would opt for a military response to the independence votes:
The United States supports "stability in the region" at all costs.

"All costs" includes billions of dollars paid to the U.S. arms industry
by governments around the world that are engaged in military responses
to the independence efforts of captive nations. In 1994 and 1995, our
country contributed $12 billion of exports annually to the global arms
trade—four times more than Germany or Russia, who are the second-
and third-largest exporters of arms, respectively. Arms manufacturers in
the United States received $7.6 billion of taxpayer subsidies in 1995, while
6395 arms salesmen employed by the Pentagon peddled their wares
abroad. Many of the arms customers insist that production facilities and
jobs be located in their own countries, with the result that American
arms deals now produce more jobs overseas than in the United States.[20]

Half of U.S. arms sales are made to Third World governments, many of whom have "separatist problems" within their borders. Several Third World countries have themselves become suppliers of small arms for such conflicts. The enormous global arms industry today props up countless economies, in both the northern and southern hemispheres, and is largely dependent on the protraction of the independence wars.

The political emergence of the captive nations, even peacefully, raises questions, of course. The growing effort to restructure the United Nations, for instance, already includes several proposals to accommodate a much greater number of members, plus stronger regional organization. In addition, the principle of human rights, certainly the crown of modern political philosophy, could be combined with the actions to correct the modern subjugation of ancient nations: The newly independent nations would be granted diplomatic recognition by the international community only if their constitutions guarantee human rights to all residents. Harrassment of ethnic or religious minorities would result in various international sanctions. What this essentially means is a return to place as the focal point in territorial claims, rather than ownership based on the supposedly pure bloodlines of the majority group who have lived there for a long while. A plurality of peoples now inhabit most places on this earth. A peaceful future requires honoring that diversity, both culturally and legally, as the new orientation for the continuing unfolding of ecosocial communities in millions of places worldwide.

The problems are not insurmountable, but their solutions can grow only from a *post*modern recognition of the moral legitimacy of self-determination for ancient nations. The independence wars are not freak events but desperate efforts at cultural survival. They are unfathomable only to those who believe *pax moderna* to be the sole rational arrangement.

A second area in which place has become a focus is the emergent challenge to the destructive effects of the globalized economy. The assumption underlying the euphoric claims for the global market, now structured by the rules of the Global Agreement on Tariffs and Trade (GATT), is that every nation will earn most of its income from exports. Nearly every conservative and every liberal party in every modern nation-state in the world today supports this model, in spite of the fact that basing one's future on conditions in distant markets is extraordinarily insecure. Advocates for the global economy, who until recently included most editorial writers in American newspapers, regard it as the bearer of unbounded potential, a rising tide that will lift all boats. True believers see it as an evolutionary triumph with spiritual overtones. Alas, it is difficult to accept that spiritual spin unless one truly feels that the universe harbors a teleological urge to have Planet Earth controlled by transnational corporations, for that is the outcome of global "free trade" as structured by GATT. Even books that tout the supposed decentralization of computerized trade as a boon for small entrepreneurs often let slip the truth about the new game: It is largely about market shares for the big boys. For example, John Naisbitt's almost delirious declaration of unlimited opportunities for anyone with a laptop—*Global Paradox: The Bigger the World Economy the More Powerful the Smallest Players* (1994)—admits that large portions of the market share for various products in, say, China are already controlled by transnational corporations.[21] When five firms control more than half of a global market, that market is considered to be highly monopolistic. In 1993, *The Economist* reported concentration ratios for twelve global industries. The greatest concentration was found in consumer durables, where the top five firms control nearly 70 percent of the entire world market in their industry. In the automotive, airline, aerospace, electronic components, electrical and electronic, and steel industries, the top five firms control more than 50 percent of the global market, clearly placing them in the monopoly category. In the oil, personal computer, and media industries, the top five firms control more than 40 percent of sales, thus showing strong monopolistic tendencies.[22]

Centralization of ownership through expansion of the biggest firms will increase under the renegotiated version of GATT, which now makes it illegal for any national, state, or local government to enforce its internal laws for environmental protection, labor protection, or community-based economics if any transnational corporation considers any of those laws to be burdensome or "prejudicial" to the sale of any of their products or services. In fact, shortly after GATT went into effect in 1994, three grievances were filed with the World Trade Organization (WTO) against the United States by foreign enterprises claiming that a U.S. law was a "restraint against free trade." Daimler-Benz argued that the American miles-per-gallon requirement is prejudicial to their most luxurious model of Mercedes-Benz; oil producers in Brazil and Venezuela asserted that the U.S. law requiring them to clean their raw oil before marketing it in this country is prejudicial against them; and the Mexican fishing industry argued that the U.S. law prohibiting the importation of tuna caught with the type of nets that also trap dolphins is an unfair restraint against their product. In each case, the grievance was decided in favor of the petitioners by the arbitration panel at the WTO in Geneva, which is neither elected nor accountable to anyone. When a country loses in a grievance decision, they must either change their internal law or pay the filer of the grievance the amount of money lost to them because of the "prejudicial" law. In short, GATT redefines "free trade" to mean that transnational corporations are free to do anything they want; no one else is.

All this was forewarned prior to Congress's approval of GATT and NAFTA (son of GATT) in a well-argued collection of essays by Ralph Nader, William Grieder, Margaret Atwood, Jerry Brown, Herman Daly, Wendell Berry, and others: *The Case against "Free Trade"* (1993). Not one newspaper or magazine in the United States reviewed that book. Nor did the media shine their spotlight on any opponents of the highly undemocratic trade agreements except for the most eccentric representative, Ross Perot. A critical examination of those trade treaties finally got a boost more than two years later, when Pat Buchanan made them an issue in his campaign for the Republican nomination for President in the spring of 1996; however, his right-wing views muddied the waters.

As the industrialized nations are gradually figuring out, the new world order imposed by the globalized economy means a race to the bottom for everyone, as jobs are eliminated in the name of global competitiveness or exported and the transnational corporations assume a level of power above any government. Even in a country like India, where 10 percent of the 980,000,000 residents comprise a new middle class that has benefited from the globalized presence of transnationals, the other 90 percent are simply not in the plan for the dazzling future. The 10 percent with disposable income constitute a large enough market to cause salivation among the global players: India is called a great success story!

Because the resources of the transnationals can crush any competition, especially with the carte blanche afforded by GATT, communities all over the world are now vulnerable to the insecurity and destructive effects of the global market. The alternative of community-based economics and regional trade, however, is rapidly gaining adherents. In the first half of the 1990s, many lending agencies, development programs, and foundations shifted their focus to micro-loans for very small-scale entrepreneurs, usually Third World women both in villages and among the urban poor. The demand for small-scale, sustainable economic development, in fact, emerged as a dominant concern at the Fourth United Nations Conference on Women in Beijing in 1995. The hypermodern dream of a globalized cyber-economy is also being challenged in the United States by a growing focus on community-based enterprises and organizations, including micro-loan programs, nonprofit corporations that build housing, and farmers' markets and other types of community-supported agriculture. The security, both economic and social, of *place* is now the countervalent focus as the global market continues to intensify. (This emergent dynamic is discussed further in Chapter 3.)

~

The knowing body, the creative cosmos, the complex sense of place—all these are asserting their true nature as we increase our abilities to see beyond the boundaries of the modern worldview. It seems inconceivable that the corrective efforts will ever regress into the ideologies of denial, that is, seeing the body as nothing but a biological machine, the biosphere and cosmos as nothing but a predictable, mechanistic clockwork, and place as nothing but background scenery for human projects. Quite the contrary, in fact: It seems unlikely that we will ever nail down the fullness of their being with our sciences. We will surely learn more about their processes, but any creative unfolding is a play of possibilities involving extremely subtle influences from the past and the present. With luck, what we will learn is awe before the real, the extraordinary source and grounding of all our human endeavors.

At the close of the twentieth century, as the mechanistic worldview gradually gives way to perceptions of a nonmechanistic reality, the influence of science—our truth mode in the modern era, for better or worse—is again driving much of the new thinking as it is adopted throughout the culture. One hundred years ago, the latest news from science also informed *fin de siècle* sensibilities, yet the gripping revelation about reality at that time was the Second Law of Thermodynamics. A fashionable despondency settled over European intellectuals in the 1890s because that law of entropy decreed that all systems lose free energy (energy capable of doing work) during the course of operating and hence run down over time. Moreover, the end result would be the heat death of the universe, an ocean of dead, lukewarm matter with all order destroyed. *Incroyable! Bring another round of cognac, immediately!*

Today, once again in a *fin de siècle* mood of reflecting on the passing century and the new one to come, we survey the crises in seemingly compartmentalized spheres of modern life and begin to see that many of the problems labeled "political" or "economic" or "psychological" or "social" are the result of enforcing a system that denies dynamic balance, creative response, and self-organization. The new understanding of those negentropic forces is now sparking a reorientation of thought and action, albeit still as a minority voice. The focus today is not the predicted disappearance of order but the abundance of it throughout the natural world. How did it come about? How is it generated and maintained? How are the self-organizing powers of the universe manifested in and around us? These are the questions pursued by complexity science.

Still, to blithely absorb the truth-claims of scientism as the guiding light once again would indicate that the "new thinking" remains situated in the prejudices of modernity. In fact, the new sciences are making such an impact because two simultaneous developments have prepared the ground. One is the postmechanistic mood in contemporary spirituality, literature, the arts, and elsewhere in Western culture. To someone who has recently discovered the creation-centered medieval mystics, such as Meister Eckhardt and Mechtild of Magdeburg, the new sciences' descriptions of a dynamic, creative world seem merely like supporting evidence for that which has long been perceived by nonmodern minds. The second relevant development is the failure of so many of the core assumptions of modernity: Poor *homo economicus* must now grapple with social breakdown, economic insecurity, and toxic waste. It wasn't supposed to turn out this way.

The resurgence of the real poses challenges and opportunities that we are only beginning to grasp. A wise response must be based on an understanding of how and why the modern assumptions arose, often for fully admirable reasons. How did we ever come to perceive body and mind as separate, nature as dead resource, and place as inconsequential? How did the problematic modern assumptions eventually lose their power to convince after several hundred years of dominance? That story is visited in the following chapter, in which I also sort out contemporary responses to modernity. I distinguish between various "postmodern" tantrums (which are actually *most*modern) and those efforts that actually correct the tragic errors in the assumptions of the modern worldview. The latter constitute an emergent postmodern transformation based on the resurgent realities of body, nature, and place.

2

THE RISE AND FALL
OF MODERN IDEOLOGIES
OF DENIAL

WHEN THE EASTERN BLOC DISSOLVED into postcommunist democracies, they were said to be in need of modernization in nearly every sector of society. It was an ironic ending for the political tradition that had prided itself on carrying forth the modern project more rationally than anyone else. "Scientific socialism" rapidly industrialized previously agrarian countries, installed productive systems of social engineering and bureaucratic management, and all but eliminated the "medieval superstitions" called "religion." State socialism could hardly have been more modern in framing its intensive destruction of ecosystems as heroic efforts on behalf of "the brotherhood of man" and technocratic progress. In the difficult transition since 1989, government officials in the new democracies have been assured by most Western advisors that the dynamism of capitalism will yield a better, more modern way of life.

They are no doubt correct on many levels, but the goal of passing through progressive stages of modernity has come into question. It has even been rejected outright as an orientation for the future by one of the most widely respected leaders of the postcommunist nations. In February 1993, Vaclav Havel, a playwright and former dissident who was elected president of the new Czech Republic, delivered an address to the World Economic Forum titled "The End of the Modern Era," which was published in newspapers internationally. He asserted that the end of communism brought an end to the modern age with its positivist, scientistic, rationalist view of life. On the Fourth of July, 1994, Havel went further, in a speech at Independence Hall in Philadelphia, which was excerpted in American newspapers. He suggested that the industrialized societies have entered a transitional, postmodern period because the modern, scientific relationship to the world has "failed to connect with the most intrinsic nature of reality and with natural human experience." Accepted dogmatically as the very essence of reality, the mechanistic orientation became misleading throughout the modern era:

> We may know immeasurably more about the universe than our ancestors did, and yet it increasingly seems that they knew something more essential about it than we do, something that escapes us. The same thing is true of the nature of ourselves. The more thoroughly all our organs and their functions, their internal structure and the biochemical reactions that take place within them, are described, the more we seem to fail to grasp the spirit, purpose, and meaning of the system that they create together and that we experience as our unique self.

Havel went on to observe that postmodern science is transcending the limits of modern science and is anchoring the human once again in the cosmos, through such discoveries as the anthropic principle in physics and the Gaia hypothesis in geobiochemistry. Turning to the political implications of this recovery of our "lost integrity," he concluded that "the basis for the new world order must be universal respect for human rights, but it will mean nothing as long as this imperative does not derive from respect for the miracle of Being, the miracle of the universe, the miracle of nature, the miracle of our own existence."

Havel, an intellectual with many contacts in the West, is conversant with various analyses of modern and postmodern conditions. The same cannot be said of most citizens in the postcommunist democracies, nor would one expect it. Their attention is claimed, for the most part, by problems of great immediacy related to the economic free fall that followed the revolutions. I learned a good deal about their situation when I was invited to give a series of talks there in the summer of 1993. I spoke over a period of five days to a gathering of young professionals held near the Mala

Fatra Mountains of northwest Slovakia, was then driven to the southwest corner of the Czech Republic to address a protest camp at the construction site of a nuclear power plant (opposed by 60 of the 62 local mayors but pushed through by the new federal government in Prague), and was subsequently driven back across the southern Czech Republic into Slovakia to address a group of philosophy professors in Bratislava. For all three audiences, I ended up putting aside my prepared lecture notes until I had addressed a subject that came up repeatedly during my stay, a perplexing paradox that seemed to weigh heavily on everyone I met.

My first inkling of the matter occurred during the thirty-minute drive from the Vienna airport to Bratislava. I was met by two members of the Green Party of Slovakia (later called the Green League)—a female biophysicist and a male engineer. After we had crossed the border into their country, they were pleased to point out among the rolling hills several picturesque villages, Baroque towns, and ruins of medieval castles on high bluffs above vigorous rivers. When we passed by the first cluster of high-rise apartment buildings jutting starkly from a distant ridge, the engineer pointed toward it and declared contemptuously over the engine noise, "That's socialism!" I, sitting in the back seat, thought to myself, "No, that's modernity. Do you think we don't have those sterile, towering boxes in Western Europe, the U.S., and Japan?" In the days that followed, as I became acquainted with more and more people living through the postcommunist experience, I saw that they regarded state socialism as a historical aberration best forgotten. Moreover, they were largely baffled that so much of the texture of daily life has remained the same since they had made that 180-degree shift from communism to capitalism, which had always been portrayed by both sides as polar opposites. An entirely different world was supposed to have manifested, a new society sparked by unleashed human potential. The implicit promise of the capitalist West had been that of a radically different existence; the proposed euphoric scenario portrayed liberation from a paralyzing malaise, followed by the unfettered dynamism of a modernized economy and the unbounded prosperity for all. Factories, banks, and retailing would have to be modernized in the former Eastern Bloc, of course, but then it would be full speed ahead. Already, by the time of my visit, Viennese ad agencies had plastered Bratislava with commercial posters, one of them so "advanced" as to skip the car altogether and feature only an attractive young woman and huge lettering: TOYOTA.

As we now know, the various postcommunist countries were fated to suffer through severe economic crises. That aspect of the new era, however, was not the main cause of the unarticulated puzzlement I encountered in Slovakia and the Czech Republic that summer. Although many people I met were facing grave financial uncertainty and possible devastation, many others were in occupations that apparently would weather the transition. Considering the profound differences between living in a communist police-state or a democracy, why, they wondered, did so much feel similar to what they had known under the old regime?

The answer lay in an understanding of the larger context: modernity. Marxism-Leninism was one of several economic systems that share the assumptions of the modern worldview. If one were to plot these systems on a spectrum of left-to-right political economies within modernity, "Marxist-Leninist socialism" and its variations would occupy the far left, to the right of which would be "democratic socialism," followed by "regulated capitalist democracies," followed by "laissez-faire (corporate-controlled) right-wing capitalist democracies," followed by "fascist corporatism in quasi-military dictatorships." Modern ideology asserts that each of these orientations shapes life in a mold that is entirely different from the others. That perception, however, reflects a central bias of modernity: economism, the tendency in modern societies to regard economics as the fundamental determinant of everything else. Such a perspective obscures the common ground shared by all of those political economies: They each subscribe to the following values of modernity.

The human is considered essentially an economic being, homo economicus. *Consequently, the arrangement of economic matters is believed to be the wellspring of contentment or discontent in all other areas of life. Economic expansion, through industrialism and computerization, is the Holy Grail of materialism, the unquestioned source from whence follows abundance, well-being, and the evolution of society. That evolution is understood to be decidedly directional: The human condition progresses toward increasingly optimal states as the past is continuously improved upon.*

Modern socialization structures our understanding of the world via objectivism, rationalism, the mechanistic worldview, reductionism, and scientism. (These dreary but arrogant "isms" are explained more fully in the Appendix.) The design and organization of work in modern societies are based on standardization, bureaucratization, and centralization. Modern interactions with nature are anthropocentric and are guided by instrumental reasoning. Above all, modern culture defines itself as a triumphant force progressing in opposition to *nature. As such, it harbors contempt for non-modern cultures, which are seen to be "held back" by unproductive perceptions such as the "sacred whole" and reciprocal duties toward the rest of the Earth community.*

Modern life is compartmentalized into discrete spheres: family life, work life, social life, political life, love life, and spiritual life, the last of which is devalued for being the furthest from rationalism. In modern societies, higher education is also tightly compartmentalized into insular disciplines. There, as in law and government, intensely agonistic modes of discussion shape all possibilities. The preference for competition and a dominance-or-submission dichotomy as the structure of relationships in all spheres of modern life reflects the extent of patriarchal socialization. Modern societies are sometimes called "hypermasculine" because "masculine" traits, such as the persona of rationalism, are valued much more highly than "feminine" traits, such as empathy.

The faces of my audiences in Slovakia and the Czech Republic lit up with recognition as I spontaneously rattled off the above characteristics of modernity. Seeing them nod and smile, I said, "This is what you were taught in school, right? It's what I was taught in school, too! Even though we were each assured in the strongest possible terms that our two systems were almost unimaginably alien to one another!"

The bloom is off the dynamo—and has been for a very long while. Modernity produced painful "contradictions" that were wrestled with throughout the nineteenth century, but our own century has witnessed the outright failure of many of the assumptions of the modern worldview. One of its central tenets—the perfectability of the human by means of rationally designed institutions—was refuted brutally in the first half of the twentieth century by the carnage of two world wars, the Holocaust, the totalitarian regime that followed the Russian Revolution, and the deployment of the atomic bomb over two cities in Japan. In each of those nightmares of recent history, the level and the intensity of destruction were heightened by the evolution of modern technology: mustard gas, torpedoes, aerial bombing, rocket attacks, and atomic bombs. In addition to technological capability, it was the convergence of several characteristics of modernity—value-free efficiency, detached rationalism, instrumental reasoning, managerial industrialism—that made possible the mass murder of European Jews in the 1940s, as Zygmunt Bauman observes in *Modernity and the Holocaust* (1989).

Yet technology has also provided the stream of benefits that characterize the modern age in most people's minds. The term "modern life" calls up images of jet planes, penicillin, laser surgery, television, telephones, cameras, photocopiers, fax machines, computers, and our strangely beloved cars. The grand conceptual promises of modernity may have proved to be somewhat elusive, but the march of technological progress has turned out to be extraordinarily dynamic and creative. Moreover, the materialist bent of the modern view of life predisposes us to perceive the worth of this vast bounty of mechanical and electronic devices as far outweighing whatever problems may exist in the areas of *liberté, égalité,* and *fraternité.* In any case, modernity holds that all problems can be solved in time through technological fixes or other aspects of "progress" that we cannot now even imagine. From inside the modern worldview, this response feels less like blind faith than realistic trust in the future that is based on modernity's track record of having solved countless problems in the past. After all, modernity has yielded devices that conquer gravity, distances, and unproductive deserts. It even defies death—at least for much longer than in past eras.

Technology, however, has created new problems while solving old ones. Modern societies have been reluctant to acknowledge those "side effects," adopting instead a surprisingly uncritical attitude toward technological change, which often brings rippling and unexamined consequences. At the core of many brilliant nature-defying breakthroughs, the seeds of new misery often lie hidden, as recent history has shown. (More about this paradox of modernity is explored in Chapter 3.)

A far greater paradox of modernity—one with the opposite proportions, that is, seeds of the positive embedded in structures of the negative—is the main focus of this book. The truly remarkable aspect of modernity is that, while its mechanistic, reductionist worldview got a great deal wrong about reality and imposed its limited, constricted view on every modern field of endeavor, the modern project also included one profoundly corrective element, one grandly idealistic value, which eventually exposed the false claims and partial truths of its own dogma: the principle of liberty. Although it has taken three hundred years, *free inquiry* in the field of science finally broke through the conceptual boundaries and revealed the shortcomings of the mechanistic worldview. The postmodern sciences have expanded the gestalt to acknowledge discoveries of a far more subtle and creative universe than the modern model allowed. In the social sphere, liberation movements, called "emancipatory projects" by Europeans, carried forth the ideal of self-determination contained in Enlightenment political philosophy. In doing so, they found that they had to challenge the enormous exclusionary areas of the new liberal idealism, which, as history has shown, could be interpreted to condone slavery, imperialism, anti-Semitism, male dominance, and rule-by-the-people when the emancipatory vanguard turned "necessarily authoritarian," on the model of Robespierre, Lenin, or Stalin. *Free inquiry* within the liberation movements, then, led to a deep questioning of problematic assumptions in the modern political worldview. Some of the emancipatory efforts argued for change that was radical on certain counts but remained ensconced in the belief system of the modern era, such as Marx's enthusiastic embrace of economism. Other movements probed more deeply into the problematic assumptions and conditions of modernity, as will be discussed in Chapter 4.

The dynamic by which the principle of free inquiry and freedom of all sorts came to be (theoretically) enshrined at the very center of the modern project was part of yet another paradox, one involving great risk and, as it turned out, tragic loss. All of the foundational movements that contributed to the birth of modernity—Renaissance humanism, the Reformation, the Scientific Revolution, and the Enlightenment—were revolutionary *reactions* against various constraints imposed by the church-state lock on power in the medieval world. The danger in a reactionary mode is that much of value is destroyed in the process of installing the new. Contrary to the Hegelian theory that history *always* proceeds by means of the violent clash of opposites, there are countless examples, in all parts of the world, of substantive change that was incorporated in ways that deftly preserved older contours of wisdom. The posture of the proto-modern movements, unfortunately, was fiercely antagonistic to all aspects of the medieval world and was blind to its accomplishments: The Enlightenment philosophers dismissed the Middle Ages as an irrational aberration in (European) civilization's grand trajectory, which began with Greek rationalism and was now being invigorated by new developments. The bold declarations of liberation were framed as sweeping and uncompromising rejections. Yet the insistence on freedom in art, philosophy, religion, science, and politics was actually embedded in an ideological context that steered the newly freed modes of inquiry in a particular direction: a radical break *from* all perceptions of organicism, holism, and interrelatedness and *toward* any works or discoveries that fit into the neoclassical, mechanistic worldview. The immediate past was to be escaped from, denied, and replaced. Only the new was of value.

The complex transition from the holistic (but hierarchical) medieval worldview to the modern mechanistic one came to be expressed as a simplistic reduction holding great allure: the passage from the Dark Ages to the Enlightenment. Has ever there been such a starkly black and white framing of history? But what a grand epic! School children have been thrilled to learn of the triumphant deliverance of society from darkness to light, from superstition to scientific knowledge, and from constraint to liberty. Deeply relieved when they grasp the outcome, students in modern schools readily identify with the winning side.

While modernity's version of its birth is a brilliantly didactic and seductive work of mythic drama, it sheds no light on the problematic aspects of the troubled world to which we have progressed. How could such brilliance have led to so much loneliness and alienation? How could such creative dynamism have led to so much ecological and social destruction wrought in dazzlingly efficient modes? Was our modern age of triumph destined from the start to be tinged with despair? The answer to such questions lies in a much fuller account of the origins of modernity than the one we learned in school, for the promise of paradise gained must be weighed with the tragedy of paradigms lost.

Each of the four movements that cumulatively created the modern worldview arose in response to a noble quest. Each challenged the status quo and courageously forged an alternative. They are justly honored for their pursuit of freedom, but the ways in which they conceived of freedom were profoundly flawed. One might say that they asked admirable questions but arrived at inadequate answers. That distinction would be an improvement over both the uncritical adulation these movements have traditionally received and the more recent rejection they have suffered. Yet it misses the deep roots of alienation in Western thought. The questions themselves were framed in ways that continued and intensified certain assumptions, resulting over time in the crises of modernity we face today. The following discussion does not attempt to document the fullness of the foundational movements but, rather, to identify their problematic aspects that led to the modern crises.

The first of these movements, the Renaissance, was not simply a "rebirth of learning," as we were taught in modern schooling, but a rebirth of *classical* learning. Even though the grand medieval synthesis forged by St. Thomas Aquinas in the thirteenth century had merged Christian theology with Greek rationalism and naturalism, resulting in recognition of the dynamic autonomy of the individual and the ontological significance of the cosmos, a growing urge to move beyond the controlling influence of the Church eventually found that synthesis inadequate. Perhaps the devastating events of the fourteenth century—the Black Death, famine, and wars—had left Europe with its fill of the Augustinian notion of humankind's fallen and sinful state, for the following century embraced a revival of pre-Christian learning that celebrated the human: *Man is the measure of all things!*

The interest in classical letters and Platonic philosophy led eventually to the establishment of secular education built on humanist values. The nobility of man [sic] was a reflection of his impressive capabilities for rational thought, creative imagination, and spiritual exultation. The cultivation of personal and civic virtue as well as powers of discernment and just deliberation were the fruits of (male) rationality, properly trained. Wishing to break free from the Church's grip on nearly everything, Renaissance humanism contrasted the Christian view of the human as prone to sin and weakness with a neoclassical sense of rational man's unbounded potential.

Yet that concept of secular potential was shot through with particular assumptions. Rational thought could be exercised only if sealed off from "corrupting" influences of the body (sensations, emotions, desires) and if properly isolated from "lowly" nature. Plato felt that we, that is, our minds, are imprisoned in the dumb matter of our bodies. Although he considered the cosmos to be sacred in its orderliness, he shared with his teacher, Socrates, a belief that nature is irrelevant to the culmination of the human race, the Greek male. In Plato's dialogue *Phaedrus*, Socrates is led by a fellow citizen of Athens beyond the city gates to a spreading plane-tree. He tells the friend that he rarely frequents such spots because nature is not his teacher. Socrates explains that he values only the knowledge of men in cities.

That simple exchange bears witness to the deep roots of the peculiar Western perception of a radical discontinuity between humans and the rest of the natural world. Socrates focused philosophy on the rational examination of human life within the Greek city-state, yet the group of philosophers who immediately preceded him, the pre-Socratics, had been engrossed with a far different subject. Between 600 and 400 B.C.E., each put forth arguments for their understanding of the natural world, the cosmological reality in which humans are embedded. Thales believed it to be essentially water. For Anaximander, it was simply "the unlimited." Anaximenes believed all existence to be essentially air. Xenophanes perceived essential reality as earth and water. Heraclitus asserted that all nature is the unity of opposites and constant flux. The common ground for all these assertions about the real was a holistic sensibility. Where did it come from?

Although nearly all philosophical surveys state that the pre-Socratics were the only philosophers in the Western canon to have no predecessors, they were in fact preserving, by threads, a rich philosophical tradition that stretched back at least twenty-five thousand years in central and southeastern Europe. Once historians of philosophy absorb the archaeological discoveries of the past thirty years concerning pre-Indo-European cultures in that part of Europe, they will see the pre-Socratic philosophers anew, as an orientation that bridged the "native European," pre-Greek sensibilities and the radically reduced focus of most of the Greek philosophy that followed. The late Marija Gimbutas and other archaeologists of pre-Bronze-Age southeastern Europe have unearthed thousands of artifacts that reflect a sense of our inherent embeddedness in the dynamics of nature: figurines that are half-human and half-bird, for instance, or female figurines incised with waves of life-giving water. The procreative powers of both nature and humans were honored with a highly developed system of symbols and a sophisticated array of artistic expression.[1] Beginning around 4400 B.C.E. in eastern Europe, however, the archaeological evidence indicates that a very different orientation arrived with nomadic tribes who migrated westward from the Pontic and Volga steppes. (Recent findings in historical gene-mapping support Gimbutas's archaeological conclusions regarding these waves of migrations, or invasions.[2]) The Indo-European tribes that eventually dominated the agricultural settlements of "Old Europe" displaced the sense of the sacred from the earth's dynamics (often expressed through a female symbol of divine creativity) to their distant thunderbolt-wielding sky-god. They also introduced a patriarchal social system, which was reflected immediately in a change in the burial patterns (from roughly egalitarian between the sexes to the chieftain-centered mode), and they brought a cult of the warrior. As they spread west and northwest across Europe, they shifted the course of neolithic European thought away from an Earth-based holism. The sky-god and those who resemble him (that is, men) were henceforth held to be ontologically superior to those enmeshed in the Earth's "lowly" realm of blood, mud, and birth. The elemental powers of the female, honored for thousands of years prior to the arrival of the Indo-European nomads, were thereafter called lowly and unclean, yet they always remained a threat to the patriarchal mentality. Masculinity became a reactive matter, an obsession with being not-female and not-nature, which eventually played a large role in the intellectual history of the West.

By the time the pre-Socratic philosophers were declaiming their sense of the real, patriarchal culture was firmly established. They did not challenge it, but they did preserve, from the pre-Indo-European era, the perception that our subtle and profound relationships with the rest of the natural world are constitutive. The nature of the biosphere matters—its flux, its water, air, and earth, its coherence—because we are it and it is us. After the pre-Socratics, this primal organicism was largely displaced by the projection of dualism, transcendent reason, and a more abstract sense of cosmic coherence. The Pythagorean school of pre-Socratic philosophy contained both the primal holism, expressed as the cosmic order evident in harmonious proportions, and a rigid dualism, expressed in their Table of Opposites. (Their positive association of determinate, fixed form with maleness and their negative association of the unbounded and changing with the female denigrated women's periodicity and gravid swellings.) Plato intensified the dualistic thought of the Pythagoreans by perceiving not only a divine order as expressed in numerical proportions and sacred geometry but also a sense that the order created by divine, or ideal, forms was radically other than the mere material world we inhabit. He established a dualism of universal and particular, of noumenon and phenomenon, of mind and body, and of spirit and matter that shaped all subsequent philosophy and religion in the European tradition. The Greek sense of reason pitted the powers of mind against the "corrupting" influences of the body, with its unruly sensations and emotions. Moreover, untainted reason was felt to bestow upon us our radical discontinuity from the rest of the natural world and our clear superiority to it. The triumph of Greek rationalism, in short, depended upon an intensely oppositional premise.

Because the early Renaissance humanists realized the dangers of going too far too fast, they sought some sort of explication that would prudently situate the new Unbounded Individual within the Christian sphere. The tension between the two views of humankind explains the enormous enthusiasm that greeted its resolution in the appearance of a body of esoteric texts called the *prisca theologica*, or "Ancient Wisdom." These texts steered the emergence of humanism in a direction that was both sacral and self-aggrandizing, for the central concept of the Ancient Wisdom was that man [sic] is a terrestrial god who can shape his own destiny and control nature.

One of the major texts of the collection, the *Corpus Hermeticum*, was brought to Florence in 1460 and immediately translated by the head of the Platonic academy, Marsilio Ficino. Its purported author, Hermes Trismegistus, was thought to have been an Egyptian magus who had been the spiritual mentor of both Moses and Plato! Such a leap of credulity reflects the desperate desire at that pivotal moment for a synthesis of the Judeo-Christian tradition and Greek rationalism that would allow for, and even bless, a far more arrogant and egotistic sense of the human than that of Aquinas's grand synthesis. Although parts of the *Corpus Hermeticum* present ancient cosmological, nature-honoring spirituality and various instructions concerning communion with the *spiritus mundi*, the sections that were more enthusiastically embraced by the new humanist mood bore an opposite message. Hermes relates that he learned in a dream that humans and nature have separate origins: God the Father instructed the Demiurge to create the natural world, but He created man Himself and made him in His image. Unlike nature, man shares a divine Father-Son relationship with God. In addition, man has the ability to discover the nature of divine power, enabling him to participate in the maintenance of cosmic order and to create a microcosmic social order. Nature provides man with the means of expressing his God-like creativity and will be restored to its original beauty, once again worthy of reverence and admiration, when man realizes his true role as magus.

Initially Renaissance humanists sought to interpret the Ancient Wisdom as a unifying core of revelations linking ancient and Christian beliefs. Eventually, however, the Promethean promise of the esoteric Hermetic texts displaced Christian "constraints" among many proponents of the new secularism. Giovanni Pico di Mirandola's famous *Oration on the Dignity of Man*, for instance, is laced with references to esoteric practices recommended in the Ancient Wisdom, although modern schooling presents Pico's oration merely as a courageous, rationalist break with the theological "dark ages." By the sixteenth century, the Ancient Wisdom was a core element in the rising call for a comprehensive reorientation of religion and politics. Its sense of the god-like powers of humans to subjugate nature and to fashion social microcosms of brilliantly rational design influenced two subsequent proto-modern movements: the Scientific Revolution in the sixteenth and seventeenth centuries and the Enlightenment in the eighteenth.

Before those further challenges to the authority of church-and-king arose, however, the second of the four foundational movements shook the very bulwarks of European culture. The Reformation may be seen as a reaction against the Papacy's attempt to finance its grand acquistions of Renaissance art and architecture by selling spiritual indulgences, which were believed to spring one from purgatory should the need arise. This practice involved the Church's transferring some of the treasury of merit, accumulated by the good works of the saints, to an individual, who then made a contribution to the Church in gratitude. Originally, the practice applied only to the removal of penalties accrued in this life and was used to raise money for the crusades and the building of cathedrals and hospitals. By Martin Luther's time, however, indulgences were being sold to shorten one's route to heaven.

The principled break from such corruption was merely the most popularly grasped element in the Ninety-five Theses that Luther posted in Wittenberg in 1517. He initially asked for clarification of the selling of indulgences because he considered it harmful to the spirit of repentance. His own theological persuasion had long held that the true meaning of God's forgiving love in Christ must be apprehended solely through faith and repentance, not through good works or ritual experiences. Eventually the Reformation moved away from the privileged *and foreign* clerical authority, establishing an individualistic focus for spiritual life: the quality of an *individual's* direct relationship with God. The community of saints, priests, monks, nuns, and fellow Christians all receded before the new theology of the individual, standing alone before his God.

Another contribution to the emergent modern worldview was the Reformation's "rationalizing" of religion. The high esteem accorded by the medieval Church to the Virgin Mary—a version of the Divine Mother symbol, with roots in European consciousness that can be traced to 25,000 B.C.E.—was abruptly curtailed. Her role of compassionate intercessor with Christ was transferred to Christ Himself, portrayed in the new theology as a loving intercessor with God the Father. Both the devaluing of the sacred womb of the female and the denial of the larger sense of the female as an honored site of Divine presence cleared the way for the masculine character of the modern worldview.

The Reformation also eliminated the sacraments of extreme unction (last rites) and penance and declared that confirmation, marriage, and ordination were no longer sacraments at all. In doing so, they made clear their rejection of the Catholic belief that grace is often experienced in the ritual practice of the sacraments; for the Protestants, grace might be bestowed by God on an individual solely because of faith and Scriptural study. (Readers interested in a cosmological sense of grace, which I understand as consciousness of the unitive dimension of being, are referred to my book *States of Grace.*)

Of the two sacraments that remained, baptism and the eucharist, the latter was cleansed of its "irrational" elements. Transubstantiation—the Catholic belief that Christ is actually present as body and blood in the communion bread and wine—was maintained by Luther but replaced by Calvin and Zwingli with a more modern semiotic interpretation: The bread and wine of the eucharist are symbols that memorialize and *remind* one of Christ's sacrifice and resurrection. Viewed through the lens of material rationalism, this was a clear improvement. Today the sensibility that was rejected, however, calls to mind the revelation in postmodern physics of a vast, unified field of subtle relatedness. The sense of an unbroken participatory field of reality was central to the primal mind as well. Traditional native peoples understand their use of symbols as participation in an unbroken field that links, for instance, the sun, the symbol for the sun, all recipients of the sun's gifts, the woman creating a beaded symbol of the sun, the garment that bears it, the person by whom it is worn, and the viewers who may gaze upon it. Perhaps, buried deep within the Church's struggle for doctrinal supremacy regarding transubstantiation was a remnant of the primal recognition of cosmological wholeness, the unitive dimension of being.

The rationalist character of the Reformation intensified in the hands of Calvin and Zwingli, shifting the emphasis even further from sacramental experience to study of the Word. Moreover, Luther's basic assertion that Scripture-based faith was the sole means by which an individual might receive God's redemptive grace was amplified by an insistence that man's innate sinfulness made independent human will ineffective and perverse. Still, the Protestant rebellion to gain "Christian liberty"—that is, private judgment and autonomy standing against monolithic institutional authority—established a focus on internal subjectivity, which became central to modern thought.

The premium placed on self-control and "rational asceticism," according to Max Weber's famous study of the legacy of the Reformation, shaped the social development of the countries in which Calvinism, Puritanism, and Pietism were predominant, leaving a legacy of methodological, self-restraining, work-oriented socialization long after the religious beliefs had faded from importance. The dissolution of worldly asceticism into pure utilitarianism contributed to a rigidly ordered, regularized, bureaucratized structure of business—that is, the structure of modern capitalism. Weber also traced the formative influence of ascetic rationalism in modern social ethics, government, humanist rationalism, culture, scientific and philosophical empiricism, technological development, and spiritual ideals.[3]

One further effect of the Reformation prepared the ground for the next of the proto-modern movements, influencing the ways in which nature would be regarded by the Scientific Revolution. Luther and Calvin asserted the theological doctrine of radical sovereignty, the belief that God's sovereignty excluded the contribution of lesser beings to his work. No "natural revelation" was possible by human apprehension of the natural world. This was a sharp rejection of Aquinas's grand synthesis and Scholastic theology, which incorporated the Aristotelian sense of the laws of nature as internal to nature itself. In the medieval view, an accommodating divine sovereignty cooperated with the dynamics of nature. The passivity of nature, argued by the Reformation in order to protect the glory of God, was subsequently adopted by the mechanistic philosophers and became central to the Scientific Revolution. The mechanists insisted that, contrary to Aristotle's claims, material bodies possess no active, internal forces but are merely acted upon by external laws and principles, such as impact, gravity, and inertia. Stripped of its cosmic majesty and now considered to be the opposite of God's transcendence, the natural world was the one area in which humans could have knowledge.[4]

The rejection of the Church's authority and its theology left a growing uncertainty about truth, valid knowledge, and a secure sense of reality. As this discomfort rippled outward from the newly Protestant countries to the adjacent lands, the need for a firm structure of knowledge that would accommodate the new mood of individual freedom became acute. Various contenders sought to advance natural science within a framework of organicism, drawing from Christian, Neoplatonic, Gnostic, or Hermetic sources, which incorporated the philosphies of Plato, Aristotle, and the Stoics, who in turn had built on the organic foundation of the pre-Socratics. The winning side, however, opted for a reductionism that located truth in that which could be measured. The orientation that came to be known as the "Scientific Revolution" declared that absolute knowledge is found solely in quantitative data, mathematical formulation, and "laws" of physical forces.

The search for a new worldview began for the best of reasons: The received perceptions of the real were seen to be inadequate. It was time to take a fresh look. Specifically, the Ptolemic cosmology, which held that the sun and all the other planets revolve around the Earth, had yielded a multiplicity of astronomical systems by the time of the Renaissance, none of which could account for or predict the planetary positions with reasonable accuracy. Because the Church needed a more accurate calendar for administrative and liturgical matters, the papacy engaged Copernicus, a Polish astronomer educated in Italy, to correct the unwieldy system. Copernicus suspected that there was an essential error in Ptolemaic cosmology. Moreover, the influence of Renaissance Neo-Platonism, with its roots in the Pythagorean perception of simple, harmonious cosmic order, predisposed him to accept evidence of an elegantly ordered cosmos, free of the clutter of projections that had accumulated in the old system. In addition, he was aware of the Scholastics' critical appraisal of Aristotelian physics.

Eventually Copernicus hypothesized a heliocentric universe in which the Earth was a planet. This new perception of celestial motion immediately explained numerous daily observations and solved problems of astronomical coherence. He presented the new cosmology initially in 1514 in a short manuscript, although he refrained throughout his life from publishing a full explication. Twenty years later, a lecture on the Copernican system was given in Rome to the pope, who approved. The new Gregorian calendar, based on Copernican cosmology, was instituted, and Catholic universities used Copernicus's *De Revolutionibus* in teaching astronomy. In doing so, they continued the flexibility in intellectual speculation that had begun in certain quarters in the medieval Church. In the fifteenth century, for instance, Nicholas of Cusa had rejected the

Ptolemaic explanation of the Earth as being above all else in the cosmic creation.

In the sixteenth century, opposition to the religious implications of Copernican cosmology came initially from the Reformation. Both Luther and Calvin declared that Copernicus flagrantly contradicted the Bible, condemning the Church's acceptance of such heresy as further evidence of its corruption of Christianity through its rapprochement with Greek thought. In contrast, they asserted that proper Christian cosmology was clearly delineated in a passage from the Psalms stating that the world cannot be moved. The sort of metaphysical interpretation of Scripture that was not uncommon in the Church in earlier centuries was now impossible because the emphatic literalism of the Reformation evoked a matching stance within the Renaissance Church.[5] Eventually it condemned the heliocentric hypothesis, but the Copernican diagrams and computations were found to be so efficacious by astronomers that the unexplained contradictions of the new system continued to intrigue them—usually in the safety of private ruminations.

One of the public advocates of Copernican cosmology was Johann Kepler, who initially defended it on the grounds of Pythagorean and Platonic sacred geometry: the perfection of a cosmos based on perfect spheres and the "dignity of the circle." He eventually discovered, however, that the planetary orbits are, in fact, elliptical. Kepler devoted the rest of his life to demonstrating the harmony of the spheres mathematically by introducing computational laws that account for planetary motion. Galileo then contributed both the inventions for astronomical observation and the establishment of the scientific method. Isaac Newton solved the final problem in the Copernican hypothesis by demonstrating that planetary motion was caused by gravitation.

At first, Newton's "laws" of motion were resisted by other scientists. How could action at a distance be possible? Surely this mysterious force Newton called universal gravitation was a regression to occult speculation, an "idol of attraction." Newton had indeed been inspired by theories of sympathies and antipathies in alchemy and Hermetic philosophy. Denying that he was making any metaphysical claim, however, he was able to demonstrate convincingly through empirical observation and deductive rigor that his three laws of motion (inertia, force, and equal reaction) explained the tides, the equinoxes, the trajectory of projectiles—and, quite simply, all celestial and terrestrial mechanisms. These behavioral laws of the cosmos completed the vision of nature as a well-ordered machine, which René Descartes had forcefully declared a few decades earlier. In support of the Copernican universe, Descartes had adapted the ancient concept of atomism, originally proposed by Democritus and then revived during the Renaissance through the works of his ancient successors, Epicurus and Lucretius. Greek atomism held that the Earth and all entities in the cosmos were composed of unchanging, invisibly small, indivisible particles that move about, colliding and combining. Descartes asserted that the Copernican system was yet another example of atomism *and* that atoms, or atomic aggregates called "corpuscles," interact throughout the universe according to mechanical principles. No qualitative changes in the imagined atoms were believed to occur through the mechanistic interactions. In short, no organicism need apply in the Newtonian-Cartesian world.

The eventual dominance of the new world picture caused a rippling effect in all directions that eventually assumed the proportions of a tidal wave. Within science itself, the "new mechanical philosophy" established the framework of acceptable observation not only in physics but also in all other sciences, which henceforth modeled themselves after Newtonian physics. The most exuberant proponent of the new science was Francis Bacon, who declared that natural science would now bring about a utopian future by employing rigorously empirical means of acquiring knowledge. In this way, all confused and prejudicial thinking would fade before the clarity and mastery that would provide man with the material and social counterpart to the spiritual redemption offered by God. Nature was now to be "bound into service" and "made a slave." She would be put upon the "rack" of scientific investigation and made to reveal her secrets. In *New Atlantis*, Bacon's explication of the utopian promise inherent in the new science includes many references characteristic of the Rosicrucian movement, which blended the Hermetic and cabalistic traditions of the Renaissance "magi" with alchemy and mystical Christianity.

Descartes also claimed that the new rationalist methodology would bring human mastery over nature and a new age of human well-being. He solved the growing crisis of skepticism regarding the certainty of any knowledge by applying a "universal mathematics" to the quantitative mechanics by which the physical world (*res extensa*) operates. Intensifying the dualism—particularly the body-mind split—that had been present in Western thought since the Pythagoreans, Descartes asserted that the thinking substance (*res cogitans*) was separate and fundamentally different from the body and the rest of the natural world. Sensations and emotions were merely confused forms or stimulators of the intellect. Through proper force of will, the rationalist intellect could ascertain reliable knowledge of the mechanics of the physical world. (The rigid mind-body split bequeathed to Western physiology by Descartes has finally been corrected by recent discoveries in neurobiology about the role of emotions in neural activity and reasoning, yet another contemporary assertion of the real over mechanistic abstractions.[6])

Newton systematically synthesized Bacon's inductive empiricism and Descartes' deductive mathematical rationalism to arrive at a scientific method even more powerful than the version Galileo had proposed. The triumph of the "new mechanical philosophy" subsequently shaped the course of Western thought. With hindsight, it is obvious that its nominally unfettered investigations and analyses had very firm boundaries indeed: Observations that did not fit the mechanistic model of the real were not admitted. Ironically, the smug assertion of pure empiricism at the heart of the new science persisted in spite of the fact that no empirical evidence existed for belief in atoms as tiny, solid bits of colliding matter. That belief in atomism was held—until the twentieth century!—simply because mechanistic reductionism felt right to the anti-organicist sensibilities of the Scientific Revolution. In addition, the modern break from the Middle Ages continued some of the most problematic assumptions: belief in a masterly source of rigidly determined knowledge and absolute truth, controlled by an elite male priesthood. The players changed, but access to "truth" remained fiercely controlled.

Eventually that sense of the truth was rejected even by some philosophers who had initally accepted scientific rationalism with great enthusiasm. Kant, for instance, lost his enthusiasm for the pure reason emanating from the Newtonian cosmology on the grounds that we can know about the natural world only what the categories of our minds allow us to realize. These categories rigidly separate our cognitive faculties, he believed, into the *formal* (conceptual, intellectual) and the *material* (perceptual, sensible). More dualism from yet another Enlightenment luminary!

Francis Bacon, by the way, used similar language while serving on courts during the witch-hunt hysteria as he did when intellectually aroused over the thought of putting nature on the rack and torturing her. The witch hunts, known today as the Burning Times, spanned the same period as the Reformation and the Scientific Revolution in Britain and on the

Continent. As European men asserted their power over the world through the new science and nascent imperialism, they also tightened their control over women. (The patriarchal dimension of European history had earlier roots, of course. For an analysis, see Appendix B in my book *States of Grace.*) New national laws denied women control of their property and earnings, barred them from higher education and professional training, outlawed their efforts to control their own fertility, and placed them under the authority of their husbands. The new modern order was enforced by a system of sexual terrorism, in which hundreds of thousands of women, mostly in the German principalities, were accused of witchcraft, tortured into signing confessions, and then further tortured in a public ritual before being burned at the stake. (Some men were also burned, but in far fewer numbers and for different reasons, usually homosexuality.) Often the women selected for persecution were older women who, while financially dependent, had authority in their communities as healers, midwives, or advisors. Frequently they were outspoken wives, who were considered monstrous shrews or unnatural traitors to their husbands. Certainly the murderous witch-hunts of the sixteenth and seventeenth centuries convinced women to keep a low profile in early modern Europe for many generations thereafter.[7]

In nearly all areas of human endeavor, the new science was accepted as the guiding authority by which a new, superior civilization would be born. The last of the four foundational movements that created the modern worldview, the Enlightenment, extended the Newtonian sense of an atomistic world operating by mechanistic laws, to a new understanding of religion, politics, economics, education, and the very nature of being human. The human was now seen as a biomechanical machine, as was the entire universe. The panentheistic medieval Christian world, wherein all creation was infused with God's presence and direction, was replaced by a sense of a clockwork-like universe that had been set in motion by God in the beginning but otherwise operated autonomously, according to Newtonian laws. From this minimalist version of Christianity, called "Deism," the further move into an entirely secular worldview was compelling for most intellectuals by the later stages of the Enlightenment.

In the emergent modern political theory, John Locke built upon Thomas Hobbes's assertion of humans' essential separateness: life as "solitary" and "brutish" in its natural state, requiring the stability of an absolute monarchy to lift human existence above a war of all against all.

Influenced by Newtonian atomism, Locke agreed with Hobbes that humans have no inherent interrelatedness but that they can come together to form a society through the understanding of a "social contract." The reasons for doing so, he felt, are to establish order and to protect private property. The social contract proposed by Jean-Jacques Rousseau terminated the natural state of humans, which he saw as noble and uncorrupted, but enabled them to enjoy political liberty and civil equality. Since he perceived society as being prior to government, rulers have no part in the social contract, as they are merely servants of the people, in whose "general will" all sovereignty resides. Other pioneers of modern political theory in the eighteenth century based their models upon "natural laws." The concept of "inalienable rights" of all (white, male) humans seemed "self-evident" to Thomas Jefferson and the other sons of the Enlightenment who framed the political structure of the United States. The Founding Fathers, by the way, were also caught up in the "Egyptian Wisdom" concerning the unbounded potential of man: They made a (Masonic) pyramid the central image in the "Great Seal" of the new political order, dated 1776, which appears on our one-dollar bills.

To enthusiasts of the Enlightenment, natural laws and self-evident truths existed in each of the separate spheres of human endeavor: science, politics, and economics. The task of the Age of Reason was to effect rational "social engineering" by redesigning all institutions and practices to properly reflect the natural laws. In this way, people could become free of the repressive conditioning of the past and experience individual liberty. Of course, social engineering also lent itself to more instrumental forms of human transformation—the training and controlling of various classes for their respective roles in the technocratic societies that would carry on both the left and right branches of the Enlightenment ideal.

The scientistic rationale was particularly influential in the creation of modern economic theory. Adam Smith began with an assumption of Newtonian atomism as the essential nature of human society: an aggregate of thoroughly unconnected, discrete beings buying or selling labor, services, or goods. Was there some sort of invisible force organizing all that interaction into a coherent social mechanism, something akin to the Newtonian discovery of gravitational action at a distance? Why, yes! It was the "hidden hand" of the market.

Smith, a Scottish professor of moral philosophy, supplied a rational, mechanistic, and confidently optimistic science of economic activity that fit perfectly with the intellectual tastes of the Enlightenment and interpreted the alarming upheavals of the Commercial Revolution as precursors to the dynamic evolution of social wealth and well-being. Beginning in the sixteenth century, with the expansion of enclosure acts, which privatized land that had long been used in common, and with the displacement of scores of thousands of farmers whose landlords had switched to raising sheep in order to export wool, the disruption of stable conditions spread throughout Britain. Premodern, Christian disapproval of the avarice of accumulation gave way to the humanist sense of unbounded human potential: Usury became acceptable, land and labor became commodities, newly centralized nation-states sought gold for their national market through foreign exploration, and the market system was born.

Smith propounded natural laws behind the new reality. The Law of Accumulation acknowledged, with some distaste, the natural greed of capitalists and all other humans. (Like Edmund Burke, Smith held a far less sanguine view of human nature than Rousseau's "noble savage.") Smith asserted that the personal drive to accumulate wealth, however, was transformed into a social benefit by the market since capital is reinvested in innovation and expansion. Competition in the market was the built-in safeguard against too much accumulation by an individual. Accumulation through dynamic expansion would be halted when the need for more workers drove up wages and eroded profits. The "natural" correction to such stagnation was the Law of Population: Laborers, like any other commodity, were produced according to demand. If wages were high, the working class would increase in number; if wages fell, the number of upcoming workers (children) would decrease. As long as the great "natural" laws of the market mechanism were not interferred with, progress for all of society would inevitably result. In Smith's view, the emergent capitalism was gloriously rational. Oddly, for a moral philosopher, he seemed unconcerned with the hideous working and living conditions of factory workers and day laborers.

Writing in an era of preindustrialized capitalism, Smith was, of course, unable to imagine the huge concentrations of wealth and power that would develop and the devastation of nature's life-support systems. His ideal was a market composed of small-scale, owner-managed enterprises located in communities where the owners resided. In spite of the fact that Smith was strongly opposed to any monopolistic power, his assertion that laissez-faire capitalism is brilliantly suited to evoking the unfettered potential of human society has long been touted by the centralizing forces of the corporate world in a constant struggle to beat back any regulation of commerce. His sense of evolutionary progress guided by natural laws and mechanistic forces was embraced by the Victorian age, including two subsequent architects of the modern worldview: Karl Marx declared that he had discovered the "laws of motion" (in keeping with the Hegelian sense of dialectical mechanism) that reveal how capitalism eventually proceeds to its doom, and Charles Darwin sought the invisible hand that determines evolution of species, locating it in the brute struggle of "natural selection."

By the end of the eighteenth century, the major components of the modern worldview and the modern condition were in place, yielding an era of technological innovation and democratic reforms that continue to shape the lives of ever-increasing numbers of people worldwide. Its successes are well known, but the ideologies of denial that were inherent in the triumph of modernity now loom large in our contemporary crises. Modern man emerged as a detached manipulator of the rest of the natural world, bringing to bear a humanist focus that located all value in human projects. His secular, rationalist sensibilities created an ideal of liberalism based on the individual pursuit of self-interest. His unsentimental recognition of *homo economicus* cleared away past restraints with a new dynamism: If each man sought his best monetary advantage, all society would benefit. Having advanced beyond the muddled, infantile beliefs of former times, modern man would be supremely poised to lead the way into unprecedented moral and material progress.

As soon as the ink was dry—on the U.S. Constitution, for instance—the assumptions of denial and exclusion buried in the elevated ideals of Enlightenment declarations became painfully apparent to a great many people who had sacrificed mightily for the new political order. The rights and privileges of citizenship in many areas of that grand Enlightenment experiment, the United States of America, were reserved for white male property owners. To the Enlightenment mind, no one else possessed the unsentimental rationality and essential competitiveness to make the new political economy succeed. Citizenship and political leadership were vested in those most inherently worthy. What could be more rational?

Even the facade of objectivist rationalism soon shattered when the French Revolution descended into the Terror. Idealistic people throughout

Europe, especially the young, had invested great hope in the French struggle to establish a new age of humankind. When they saw the dream defeated by the worst traits of human behavior, many of them reconsidered the premises of the Enlightenment project. The English Romantics, for instance, concluded that political change devoid of spiritual transformation would always collapse back into destructive patterns. The Romantic movement, in fact, mounted a comprehensive critique of the mechanistic, reductionist, and solipsistic humanism of the modern worldview. This and subsequent oppositional movements, which are considered in Chapter 4, succeeded in convincing people in limited circles of the need for corrective efforts, but it was the emergent realities of the modern condition itself that caused the greatest range of disillusionment with modernity.

Only a few decades after the persuasive boosterism of Adam Smith's *The Wealth of Nations* had appeared in 1776, belief in social evolution through market forces had yielded to the social crises and disruptions caused by industrialism, exploitation, and the political struggle between the landlords of vast agricultural tracts and the factory owners in the new manufacturing sector. Everyone but the owners of the "dark satanic mills" saw the polluting factories that devoured childen as well as parents as a blight upon the Midlands. Everyone realized, eventually, that the ravages of industrial*ism*—an emergent ideology in its own right—might be managed and ameliorated through hard-won reform and regulation, or even revolution, but would forever be a problem in our midst. Whether politically right or left, all modern institutions would conform to the needs of industrialism and the logic of its expansion.

In the nineteenth century, economic expansion through imperialism was seen as the panacea for the mounting social problems. This focus created new problems, however, such as German anger in the period leading up to World War I over the short shrift Germany had been given in the Europeans' carving up of Africa. The Great War itself, devouring almost an entire generation of young men in Germany, France, and Britain, signaled the end of most Europeans' belief in the Enlightenment dream: the perfectability of the human through social engineering and the modern state. All those lofty ideals and principled declarations had led to unprecedented carnage in the trenches. In the decade that followed, a mood of extreme pessimism settled over Europe.

In Germany, widespread economic hardship, resentment over the terms of the Treaty of Versailles, and disgust with the political chaos of the Weimar government fanned the flames of growing discontent over the disruptive effects of industrialism and modernization. Those effects were particularly intense because Germany had industrialized comparatively late but very rapidly, increasing its coal production fourfold and its steel production tenfold between 1880 and 1913. Population had increased rapidly, and millions had moved to the cities. The loss of authentic community (*Gemeinschaft*) was linked to the spreading influence of the impersonal, abstract commercial society (*Gesellschaft*). From these currents of dissatisfaction the National Socialist German Workers Party (Nazis) emerged, faltered, and then finally gained control of the government. Because their self-declared propaganda so successfully manipulated people's discontent with modernity, their tactics comprise a cautionary tale. However, it is quite possible to draw the wrong lessons from the rise of the Nazis. In Germany today, members of the left and other rationalists, for instance, insist that Nazism resulted from "the natural progression of capitalism" plus the influence of "the irrational" (spirituality that honored nature, body, and community in ways that replaced rational politics). Therefore, any talk of spirituality or a sacred dimension of nature will lead us straight back to fascism, according to these "politically sophisticated" analysts.

I find it fascinating that an analysis with such a gaping hole at the center could gain such popularity, much like the similar conclusion that opposition to modernity is inherently reactionary and leads to fascism. Both of those conclusions ignore the ways in which people's discontents with modernity were *used* by the Nazis in their quest for domination. What was the solution to social atomism and alienated liberal individualism? One should submerge personal identity in the greater entity, the German *Volk*, whose spirit is expressed in the *Völkisch* Nazi party. What was the solution to the spiritual barrenness of the modern, materialist view of nature? The realization that German forests, German soil, and German bodies were sacred and were an especially graced part of the larger cosmic order. What was the solution to the reductionism of liberal-rationalist thought? The understanding that Greek, French (Enlightenment), and British (Adam Smith) bases of rational thought were being imposed on Germany when, in fact, true German rationality was unique to the German *Völkisch* experience.[8] What was the solution to religious sectarianism that was powerless in the face of the destructive dynamics of modernization?

The redirecting of one's faith to "Positive Christianity," or the "religion of blood," and to the inseparable trinity of state, movement, and *Volk*. What was the solution to the "spiritual bankruptcy" caused by the material "progress" of capitalist industrialism? The (early) Nazi call for profit-sharing for workers, an end to profiteering, and the coherence of all work in service to heroic nationalism that would lead the world. What was the solution to the transcendental rationalism that supposedly guides modern European democracies but had actually sapped the strength of the German spirit, making it "effeminate" and powerless to compete in modern geopolitics and economics? A radical renewal of the spirit of the *Volk*, drawing upon the "fire spirit" of pre-Christian Germanic myths and the Nazi ideal of "Strength through Joy." How could the West be saved from the disintegrative forces of selfish individualism, materialism, rationalism, and industrialism? Only if Germans would make the sacrifices called for by their unique historical role during the Weimar crisis of modernity and establish the glorious Thousand-Year Reich.

All concerns about modern life were supposedly resolved by National Socialism. The concerns themselves and the articulation of them did not "lead to fascism." Rather, fascism triumphed because sufficient numbers of people enthusiastically accepted one cynical party's ideological response to those concerns. Of course, after the mid-1930s the party leadership did not hesitate to focus its efforts on the enormous industrial task of building up a modern arsenal. The modern mindset also figured largely in the monstrously efficient mass-murder of six million Jews: the detached, instrumental rationality that had been instilled by modern bureaucratic institutions; the death camps as managerial industrialism; the rational engineering solutions to physical problems; the bureaucratic thoroughness in accomplishing evacuation from Jewish homes; the efficient use of mass transport (railway freight cars) to move large numbers of people; and the medical experiments performed on prisoners to advance modern science. These elements led the sociologist Zygmunt Bauman to conclude, in *Modernity and the Holocaust* (1989), "The 'Final Solution' did not clash at any stage with the rational pursuit of efficient, optimal goal-implementation. On the contrary, it arose out of a genuinely rational concern, and it was generated by bureaucracy true to its form and purpose."[9] He further concludes that the rules of instrumental rationality are incapable of preventing "Holocaust-style phenomena" because there is nothing in those rules that disqualifies "Holocaust-style methods of 'social engineering' as improper or the actions they serve as irrational."[10]

The cold-blooded dimension of instrumental rationality also became painfully apparent to millions of people in modern nation-states committed to "scientific Marxism." After the break-up of the European empires following World War II, however, a different sort of disillusionment with modernity gradually emerged, this time from the Third World. (The Third World is also called the "Three-Quarters World," as a reminder of the portion of the world's population who live in the "developing" and indigenous nations; the figure is actually closer to 85 percent.) The postcolonial societies, for the most part, were not subjected to the totalitarian hell of concentration camps or gulags. Theoretically, they experienced the very best side of modernity through exposure to the dynamism of European commerce, rational governance, and indominable science. Something vital was lost, though, when the modern scientistic worldview pushed aside all vernacular knowledge of body, nature, and place. The loss was not some sort of ethereal *Volkgeist* but, rather, extremely pragmatic knowledge situated in a web of living relationships.

One example of this critique is an anthology from India titled *Science, Hegemony, and Violence: A Requiem for Modernity* (1988).[11] In an essay called "Reductionist Science as Epistemological Violence," the physicist Vandana Shiva deplores the sweeping dismissal of local knowledge— about agriculture, for instance—that is enforced by the scientific arrogance inherent in the modern model of development. She traces the "structural violence" resulting from a rigidly reduced range of acceptable knowledge, not only among the "alleged beneficiaries" but also among scientists themselves. In "Science as a Reason of the State," Ashis Nandy asserts that the legitimacy of the postcolonial state rests on the unrestrained authority of scientists, national security experts, and development specialists. He asks, "Can one not go beyond shedding tears copiously over the misuse of modern science by wicked politicians, militarists and multinational corporations, and scrutinize the popular culture and philosophy of modern science? May the sources of violence not lie partly in the nature of science itself? Is there something in modern science itself which makes it a human enterprise particularly open to cooptation by the powerful and the wealthy?"[12] Like many other Third World critics of modernity, these Indian analysts advocate not a rejection of modern science but a creative option that would integrate significant knowledge from premodern, nonmodern, and postmodern science as well.

A critique of modernity has also arisen in recent years from within indigenous nations as part of the effort to "decolonize" their cultures. Much of this thinking avoids both an uncritical acceptance of the modern worldview (being "good subjects") and a reactionary rejection of all things modern, a constant rebelling within the parameters of the colonizing world (being "bad subjects"). Instead, the goal is to become "non-subjects" by thinking and acting in ways that are far removed from those of the modern West and that honor the native worldview as a legitimate frame of reference from which dialogue with other cultures may take place.[13] One of the groups developing this option is *Proyecto Andino de Technologias Campesinas* (PRATEC) in the Peruvian Andes, a non-governmental organization (that is, an NGO recognized by the United Nations) devoted to research and writing about Andean technologies, knowledge, and worldview. Its members advocate neither a cultural fundamentalism nor a "hybrid" culture of modern and nonmodern but, rather, "cultural affirmation" that questions the evolutionary inevitability of "progress" and modernization. At the heart of their dialogic openness is a spiritual conversation of remarkable attentiveness to all beings of the Earth community—rivers, animals, other peoples.[14]

Inside the Western tradition, a different sort of critique of the modern era has emerged over the past two decades, involving a surprising number of intellectuals in a circumscribed rebellion that the above-mentiond native theorists would surely perceive as "bad subjecthood" because it rebels within the worldview it attacks. The critical orientation known as "deconstructive postmodernism," "constructionism," or "constructivism" asserts that there is *nothing but* "social construction" (of concepts such as language, knowledge systems, and culture) in human experience. That is, humans have *no* experiences or sensations that are not the result of social construction, all of which form a mesh of relationships established so as to achieve and maintain power on behalf of the dominant forces. We can know nothing of nature or our bodies, for instance, except what our received cultural constructions project onto them. After all, our thoughts are structured by a particular language. Since all knowledge and "truth" are relative, our actual reality is utter groundlessness. Modern selfhood is created and regulated by institutions, child-rearing, and ongoing socialization that enforce the modern order. The trouble with modernity, say the deconstructionists, is its oppressive—if often subtle—power mechanisms, which "totalize" the particular and the individual with the ploy of "fictive unity," such as "metanarratives" about the "brotherhood of man" or the "scientific temperament" of modern man. Every belief or concept in modern life can be "deconstructed" to reveal the machinations of power and control behind it. Systems of knowledge, or anything else, are actually a power play, according to deconstructionists.

The philosophical core of deconstructive postmodernism is the rejection of any sense of the "Real," as is illustrated by the following composite declaration drawn from leading theorists by Jane Flax, a proponent of this orientation:

> According to postmodernists, Western philosophy has been under the spell of the "metaphysics of presence" at least since Plato. Most Western philosophers took as their task the construction of a philosophic system in which something Real would and could be re-presented in thought. This Real is understood as an external or universal subject or substance, existing "out there," independent of the knower. The philosopher's task is to "mirror," register, mimic, or make present the Real. Truth is understood as correspondence to it.
>
> For postmodernists, an unacknowledged will to power lies concealed within and generates claims to truth. The quest for the Real conceals most Western philosophers' desire, which is to master the world once and for all by enclosing it within an illusory but absolute system they claim re-presents or corresponds to a unitary Being beyond history, particularity, and change. To mask his idealizing desire, the philosopher must assert that this Being is not the product, artifact, or effect of a particular set of historical or linguistic practices. It can only be the thought of the Real itself. . . . In addition, they [deconstructive postmodernists] claim there is no stable, unchanging, and unitary Real against which our thoughts can be tested. . . . . Unity appears as an effect of domination, repression, and the temporary success of particular rhetorical strategies. According to postmodernists, all knowledge construction is fictive and nonrepresentational. . . . We need to learn to make claims on our own and others' behalves and to listen to those that differ from ours, knowing that ultimately there is nothing that justifies them beyond each person's own desire and need and the discourses which both generate and support such desire.[15]

I cannot help but notice that the deconstructionists have thrown out the baby with the bathwater. Instead of denying human access to the real, why have they not focused their railing for the past twenty-five years on *the violation of the real* by various philosophers' claims that it is an external substance that exists separately from us? Why have they not directed their indignation at the *diminution of the real* to "an illusory but absolute system" proclaimed by certain philosophers? Why have they not poured their scorn upon the *distortion of the real* in Plato's anti-ecological sense of a "stable, unchanging" entity? Why do they express contempt for any correspondence theories of epistemology that involve attentive engagement with the real? *Because the deconstructionists are moderns.* They have been socialized and educated in the scientistic-humanist worldview, which is dedicated to the denial of the power and presence of nature. The myriad ways in which "social construction" and the deconstructionists' own individual experiences are embedded in the processes of the real—the dynamic physicality of the cosmos—have, in all likelihood, never crossed their minds. Consequently, when they perceive that self-aggrandizing patriarchal philosophers have installed "logocentrism at the heart of Western culture" based on the "collapsing of Reason and the Real," they experience not the slightest hesitation in dismissing the real along with the power plays.

This supposedly radical form of postmodernism captured the hearts and minds of hundreds of thousands of modern academics and other intellectuals because it stays comfortably within the essential parameters of the modern worldview by failing to challenge the core discontinuities imposed, or intensified, by that worldview: between humans and nature, body and mind, and self and the rest of the world. Modernity situates humankind in a glass box *on top of* nature, insisting on a radical discontinuity between humans and the rest of the natural world. It frames the human story apart from the larger unfolding story of the Earth community. To be truly *post*modern is to reject that discontinuity by opening the box to connect anew with our larger context: the Earth, the cosmos, the sacred whole. Yet the deconstructionists move in the opposite direction, taking the focus down from the level of human projects to the level of "language games" (construction of concepts). They uphold the modern body-mind split by asserting an inner version of social construction whereby culture (mind) projects assumptions and other concepts onto dumb matter (the body)—the usual one-way construction of meaning, according to both Cartesian and deconstructionist thought. The inauthentic individual, trapped by the language games and power plays of his or her culture, feels more acutely than ever the radical discontinuity between self and the rest of the world.

Besides the fact that deconstructionist postmodernism continues some of the most problematic strains of modern thought, its widespread embrace as a radically *new* analysis of the modern condition is exceedingly puzzling. When an aspect of my previous book required that I immerse myself in deconstructionist-postmodern works in the late 1980s,[16] I was often reminded of the response made by Samuel Johnson after reading a manuscript: He was pleased to tell the author that he found the work both good and original, adding that, regrettably, what is good is not original and what is original is not good. As I have noted, the deconstructionists' central assertion that there is *nothing but* social construction in human experience is "not good" because it is astoundingly solipsistic (on the collective level of a society rather than an individual). Surely their replacing biological determinism with social constructionism presents too limited a dialectic. On the other hand, the deconstructionists have contributed a number of significant insights about the ways in which power dynamics are structured—while rarely, if ever, acknowledging that that sort of analysis was begun long before the new theory arrived from Paris, spreading through the British and American groves of academe with much bravado in the early 1970s. For many years the deconstructionists cited chapter and verse of Derrida, Foucault, Lyotard, and other "indefensible French"[17] without ever mentioning the anti-foundationalism present in certain quarters of Western philosophy since the Greeks, the loss of faith in scientific positivism that began in the late nineteenth century, the cantankerous perspectivalism of Nietzsche, the totalizing "language games" illuminated by Wittgenstein, the sociology of knowledge, and the various political critiques of rationalist, patriarchal, racist framings of reality that were put forth by grassroots movements of the 1960s.

Today the aggressive presence of deconstructionism that shook up so many academic departments in the 1980s has receded. In some areas, it has disappeared altogether but often for reasons other than a substantive critique of its shortcomings. Sometimes—in the art world, for instance— the deconstructionists' perspective simply reached the saturation point and lost "the shock of the new." Sometimes opposition came in the form of fellow leftists defending modernity. (The ranks of deconstructionism included many formerly Marxian academics because it was an easy step from viewing all social relationships as "mysifications" masking the "forces and relations of production" to viewing them somewhat more broadly as masking "social construction" in order to hide the power dynamics.) Left theorists such as Juergen Habermas assert that the "modern project" is merely incomplete, not deserving of rejection by the deconstructionists. Marshall Berman insists that modern, left politics carries on the courageous smashing of the status quo to assure that the new can be born. He sees any rejection of the ideologies of modernity as a collapse into the spiritual and as an immature desire for "a secure place in the universe."[18] Other left activists bristled at deconstructionism's attack on science as largely a social construction, for that sort of critique severs the comforting association of rationalist socialism and rationalist science as the guiding lights of the modern project. One left physicist, in fact, went so far as to submit a deftly satirical article on the social construction of *pi* and other scientific concepts to a left-deconstructionist journal, *Social Text*. The editors unwittingly published the spoof in spring of 1996, mistaking it for the standard deconstructionist "revelation," put forth this time by a scientist who had apparently seen the light. When the author explained his hoax, in a different journal, as a defense of the noble socialist-rationalist-scientific trinity, the deconstructionist folks were unamused.[19] A far nastier attack on deconstructionists was mounted by two left academics in *Higher Superstition: The Academic Left and Its Quarrels with Science* (1994).[20]

Another reason deconstructionism has lost steam is that those among its proponents who are concerned with extending social justice came to realize the reactionary nature of "subverting" all theory on the grounds that any overarching "metanarratives" are odious because they crush internal differences and particularities. All analyses of patriarchal socialization, corporate machinations in the Three-Quarters World, or the maintenance of racism were suddenly declared not only unsophisticated but inherently oppressive.[21] In addition, the deconstructionist exposé and celebration of the self as being nothing but multiple, shifting identities wore thin, as adherents gradually concluded that such a model plays into the "logic of late capitalism" in that individualist expressionism is the linchpin of the manipulation of desire by advertisers in a consumerist culture. It was finally determined that a little internal coherence was necessary for a self to resist such manipulation. "Reconceptualizing" one's thoughts as often as possible, as deconstructionists used to recommend, just wouldn't do. Both of those internal rejections of deconstructionist ideology address only strategic problems with the position. It is rare to encounter a deconstructionist who can break out of that closed circle of assumptions and counter it with *felt experience of the real* that contradicts the theory that there is nothing but fragmentation and particularity in human experience. Surely some internal coherence has been experienced by even the most staunchly deconstructionist self, yet the ideology of denial forbids that realization.

The assumptions underlying the deconstructionist view of reality linger on in surprisingly wide circles of influence in the 1990s. People who would never label themselves "deconstructionist" now accept as obvious truth the notion that human interaction with nature is a one-way process of projecting concepts, that any talk of coherence in the biosphere is a projection, and that beliefs and values are merely relative and have no validity other than their own invention. These perspectives—and the enormous body of theoretical work from which they are derived—are based on a *formalist* critique of modernity. The *forms* of organization, power, control, coercion, and all modes of social construction are the focus. Every relationship is seen to be political—that is, about power. While I agree wholeheartedly with the need to comprehend the power dynamics of our era as thoroughly as possible, an analysis that ignores the *content* of the modern worldview, especially the core discontinuities, is surely skewed in an odd direction.

While deconstructionists reject modernity simply because it makes use of "metanarratives" (never mind their content, they say, since all universals must be false), other critics today do indeed analyze the ideological content. Stephen Toulmin, for instance, argues in *Cosmopolis: The Hidden Agenda of Modernity* (1990) that the first of modernity's four foundational movements, humanism, was entirely admirable but that things went very wrong with the advent of the Scientific Revolution and its "mechanical philosophy." He admires the openness and curiosity exhibited by Renaissance humanists with regard to all things human, ranging from "exotic" cultures to "local, timely, practical issues." He deplores the shift to a philosophical research program with an exclusively general, timeless, and theoretical focus. The "hidden agenda" was not only to resolve the "quest for certitude" about valid knowledge with a rigid, scientistic determination of truth but also to provide a new political order for modern nation-states emerging from the Thirty Years War. The new scientistic rationalism provided proof of a cosmopolis (a rational social order in accord with the structure of nature) that is based on stability and hierarchy, from the astronomical universe to the patriarchal family. While this political dimension of Toulmin's interpretation is accurate, the notion of humanism and "mechanical philosophy" being oppositional is belied by their happy marriage in the Age of Enlightenment. In turning to Greek philosophy for their orientation, the Renaissance humanists rooted their bid for intellectual freedom in the core discontinuities, which were not only maintained but intensified by the new science and its new philosophy. Even those humanists who paid some attention to nature did so with the sensibility of detached observers because a deeper connection had long since been lost.

Toulmin's book is but one example of the growing number of analyses of modernity and suggestions for corrective efforts. At conferences on this subject I have noticed a few patterns in all the intellectual fervor. First, a certain level of critique of modernity is almost universally acceptable as the sophisticated position in such circles, but a deeper challenge to the core assumptions is often met with an angry defensiveness—and not only from left academics who still cherish poor, bruised modernity as the noble achievement of scientific rationalism. Second, in the defensiveness about modernity a gender correlation is not uncommon. The ideal of the free-wheeling Autonomous Individual and the socialization of boys in patriarchal societies has always been a cozy fit. The fact that even the crown jewel of Enlightenment political thought—the concept of universal human rights—was purposively withheld by legal fiat from applying to women's beatings, loss of property, exploitation, and disenfranchisement *for two hundred years* of Enlightenment "bliss" inclines women to conclude that something is very wrong at the heart of the rationalist modern worldview.[22] African-Americans, Asian-Americans, and native peoples tend to share an experiential sense that the problem with modernity is far deeper than mere oversight.

A third pattern of division among content-based critiques of modernity is the matter of whether the analyst feels that anything was lost in the passage from premodern to modern. Many people in the social sciences, whether they are deconstructionists or not, remain within the Marxian ideological framework that was prevalent in the sixties and seventies: Modernity was preceded by a swamp of superstition (religion) about which a rational person today need not think twice. Others, however, share Max Weber's regret that the premodern spiritual richness was replaced by the rationalist ethic in Protestant asceticism, an ideal of self-control that eventually spawned a rigidly ordered, regularized, bureaucratized structure of modern institutions in both the public and private sector. In 1905 Weber observed that "the rosy blush of religious asceticism's laughing heir, the Enlightenment, seems also to be irretrievably fading." He summarized twentieth-century modernity in this way: "Specialists without spirit, sensualists without heart; this nullity imagines that it has attained a level of civilization never before achieved."[23]

The recent work of an admirer of Weber is particularly relevant here because his historical study of the making of the modern self has become widely influential.[24] Charles Taylor, a professor of moral philosophy, sees modern identity as shaped by both the disengaged, instrumental rationalism of the Enlightenment *and* the orientation that arose to challenge it: Romantic "expressivism." Like Toulmin, Taylor believes there is something amiss in our modern disconnection from nature. He goes even further, wishing we could reconnect with a sense that "the world is not simply an ensemble of objects for our use, but makes a further claim on us." He cites the example of Rilke's phrase "making inward" as an ontological and spiritual "demand" emanating from the world for attention, scrutiny, and respect toward what is there[25] Yes! How poignant, then, and how reflective of the grip of the core discontinuities on our modern minds that even this sensitive pilgrim arrives at a solution that maintains the split between self and the rest of the world: Declaring that we are now in an age in which "a publicly accessible cosmic order of meanings is an impossibility," our only hope for correcting the disengaged consciousness of modernity, according to Taylor, is to focus on new languages of "personal resonance."[26] The self as Lone Cowboy also informs his modern interpretation of the goals of Romanticism and Transcendentalism: "self-expression, self-realization, and self-fulfillment, discovering authenticity." Those were indeed the *forms* of Romantic activity, but the *content* was spiritual communion with the sacred whole. The Romantics, like Taylor, take as a given the modern, Western sense of the discrete individual. Admirably, they believe that the Lone Cowboy can act in such ways as to engage spiritually and ontologically with our larger context: nature and cosmos. Regrettably, however, that approach keeps us trapped in the core discontinuity.

As will come as no surprise by now, I believe that the trouble with the "radical break" effected by modernity in the fifteenth through eighteenth centuries is that it was not nearly radical enough. It continued and inflated the bad habits in Western thought begun with the Greek rationalist and idealist separation from the earlier organicism and holism. Since the core discontinuities informed every single creation of modernity's four foundational movements, the only sort of *post*modern transformation that stands a chance of correcting the tragic errors is one that is profoundly *ecological.* By the term "ecological," I do not have in mind its common reduction to "environmentalism" or even a fuller sense of "ecology" that still lacks historical, political, and philosophical knowledge of the crises of modernity. Nothing short of a broad and deep engagement with the real will do. The sort of postmodernism I have in mind could just as easily be called "cosmological" since all Earth processes are also cosmological processes. The difference is merely one of scale and perspective. Yet "cosmological" carries connotations of the remoteness of astronomy, whereas "ecological," though often misunderstood in narrow and shallow ways, has the ring of the familiar and the immediate.

Foremost, "ecological postmodernism" changes the essential gestalt. Instead of perceiving ourselves as social "atoms" colliding and combining with other discrete "atoms" in a human society that uses and projects concepts onto its background matter (nature), we perceive an unbroken continuity of cosmos/Earth/continent/nation/bioregion/community/neighborhood/family/person. These are the extended boundaries of the self. Our field, our grounding, and our being is the cosmos. Moreover, we finally slough off the modern obsession with escaping from nature and realize that all human endeavor is derivative of the Earth community, not the other way around. As the "geologian" Thomas Berry reminds us, the Earth is the great economy, the great educator, the great healer, the great organizer, the great artist and storyteller, the great experimentor, and the great blend of cosmic novelty and continuity. Our institutions and actions can fit well or badly into that larger context, our extended sense of being. Ecological postmodernism, then, replaces groundlessness with groundedness, supplanting freedom *from* nature with freedom *in* nature. This orientation acknowledges the enormous role of social construction of concepts in shaping human experience, but it also acknowledges our constitutive embeddedness in subtle bodily, ecological, and cosmological *processes*.

The following comparisons with modern and deconstructionist-postmodern thought serve to situate ecological postmodernism. I have included a column of deconstructionist thought, even though its influence is fading, in order to clarify that its version of postmodernism is only one subset. Unfortunately, many people use the word "postmodernism" as a synonym for "deconstructionism."

Modern	Deconstructionist Postmodern	Ecological Postmodern
Metanarrative: salvation, progress	None (They're all power plays.)	The cosmological unfolding
Truth mode: objectivism	Extreme relativism	Experientialism
World = a collection of objects	An aggregate of fragments	A community of subjects
Reality = fixed order	Social construction	Dynamic relationship
Sense of self: socially engineered	Fragmented	Processual
Primary truth: the universal	The particular	The particular-in-context
Grounding: mechanistic universe	None (total groundlessness)	Cosmological processes
Nature as opponent	Nature as wronged object	Nature as a subject
Control over the body	"Erasure of the body" (It's all social construction.)	Trust in the body
Science: reductionist	It's only a narrative!	Complexity
Economics: corporate	Postcapitalist	Community-based
Political focus: nation-state	The local	A community of communities of communities
Sense of the Divine: God the Father	"Gesturing toward the sublime"	Creativity in the cosmos, ultimate mystery
Key metaphors: mechanics, law	Economics ("libidinal economy"), signs/coding	Ecology

The label for an orientation such as "ecological postmodernism" is less important than the fact that the perspective is emerging from many directions. In addition, ecological postmodernism shares common ground with other nondeconstructionist forms of postmodernism, as I discovered after I proposed this version in *States of Grace* in 1991. David Ray Griffin, a process philosopher and theologian in the tradition of Alfred North Whitehead, has edited a groundbreaking series of books on "constructive postmodernism" with the State University of New York Press.[27] Richard Falk, a scholar of international law and grassroots political movements, has developed a rich, nondeconstructionist sense of postmodern possibilities in his work.[28] Charles Jencks, an architectural historian, has presented a substantive and energetic overview of such developments in the 1996 edition of *What Is Postmodernism?*[29] In 1992, Jencks and his wife, the late Maggie Keswick Jencks, drew together Griffin, Falk, and myself as the planning group for a series of eight small conferences on the sort of postmodernism we call "reconstructive" or, to use Maggie's term, "restructive." During the course of these conferences, we have witnessed a good deal of interest, including some from formerly intense deconstructionists, in a postmodern option that recognizes the role of social construction but also includes the cosmological, the spiritual, *and* a pragmatic alternative to destructive aspects of modern politics and economics. These dimensions of ecological postmodernism will be considered later on, but I will close this chapter by presenting some of the recent work within this orientation that is nudging aside the old conceptualizations by asserting the real. Such work presents new understandings in answer to very basic questions.

• *What is the nature of language and meaning?*

The modern, objectivist sense of language and meaning derives from the objectivist sense of reality: The world consists of objects that have properties and that stand in various relationships independent of human understanding. Reality has a rational structure, and correct reason mirrors that structure. Words are symbols that gain meaning by directly referring to things in the world, and rational thought is the algorithmic manipulation of such symbols.[30] This orientation is also known as "foundationalism." Its opposite is the extreme relativism espoused by deconstructionists: Language is just a self-referential system of arbitrary symbols (letters and words), and all concepts constructed of those symbols are themselves merely arbitrary social constructions of particular cultures. Meaning is totally relative since all concepts and definitions are simply invented in a certain time and place.

During the past decade, various philosophers have grappled with the problematic assumptions inherent in objectivism, while trying to avoid the slide into extreme relativism. From the vantage of ecological postmodernism, the most interesting work on this subject is the *experientialist* insights developed in collaboration by George Lakoff, a professor of linguistics, and Mark Johnson, a professor of philosophy, as well as the separate work of the phenomenologist David Abram. The context for their work is the sense of language that has prevailed since the seventeenth century until recently—the belief that logical thought processes consist of the rational application of rational concepts. In contrast to conceptual or abstract thought, metaphor was employed for decorative use by poets; traditionally it was considered a "deviant linguistic expression" of no great importance. Lakoff and several others in his field have demonstrated, however, that nearly all conceptual and abstract thought is structured metaphorically. Moreover, he and Johnson have shown that, far from being arbitrary, most of those metaphors derive from *bodily experience in the world*. For instance, cross-culturally, the word "more" (meaning an "increase") is metaphorically oriented to "up" because the level goes up if you add liquid to a vessel or objects to a pile. Numerous examples are categorized into schemata in their jointly authored book *Metaphors We Live By* (1980) and in Johnson's *The Body in the Mind: The Bodily Basis of Meaning, Imagination, and Reason* (1987).[31]

In addition, Lakoff and Johnson develop an experientialist understanding of meaning as grounded in our imaginative projections, including metaphors, that derive from our embodiment. Their sense of "imagination" counters the notion of it as either idiosyncratic and private or a creative breakdown of logical sense. Their central revelation is "embodied understanding," the way in which we make sense of our world by co-constituting meaning through the creative development of conceptual organization that corresponds with our basic level of experience. Objectivity must fit with our "experiential beliefs." (Lakoff and Johnson's contribution to the accumulation of labels for various nondeconstructionist postmodernisms, by the way, is "harmonious postmodernism," based on the experientialist orientation, as distinct from "alienated postmodernism," the better known, relativist orientation.)

The ecological-postmodern realization that perception and language are acts of *participation in nature* is beautifully explored by David Abram in *The Spell of the Sensuous* (1996). Yet another bulwark of the humanist and Enlightenment worldview—that humans are set apart from other species and dumb nature by our capacity for complex language—takes a tumble here. Abram exhibits great sensitivity and insight into the essential reciprocity between our human senses and the sensuous earth. He stresses that language emerged in interaction with the animate world and, as Lakoff and Johnson demonstrate, remains dependent on that world for its coherence. Even though our modern socialization trains us to be detached observers perceiving predictable presentations of reality, Abram lays before us the possibility of effecting a recuperation of our full sensorial dimension of being. We then discover that our sensory perceptions are part of a vast web of sensations and perceptions borne by countless other bodyminds. The biosphere is then "experienced and *lived from within* by the intelligent body" rather than seen as an abstract, objectifying concept borrowed from science.[32]

• *What is the nature of the human psyche?*

As we have seen, the dominant Western view melded Greek rationalism and Augustinian Christianity, arriving at a dualistic perception of the human mind, torn between its rational and spiritual capabilities, on the one hand, and the "corrupting" influences of its senses and emotions, on the other. This dualism was nestled inside a larger, but parallel, version: the split between humans and nature. Modern psychology has presented an array of theories and ministrations for the poor, beleaguered Western mind, but they all "stop at the city limits," as the cultural historian Theodore Roszak has noted. In *The Voice of the Earth* (1992), he proposed a new orientation called "ecopsychology," which has met with an enthusiastic response, perhaps because it has been badly needed for 2500 years. Roszak's initial sketch of this new field addressed the "ecological repression" of industrialized society, the deep root of the collective madness that has polluted and destroyed physical conditions necessary for survival. The alienation this therapy seeks to heal is the fundamental one: alienation between the person and nature. The "ecological ego" matures toward a sense of ethical responsibility toward the planet that is vividly experienced as our ethical responsibility to other people.[33]

From these seeds have grown a crop of books, including a thoughtful anthology titled *Ecopsychology: Restoring the Earth, Healing the Mind* (1995), edited by Roszak and two colleagues. In an essay in that collection, "Where Psyche Meets Gaia," Roszak reflects on the modern sense of boundaries of the self:

The preecological science of Freud's day that became embedded in modern psychological thought preferred hard edges, clear boundaries, and atomistic particularity. It was predicated on the astonishing assumption that the structure of the universe had simply fallen into place by accident in the course of eternity. Accordingly, the psychiatry of the early twentieth century based its image of sanity on that model. The normally functioning ego was an isolated atom of self-regarding consciousness that had no relational continuity with the physical world around it. As late as 1930, well after the Newtonian worldview had been significantly modified and the very concept of atomic matter had been radically revised, Freud, still a respected authority, could write in one of his most influential theoretical pieces: "Normally, there is nothing of which we are more certain than the feeling of our self, of our own ego. This ego appears as something autonomous and unitary, marked off distinctly from everything else . . . . One comes to learn a procedure by which, through a deliberate direction of one's sensory activities and through suitable muscular action, one can differentiate between what is internal—what belongs to the ego—and what is external—what emanates from the outer world. In this way one takes the first step towards the introduction of the reality principle which is to dominate future development."[34]

"One comes to learn a procedure . . . ." These are among the most fateful words Freud ever wrote. Whatever else has changed in mainstream psychological thought, the role Freud assigned to psychotherapy, that of patrolling the "boundary lines between the ego and the external world," remained unquestioned in the psychiatric mainstream until the last generation. Moreover, his conviction that the "external world" begins at the surface of the skin continues to pass as common sense in every major school of modern psychology. The "procedure" we teach children for seeing the world this way is the permissible repression of cosmic empathy, a psychic numbing we have labeled "normal." Even schools of psychotherapy as divergent as humanistic psychology could only think of "self-actualization" as a breakthrough to nothing more than heightened personal awareness. As for the existential therapists, they were prepared to make alienation from the universe the very core of our authentic being.[35]

Rather than the modern belief that sexual and aggressive instincts are the deepest roots of the psyche, ecopsychologists see the psyche as rooted inside a greater intelligence once known as the *anima mundi*, the psyche of the Earth, nurturer of life in the cosmos for billions of years. When our larger identity is realized, the result is spontaneous loyalty . . . and even love.

• *Like psychology, do not all the branches of Western philosophy need to be reconceptualized now that the mechanistic view of human existence is being replaced by scientific and other perceptions of our subtle embeddedness in the cosmological processes?*

I'll say! The analytical and deconstructionist reductions of the human to a language machine should meet with the same epistemological skepticism that dethroned earlier claims of innate ideas and innate reason. If there is anything innate in human experience, it is surely the enormously complex dynamics of embodiment and embeddedness in the cosmological web of processes and relationships. Rather than ignoring those, as has every school of philosophy since the pre-Socratics (except the Stoics and, much later, the phenomenologists), why not bring the fullness of the real to bear on our understanding of ontology, metaphysics, epistemology, ethics, aesthetics, moral philosophy, and political philosophy? The isolation of the new branch called "environmental ethics" merely maintains the anthropocentric boundaries of the traditional branches of philosophy. What is needed, in any case, is a far more radical revisioning than "environmental ethics" is likely to provide. A new challenge to philosophical reductionism has already been issued by a few philosophers who make central our *grounding* in physical reality: Maxine Sheets-Johnstone, Luce Irigaray, Carol Bigwood, David Abram, Mark Johnson, Linda Holler, and others.[36]

Why now? It seems odd, at first thought, that modernity's interlocking ideologies of denial could have held sway for so long, as they reject or devalue a vast amount of human experience. Since those ideologies are the basis of all modern institutions, though, challengers were usually slapped down by guardians of the status quo. Even now, *some* critics of modernity are kept sidelined by others. Take, for instance, this partial list of the "tropes of 'the other of order'" from Zygmunt Bauman's interesting study of modernity, *Modernity and Ambivalence*, in which he concludes that modernity is the obsession with order over (the fear of) looming chaos: illogicality, irrationality, indecisiveness, and ambivalance. At no time does he mention in his analysis that these are traits associated in patriarchal culture with women! (Bauman is merely typical of many male critics of modernity in this respect, not singular.) The roots of the modern ideologies of denial are deeply entwined with, though not limited to, imposing order over *nature and women*. Hence to be truly *post-modern* is to be, among other things, *ecological and feminist*—a calling open to all.

3

PROMETHEUS
ON THE REBOUND

IN THE SOAP OPERA OF OLYMPIAN MYTHOLOGY, Prometheus stole fire from the gods and gave it to humankind. This simple story line was elaborated in the works of Hesiod, Aeschylus, Lucian, Ovid, and others. The fullest treatment during the classical era was Aeschylus's tragic drama *Prometheus Bound,* which opens with the heroic titan being chained to a rocky slope in the Caucasus as the punishment Zeus has imposed for the theft.

Two thousand years later, Renaissance humanism trawled the classics to effect a rebirth of secular learning that would energize its gradual separation from the church. Prometheus was embraced as the man of the hour, for his heroic deed could be emphasized in either of two ways: as a successful strike against tyrants and corrupt institutions or as a bold defiance of divinity itself. Over time, his story became emblematic of the spirit of the modern age.

The Promethean impulse was widely felt to be guiding the Scientific Revolution and the Enlightenment. The antireligious fervor spread to Germany and was expressed by young men in the 1770s through a posture of *Sturm und Drang,* in which the youthful Goethe wrote a prologue for a planned drama about Prometheus, who showered contempt on Zeus and cherished only man-made accomplishments.

Nearly fifty years later, two leading figures of the Romantic movement challenged the triumphalist version of Prometheus's ongoing tale. Mary Shelley's *Frankenstein* was originally subtitled *The Modern Prometheus.* In that novel, science proudly separates matter from spirit and degrades the sanctity of life in its unending quest for power and immortality. Percy Bysshe Shelley then wrote a four-act drama in verse, *Prometheus Unbound*, asserting that a miracle was necessary to redeem (European) civilization in the wake of the mechanistic worldview and the bloody failure of the French Revolution, which had initially been hailed as the most glorious effect of the Enlightenment. In Shelley's play, Jupiter (Zeus) is the spirit of evil and corrupt values. He is overthrown by Prometheus (here the spirit of humankind), who is redeemed through unselfishness, love, and his association with the "Earth Spirits," "Panthea," and other influences.

In this endeavor, as in others, the Romantics did not carry the day. The modern use of Prometheus, slightly updated as a Nietzschean agent of creative destruction and destructive creation, was maintained even into our time. Along the way, various heroes of modernity, such as Gropius and Picasso, overtly identified their self-image as Promethean.

But where is that forceful symbol of modernity today? Certainly not bound. Nor is he triumphantly unbound, a victorious conqueror of body, nature, and place, a freewheeler long since rid of the divine. He is, I believe, bounding between failure and success, bravado and doubt. The outcome of this transitional period is unknown, but the forces pushing and pulling at various possibilities can be discerned. In economics, politics, science and technology, religion, and culture, the smug certainties of modernity are being shaken to their core.

The reaction of modern institutions to current challenges and resistance are strikingly contradictory, even schizophrenic. In the economic sphere, for instance, the World Bank finally responded to grassroots pressure in 1994 by granting its first micro-loans to small-scale entrepreneurs (rather than its usual massively disruptive development schemes, about which more will be said presently)—but 1994 was also the year the renegotiated version of GATT and its new enforcement arm, the World Trade Organization, were approved. (GATT and the WTO, like the World Bank, are descended from the Bretton Woods agreements made shortly after World War II). Under GATT, transnational corporations (TNCs), with their superior size and resources, can easily and quite legally wipe out any competition from local entrepreneurs anywhere in the world. Extending micro-loans for "people-centered development" while enforcing new laws that favor TNC development makes no sense.

In any case, the economic sphere is not the only source of surprising responses to various discontents these days. The scientific establishment is gravely concerned about three developments that undercut its authority: the growing disgruntlement with destructive effects of science and technology, the growing public interest in "supernatural" phenomena, and the growing critique of science as "socially constructed" rather than value-free and culture-free. To address these concerns, the New York Academy of Sciences held a conference in June 1995 titled "The Flight from Science and Reason," which attracted considerable attention from the national media. Since I, too, find it odd and even worrisome that bizarre tales that once would have been relegated to "Ripley's Believe It or Not" in the comic pages are now the subject of sensationalist documentaries on the major television networks as well as cable programming, I share the scientists' concern over such developments. Yet a far larger problem for them is that the modern public has lost a good deal of faith in science as the truth-mode of the modern era. I would think that a public statement from the scientific establishment in 1995, such as that widely publicized conference, would have said something like the following:

Fellow citizens, reality has turned out to be a lot more complex than we thought. Our tradition, always conscientious and hard-working, clung so fiercely to the mechanistic, reductionist model of the natural world for 300 years that we got a lot wrong. Throughout this century, however, we've been gradually correcting our orientation. Now, with the breakthroughs of the new sciences, we're making many exciting discoveries about the subtle interconnectedness in and among our bodies, nature, the biosphere, and the whole universe. This brings us a new respect, which we hope you'll share, for other traditions that perceived that sort of interrelatedness all along, such as religion, art, and native peoples' worldviews.

Just because the natural world is composed of all kinds of subtle processes, however, is no reason to be taken in by people claiming to have superhuman connections to that level of reality. Please be wary of such charlatans, who seem to be on the increase recently.

Our whole society is going through a postmodern transition, a massive sorting process in which we scientists are applying our new knowledge to all kinds of phenomena that were simply denied by the mechanistic model.

The complexity of nonlinear systems! *Who'da thunked it, eh? We're in a real learning mode these days, but we want to proceed carefully. We want to be more open-minded than the mechanistic model allowed us to be in the past, but we will remain rigorous in our reexamination of our perceptions of the natural world. We hope you'll appreciate that rigor because we don't want to replace old misconceptions with new ones.*

Finally, we want to drop the pretense that science is beyond human foibles, as if the scientific method were some sort of transcendent mode of gaining knowledge. Like all other fields of human endeavor, science is subject to political pressures, internal trends, and cultural influences. Moreover, there's no getting around the fact that science sold itself *to political ideologies, militarism, and corporate interests on many occasions. Yet we have the same split within our profession as that in the general public about the morality of such projects: Are they high-minded patriotism or mere opportunism with a Faustian zing?*

Also, we no longer want to claim that scientific knowledge is the only valid kind. Our past arrogance was unwarranted and insulting to nonscientists. Clearly, any grandmother in the ghetto knows more about child development than did the Skinnerian behaviorists, to cite just one example of our "misplaced concreteness."

Our hope is that scientific knowledge will be recognized and honored as a well-intentioned and painstaking exploration of the Earth community and the universe. As we enter the new millennium, we hope to do a better job of sharing with the public all the amazing things we are learning about nature—from the "memory" in cell behavior, to the moons of Jupiter. We believe that art, religion, and science are all humble explorations of our awe-inspiring cosmos. They need not be strangers any longer.

How far is this hypothetical message from the one actually expressed by the conference? Only a few thousand light years. To my utter amazement, the leading scientists quoted in the press coverage of the conference dug in their heels *in the seventeenth century*, declaring that objectivism and positivism are alive and well—particularly in their possession. Most unequivocally believe that there is one path to truth, and that path is science. Venturing into the eighteenth century, several of the scientists linked the supremacy of science with the survival of democracy. Never mind that philosophical training in logic is another source of critical thinking skills. Surely a true democracy also depends on such values as responsibility, caring, ingenuity, and the art of compromise. Is the kind of thinking required for scientific experimentation the same kind required for civic virtue? A forceful *yes* was the answer given to the second question by conference participants who view contemporary scientists as the guardians of "Enlightenment values." This is rather interesting. They do not speak of defending the values of the Scientific Revolution but, rather, those of the subsequent stage of emergent modernity, in which scientific rationalism was extended as the guiding force in all areas of human endeavor, from social engineering to garden design. The Enlightenment was, above all, a scientistic reforming of society.

"The Flight from Science and Reason" conference was actually designed with dual opponents in mind. "Faith healing, astrology, religious fundamentalism, and paranormal charlatanism" was a cluster easily dispensed with.[1] The far larger concern was the current attack by academic critics on science's traditional claim to be a value-free, culture-free method of determining truth. Debunking the debunkers involved citing the most extreme, out-of-context statements from critical philosophers of science and others so that they were made to seem like deranged eccentrics.[2] Limiting the response to straw-man arguments constituted something of a controlled experiment, one might say. Perhaps that tone was encouraged by the initiators of the conference, however, who had adopted a similar methodology in their book, *Higher Superstition: The Academic Left and Its Quarrels with Science* (1994).[3]

Collectively, such skirmishes have become known as the "science wars." The battleground is a new academic field called "social studies of science and technology," often shortened to "science studies." Scholars from various disciplines—many of them deconstructionists—seek to understand how modern science and technology work by analyzing its practices, institutions, metaphors, and assumptions. What could be more *post*modern than probing the hitherto sacrosanct inner workings of science? As elsewhere, though, there are two types of postmodernism involved: the deconstructionist variety and a more grounded, ecological version. Understandably, scientists bristle at investigations by the former because deconstructionists approach any situation with their conclusion already drawn: All systems of knowledge are nothing but a social construction with their own internal logic. As such, science tells us nothing about (the concept of) nature, say the deconstructionists, but only about its own ever-changing narrative. A far less ideological examination of science—one that predates deconstructionism and emerged from the disciplines of philosophy, history, and sociology—is based on the commonsense recognition that our interactions with the rest of nature and our scientific explorations of them are far more than mere social construction of concepts, yet they *are* culturally influenced.[4] So many scholarly, non-deconstructionist studies of the economic and political influences (including patriarchal anxieties) on the history and practice of modern science have been published by now that it seems unbelievable that defenders of science would simply dismiss all of it as moronic gibberish. The choice of models, metaphors, and relevant data is obviously influenced by a number of assumptions that deserve study.[5] Sometimes, buried deep within even the most dismissive counterattacks on critics of science, one finds surprising patches of common ground with "science studies." An example is Gerald Holton's discussion of the crucial role in scientific practice of "the visual imagination," "the metaphoric imagination," and "the thematic imagination" in his most recent book debunking the current "Romantic rebellion against science."[6]

As if barbarians at the gate were not trouble enough, a haunting fear seems to be rippling through the scientific community these days—that all the fundamental discoveries about the biosphere and the universe have now been made, leaving nothing heroic to be done. This anxiety is engagingly explored in a collection of interviews conducted by John Horgan, *The End of Science: Facing the Limits of Knowledge in the Twilight of the Scientific Age* (1996). Although most of the scientists he questions have already made their mark and seem little bothered by the possibility that humans have figured out almost as much about physical reality as we ever will, the horror that they have arrived too late to do truly important work is said to hang over the heads of younger scientists. Not to make light of the suffering of others, but as a mere observer of such angst, I find it rather exasperating that all that brainpower feels thwarted when society is, in fact, up to its eyeballs in enormously serious and seemingly intractable problems that should be attracting heroic ingenuity. Must we add another Nobel Prize in science, one for enabling the survival of the species and the Earth community?

The future of science lies less with its petulant warriors than the visionary scientists who are enlarging the integrity of their profession by expanding the very meaning of the scientific endeavor. An example is C. J. S. Clarke's *Reality through the Looking-Glass: Science and Awareness in the Postmodern World*, as well as *The Reenchantment of Science:Post-modern Proposals*, edited by David Ray Griffin, and *New Metaphysical Foundations of Modern Science*, edited by Willis Harman with Jane Clark.[7]

I expect that science will, after all, take care of itelf quite well. The rest of this chapter turns to three larger areas: the ways in which the Promethean assumptions of modernity, now played out with hypermodern intensity, are causing detrimental transformations of economies, governance, and education. The new conditions in each of these spheres are related to the even larger transformation in which they are embedded,—globalization. Made possible by computerization, satellite-based communications, and other technology, the globalization of various areas of human activity is the most far-reaching reconfiguration since the Industrial Revolution.

Any consideration of the current fate of the Promethean dream must, of course, begin with the sphere considered central in modern ideology—the economy. The following composite description of the new, globalized economy should be familiar to anyone exposed to editorial pages, political speeches, or explanatory statements from corporate executives (often expressed through their ad campaigns) in modern or modernizing societies.

The emergence of the global economy is the most significant development of the post-Cold War era. Since prosperity is linked to economic growth and trade, the global opportunities for each country are now enormous if it restructures its particular economy in ways that will allow it to be globally competitive. This requires vision and leadership sufficient to remove obstacles to steady growth as well as gains in efficiency and productivity related to global integration and technological advances. Political will is necessary to guide societies through the temporary structural adjustments during this transitional period.

The new possibilities have been facilitated by the passage of GATT and NAFTA, which disallow the protectionist barriers that caused devastating trade wars in the past. These new trade treaties have leveled the playing field for everyone in the market: They have established democracy in the global business world. Sustainable growth in the global economy through free trade is a rising tide that will lift all boats.

In the developing countries, prudent loan programs from the International Monetary Fund and the World Bank will continue to encourage structural readjustments in government spending and to help them establish and expand their export industries. In addition, the new presence of global corporations will provide new jobs and, hence, new markets of consumers.

In the developed countries, companies must become globally competitive by downsizing their operating expenses and increasing efficiency and productivity. Their success in doing so will create wealth and expand the economy. It will create new opportunities at home and abroad for those willing to acquire technological skills and retraining.

The more interconnected the peoples of the world become through free trade, the less probability there is that wars will break out. Therefore, national governments can best bring about security and prosperity for their citizens by facilitating the growth of globalized trade. This includes enforcing the terms of GATT, which protect intellectual property rights and disallow unfair restraints. There lies the best hope for lifting the poor from their misery in stagnant, constrained economies. Continuing progress in industrial agricultural and other technologies will provide abundance in place of backward methods and modest yields. The global market will also bring the global village closer together through global media and communications. Never have opportunities been greater for so many people.

What's wrong with this picture? It is full of positive, constructive terms like "growth," "integration," "free," "efficiency," "abundance," and "interconnected." In spite of the upbeat packaging, however, the number of false claims and incorrect assumptions one can spot in this all-too-familiar litany might well serve as an indicator of *post*modern economic awareness. If your count is less than twelve, please read on as I decode the hypermodern hoopla.

The underlying premise of the global market ideology is that every country will earn most of its income from exports. The economic security and well-being of every nation will be dependent on the stability of conditions in distant markets—free, one must hope, of political conflicts, ecological collapse, drought or flooding, social upheaval, or countless glitches in the logistics of such long-distance operations. Obviously, the only enterprises that could do well in such a situation would be those large enough to be located in several countries so that market disruptions could be absorbed and balanced by uninterrupted profits elsewhere. To do really well, those large enterprises—transnational corporations (TNCs)—would have to be given maximum freedom and control. This they attained by being the chief consultants in the rewriting of the Global Agreement on Tariffs and Trade (GATT), which now overrules any national or local laws that hinder the operation of the TNCs. In the new world order established by GATT, such laws are called "restraints against free trade."

With national laws protecting labor, the environment, or community-based economics out of the way—except for the extremely minimal standards included in GATT—the big players are free to follow the internal logic of the global market: maximum production with the fewest possible employees, at locations accepting the lowest wage-scales in the world and the weakest levels of protection of the environment and labor. To be attractive to the TNCs as manufacturing sites, communities around the world must compete by offering far weaker regulations than even GATT requires. Unions are kept out by police action and other governmental deterence. For these reasons, the industrialized North (that is, the northern hemisphere) and the "developing" South are both coming to realize that "free trade" as structured by GATT means a race to the bottom for everyone.

The one exception are the owners and managers of the processes of globalization: the TNCs and those who provide professional services to them—accountants, financiers, advertising agencies, lobbyists, compliant politicians and bureaucrats, computer and robotics suppliers, and so forth. As mentioned in Chapter 1, a handful of TNCs in almost every industry have a near-monopolistic control over their market. Their profits increase as they continue to shed expensive workers in the North and to exploit desperately poor workers in the South, while stepping up levels of environmental destruction to feed continuous growth of production as well as the increased long-distance transport of raw materials and finished products. In recent years, ownership has become increasingly centralized, such that a few "core corporations" dominate each industry. They often "outsource" their manufacturing to smaller contractors and suppliers, who must compete with each other and take whatever price the core corporations offer. Hence, everyone is financially vulnerable and insecure except those close to the center of the corporate sector. Their positions are so insulated and their lifestyles so opulent compared to those of the sinking middle and working classes that David Korten, author of *When Corporations Rule the World* (1995), calls them the "stratosphere dwellers," or "Stratos," a global class of elites whose essential affiliation is with the networks of the corporate globalized economy.

Korten, who comes from a conservative background and acquired mainstream economic training at Stanford University before teaching at the Harvard Graduate School of Business, went into development work thirty years ago and eventually realized, to his surprise, that the modern model of development was deepening poverty in the Three-Quarters World (or "Third" World) instead of alleviating it. That model was shaped by two institutions founded at a meeting of forty-five nation-states in Bretton Woods, New Hampshire, in 1944: the International Bank for Reconstruction and Development (known as the World Bank) and the International Monetary Fund (IMF). (GATT was formed at a subsequent meeting.) For several years there was little interest in loans from the World Bank because the Marshall Plan covered most of the assistance necessary in the rebuilding of Europe—with strings attached, of course—and because a strong sector of businesspeople in the Three-Quarters World believed that foreign economic entanglements should be minimal so that their national economies could be built up. Such economic nationalists favored import-substitution strategies that reduced the need for foreign currency by producing vital goods domestically. They were opposed by transnationalists, businesspeople with links to transnational banks or corporations, many of whom had been educated in the North. The latter eventually came to dominate because the World Bank—like the corporations of the 1800s, which faced a frugal society—discovered a way to create a need for their product, in this case, loans. The Bank gave priority in the 1950s to "institution-building" projects aimed at creating autonomous governmental agencies that would become regular World Bank borrowers. The Bank also increased its leverage over policy in the "developing" countries by forming donor groups that promised substantial increases in aid if countries would abandon import-substitution and move to more export-oriented, "free trade" economies.

The effect, as is now painfully clear in the Three-Quarters World, was to deepen the dependence of low-income countries on the global economic system and then, when they were swamped with debt, to open their economies to corporate colonization. Moreover, the development schemes favored by the World Bank, such as large-scale dams, were often enormously disruptive and were usually centralized, capital-intensive, and ecologically destructive. Even worse, there is evidence that a majority of the World Bank projects failed to achieve their objectives.[8] Whether projects were failures or not, the loans must be paid off, as the Bank bears no liability. By the late 1970s, most "developing" countries had had to take out even more loans from Northern banks just to pay the interest on the earlier loans. In a desperate attempt to earn foreign currency, most of those countries sacrificed their age-old systems of subsistence agriculture to convert to giant export plantations, which enriched a small class of elites. Even though billions of dollars in interest payments were flowing from the impoverished South to the rich North every year (and still are), it looked as though an enormous loan default was about to take place in the 1980s. The World Bank, backed by other Northern banks, then stepped in and required debtor nations to establish Structural Adjustment Programs in order to secure further loans. The free-market reforms called for by Structural Adjustment Programs include severe cuts in government spending on healthcare, education, and housing, plus the elimination of agricultural subsidies and the expansion of plantations growing cash crops for export. Consequently, the real effect of modern "development" policies on the poor has been a substantive increase in their suffering. In Africa, for instance, the "austerity measures" imposed by the World Bank on social-service budgets have created economic devastation for millions of families, causing social repercussions such as the boom in child prostitution in the mid-1990s.[9]

As the poor have struggled to survive under the World Bank "restructuring" programs, the globally linked Third World elites have remained the major benefactors of economic growth. All the while, "development" policies continue to make matters even worse. The chemicalization of agriculture through the "green revolution" in the South left the soil brittle, the water contaminated by toxic runoff from the fields, and the biodiversity of cultivar plants much reduced. The current transformation of agriculture through the new biotechnologies replaces a common resource (self-generative seeds) with a commodity: seed that does not regenerate and thus must be purchased every year from a TNC, such as gargantuan Cargill, and that has been designed to be more responsive to chemical fertilizer.[10] After studying this situation and similar ones, Vandana Shiva, an Indian physicist, concluded that "maldevelopment" is the correct term for the results of the modern model.

A far worse surprise is in store for the Southern countries now dependent on export commodity crops: the impending development by Northern chemical companies of artificial replacements for many of those crops. Natural vanilla, for instance, sells on the world market for about $1200 per pound and is grown almost exclusively on three small islands in the Indian Ocean. It is expected to be replaced by a genetically engineered substitute that sells for less than $25 per pound.[11] According to a Dutch study, ten million sugar farmers in the Three-Quarters World may lose their livelihood to laboratory-produced sweeteners in the next several years. Similarly, tissue-culture substitution could push economies based on export crops into collapse. The plan calls for planting fields with only biomass perennial crops that would be harvested and converted with enzymes to a sugar solution, from which tissue culture would yield pulp that can be reconstituted and fabricated into different shapes and textures mimicking traditional crops. The factories involved would be highly automated and require few workers.[12]

Yet another hypermodern blow to traditional economies in the Three-Quarters World is the imposition, under GATT, of new rules for Trade-Related Intellectual Property Rights (TRIPS). These laws allow Northern pharmaceutical and chemical companies to patent substances that are obtained through a slight alteration to plants having uses that have been discovered, over time, through local experimentation. For example, several U.S. patents have been granted for stable neem-based solutions and emulsions derived from the neem tree in India, whose potent compounds have been used for centuries for medicine, toiletries, contraception, timber, fuel, and agriculture. As the effects of TRIPS became clear, public demonstrations and riots in India urged the government to reject these provisions of GATT.

Although the United States asserts that its corporations lose billions of dollars annually because U.S. patents are violated in Southern countries, a Canadian study determined that if the long history of plant breeding by indigenous farmers of the Three-Quarters World were taken into account, along with the discovery and care of plants with pharmaceutical properties, the United States would owe the Southern farmers $302 million annually for royalties on farmers' seeds now used in this country and $5.1 billion for pharmaceuticals now sold in U.S. drugstores.[13] Traditional knowledge, as we have seen, is inconsequential in the modern scientific worldview.

All these detrimental effects on rural, traditional communities—plus

the displacement of native peoples from their previously protected lands—
were brought to public attention by the uprising of the Zapatistas in Chiapas, Mexico, on the day the North American Free Trade Agreement went
into effect (January 1, 1994). Their initial spokesperson, Subcomman-
dante Marcos, subsequently described the rebellion in this way: "Thousands of Indians, armed with truth and fire, with shame and dignity, shook
the country from the sweet dream of modernity."[14] Elsewhere, he has referred to the uprising as a *postmodern* action, which made no sense to
journalists, who take "postmodern" to mean solely deconstructionism.[15]
The hypermodern global integration of control by the corporations and
banks of the "developed" world, however, is exactly what he had in mind.
In the United States, media coverage of the Zapatista uprising has presented it simply as the usual sort of protest by the poor against the ruling
authorities, one that just happened to occur in Mexico on that particular
date. Like the devaluation and collapse of the Mexican peso beginning in
December 1994, however, the Zapatista revolt—by Mayan activists—was
a clearly focused reaction against NAFTA and the changes in Mexican
law that had been pushed through by President Carlos Salinas de Gortari.
He succeeded in changing the Mexican constitution so that previously protected preserves for native peoples in the eastern highlands and elsewhere
could be broken up and sold whenever foreign or Mexican interests waved
a wad of money before the poor. He also kept the value of the peso artificially inflated prior to the NAFTA vote. Both of these actions, as well as
others suppressing protection of the environment and the extension of
labor organizing to the new TNC factories, allowed the U.S. corporate
and financial sector to see what they wanted to see in Mexico: a hungry,
"emerging" economy ready to play by the neoliberal rules and the discipline of "free trade." An extremely modern society, complete with skyscrapers and chic discos, was the image of Mexico projected in television
ads paid for by the Mexican government and aired in the United States
prior to the vote in Congress on NAFTA. There was no mention, of
course, of the hundreds of thousands of farmers who would be displaced
as transnational agribusiness moved in. Such effects are considered mere
structural adjustment anyway, as the displaced workers can, theoretically,
uproot and find jobs (with Dickensian conditions) in the *macquiladoras*—
factories in the highly polluted manufacturing zone that runs along the
Mexican side of the Rio Grande, the border with the United States.

When the balloon burst, things went very wrong very quickly. In the wake of the uprising in Chiapas and the initial flight of some foreign speculative capital, followed by the peso devaluation and the massive flight of foreign capital, the banking crisis, and the severe recession, there were calls to bring former-President Salinas back to Mexico to face prosecution for the ill-conceived policies he and his administration had forced through. Where was Salinas at this time? Why, in Europe, informally campaigning to be elected head of GATT's new World Trade Organization in Geneva on the basis of his great success in bringing Mexico into the global economy! When his successor, President Ernesto Zedillo, sent federal army troops against the poorly armed Zapatista rebels in February 1995, his action was linked in the press with a recent memo that had been released to investors at giant Chase Manhattan Bank, calling for swift, authoritarian action by the Mexican government against the Indian protesters. The memo further suggested that not all democratic victories at the ballot box should be allowed by Zedillo.[16]

Like many "emerging markets," Mexico was battered by the rapid inflow and outflow of "hot money," or "quicksilver capital"—international investment money moved restlessly around the globe in search of the highest, fastest profit through speculation on interest rates, currency valuation, or stocks and bonds. All of this takes place within computer networks at split-second speed. Every day, billions of dollars ricochet around in the globalized economy. If interest rates rise in New York, investment managers immediately pull capital out of "emerging markets" to bring it home for a while for some high yields. In the aftermath of the Mexican crash, an enormous amount of Northern speculative capital was pulled out of scores of "emerging markets." Moreover, uncertainty that the "Stratos" would successfully prevail upon President Clinton and the U.S. Congress to approve the $50-billion bail-out to Mexico (designed to save Wall Street's major investments) caused further sell-offs of U.S. investments in "developing" countries. Even the *Wall Street Journal* (January 30, 1995) was sufficiently alarmed to admit on its front page that the long-standing insistence by the IMF and the World Bank that Third World development is reinforced by foreign capital must surely be reconsidered. Commenting on the rapid withdrawal of "nervous" hot money, the *Journal* concluded, "The dizzying reversal leaves the Cinderellas badly shaken and raises new questions about whether unfettered private-capital flows really facilitate long-term economic development." The major concern of the Stratos, of course, is the problematic instability for their investments rather than the "domestic concerns" in the Three-Quarters World. For working people in Mexico, in contrast, the situation is severe: Real wages, as of mid-1996, are below what they were in 1981, and the extreme disparity of income between rich and poor continues to worsen.

Was the *Wall Street Journal* chastised by fellow Stratos for expressing such a sympathetic position toward the badly "whacked" Third World countries and even proposing—*horrors*—that they should "establish restraints on capital flows"? Two weeks later (February 13, 1995) the *Journal* ran another front-page article on the subject, concluding this time that the problem is not global-market reforms but failure on the part of developing nations to push beyond partial reform. "What could turn difficulty into disaster would be a wave of 'reform fatigue' in the developing countries themselves . . . . Signs of backsliding abound," warned the *Journal*. The World Bank's chief economist for Latin America hauled out the Stratos' usual bludgeon for opponents of the modern model of development, dismissing them as the "forces of protectionism": "We're seeing in a number of countries, in Latin America, Eastern Europe, and Asia, people arguing that opening up to international trade and investment isn't the way to go." Small wonder!

As is readily apparent to most people in the industrialized countries, the ideology of the global market is an extension of themes of the corporate sector that have been familiar for the past century. The "new economy" is an enlarged and intensified version of the very arrangements that have caused so many problems in the North, including extensive ecological damage. Antitrust legislation finally broke up monopoly cartels in the United States at the beginning of this century, but today's core corporations have absorbed or knocked out so much of their previous competition that they exercise the very same control over a market as did the old cartels. The megaretailers—Wal-Mart, Kmart, Toys "Я" Us, Home Depot, Circuit City, and others—play their suppliers against one another and abruptly shift their sourcing to countries with the cheapest labor. Just as millions of independent retailers have been pushed out of business, so have eight of the ten million farms that existed in 1950 in the United States. The permanent elimination of jobs now haunting the global economy was first experienced in the industrialized countries—always in the name of efficiency, economic growth, and modernization. In an economy that is owned by a relative few, economic growth benefits those few, not society at large. During the last five years of the Reagan administration, for instance, the nation's wealth grew by 8 percent (compared with 31 percent between 1975 and 1980), but the distribution changed drastically: Income for the wealthiest 1 percent of the population rose by 74.2 percent between 1977 and 1987; income for the poorest 10 percent fell by 10.5 percent. The top 1 percent now own 42 percent of the national wealth. Today the United States ranks last in economic equality among industrialized nations.[17]

The centralization of wealth and ownership on the global level is having the same sort of disempowering effect on the majority of people worldwide as it has had in the United States. According to the UN Human Development Report of 1996, eighty-nine countries were worse off economically than they were a decade earlier and, in seventy "developing" countries, incomes were lower than they were in the 1960s or 1970s. With the gap between rich and poor widening both within and among nations, more than half of the human population worldwide (more than three billion people) now live on incomes of less than two dollars per day. An administrator associated with the report noted in an interview that the "two-class world" is a breeding ground for hopelessness, anger, and frustration among the poor.[18] The social strains that accompany the hard realities of modern "development" have led David Korten to conclude, "We are now coming to see that economic globalization has come at a heavy price. In the name of modernity we are creating dysfunctional societies that are breeding pathological behavior—violence, extreme competitiveness, suicide, drug abuse, greed, and environmental degradation—at every hand. Such behavior is an inevitable consequence when a society fails to meet the needs of its members for social bonding, trust, affection, and a shared sense of meaning."[19]

Even with all the devastated families and communities piling up as statistics, the corporate cheerleaders urge the public to be "realistic," reminding us that no one can turn back the tide of progress. An editorial in my hometown newspaper, the *Columbus Dispatch* (August 1, 1994), scolded rural readers for "sentimentality" over the demise of the family farm and advised enthusiasm for the new megafarms that operate on contract from agribusiness corporations and provide new opportunities for export. An example cited was a proposed 2.5-million-hen "egg farm." The editorial scoffed at worries from neighbors about pollution, stench, and falling property values. Likewise, it dismissed concerns from the Ohio Farmers Union about the dangers of monopolies and vertical integration of markets. In a conclusion that is utterly typical of this genre, the inevitability of globalization and centralized corporate ownership was stressed: "Agriculture cannot be exempt from the changes that are reshaping the national and global economies."

That very inevitability is being challenged today by the accumulation of disastrous effects on body, nature, and place. A global corporate-industrial sector freed of "unfair" restraints is likely to bring us more plummeting sperm counts due to pesticide residues, more abnormally early menarches due to hormones in hamburgers and other foods, and more disease caused by toxic manufacturing and farming practices. It is likely to cause more poisoning and depletion of groundwater, more deforestation and flooding, more loss of precious topsoil, and even faster rates of species' extinction. As for place, communities in the North will feel the increasing effects of economic depression and social strain as the global economy continues to relocate its manufacturing jobs—as well as white-collar jobs such as software design—to countries with far cheaper labor. Communities in the South will continue to suffer colonization by the TNCs and by the Stratos in their own society who sacrifice small-scale livelihoods and self-reliant economies in order to expand the export-based model of economic development.

The inevitability of the globalized economy is also being challenged by critics in the North and South who are framing alternatives such as "fair trade" and "community-based economics." For more than twenty-five years, a handful of economists and other analysts have pointed out that not only is the modern model of development and globalization deleterious for the majority of people, but the means of measuring its success is ludicrous. Nonexistent *homo economicus*, the Lone Cowboy of modern economic theory, who is thoroughly isolated and makes all decisions in life on the basis of his simple self-interest, is trotted out once again, in the form of *per-capita income*, as the measure of successful development.[20] Does the average income of a country reveal anything about the state of families and community, social cohesion and civic well-being, or ecological health and long-term viability? It tells us no more than the absurdly reductionist Gross National Product (GNP, also known as "Gross Domestic Product"), which supposedly measures how well a country is doing according to how much money is paid out for goods and services *of any kind* in a year. Through the lens of the GNP, oil spills boost the economy since the massive cleanup efforts generate temporary jobs, increasing rates of disease run up healthcare spending, and crime is great for the security industry. In fact, a family going through a divorce is just about ideal in this system of measurement, as real estate transactions are generated, moving services are probably needed, and long-term psychotherapy for the children, and perhaps the parents, is often involved. Business booms . . . as people and nature are pummeled. Indexes that would measure far more than monetary exchange in order to gauge the well-being of a society have been emerging for nearly twenty years, but such "quality of life" measurements did not attract mainstream attention until the mid-nineties. Some examples are the Human Development Index (created by the UN Development Programme), the System of National Accounts (sponsored by the World Bank, the IMF, and others), the Country Futures Indicators (created by Hazel Henderson), the Index of Sustainable Economic Welfare (created by Herman Daly and John B. Cobb, Jr.), and the Genuine Progress Indicator (created by Clifford Cobb and Ted Halstead).[21] Nearly all of these new indices are part of a larger effort to redefine wealth and well-being.

As critics since Carlyle and Ruskin have noted with exasperation, the isolated model of *homo economicus* in modern economic theory is about as far from the real dynamics of life as is theoretically possible. Humans are social animals. We need sustenance and a viable habitat, but we also need social cohesion and *connection* of all sorts. Community-based economics, a pragmatic alternative to the global economy, is proving successful in towns and cities across the country because it rebuilds and creates community bonds while addressing economic needs. The premise is simply that keeping money circulating largely within a city or region yields greater stability and security than having capital continuously sent out of the area to distant corporate headquarters. One of the reasons poor neighborhoods remain poor is that a very high percentage of money earned goes out of the community at the very first retail transaction. Community-based economics adopts several elements from the only long-term model of successful sustainability that we know: nature. Principal among these is the adaptability and security that results from diversity. Encouraging a wide range of economic activity in a town is a safer bet than trying to attract a TNC factory by promising tax breaks, spending millions of public dollars on extending the municipal infrastructure to the new plant, and then hoping that operations are not abruptly moved to a country with cheaper labor.

When one patronizes a mega-retailer, not only does the profit on the item purchased go directly out of the community, but so do payments for business services such as advertising and accounting, which are usually handled by corporate headquarters. Why buy cookies, for instance, that have been shipped thousands of miles across the country, contributing to resource depletion, pollution, and wear-and-tear on the bridges and highways, when cookies are available in locally owned bakeries? Those local bakeries buy supplies and services from other local businesses. The creation and expansion of such enterprises are facilitated by local credit unions and enlightened banks, which extend loans to community and regional businesses rather than sending it out to the global economy's games of speculation. Wealth and ownership are spread by profit-sharing with employees, employee-owned businesses, and cooperatives.

Some towns have gone further and established a local currency, which is quite legal as long as it is not used beyond state lines. The best known example of local currency is the Ithaca HOUR, which was begun in 1991 in Ithaca, New York. As of mid-1996, over $57,000 of local currency had been issued to over 1000 participants, who have used it for the equivalent of $2 million worth of transactions: plumbing, carpentry, electrical work, roofing, nursing, chiropractic, child care, car and bike repair, eyeglasses, firewood, gifts, rent, groceries, restaurant meals, admission to movie theaters, and mortgage payments to the credit union. The Ithaca HOUR is Ithaca's ten-dollar bill because ten dollars is the average hourly wage in their county. Everyone who agrees to accept HOURS is listed in a newsletter, *Ithaca Money*, and is paid four HOURS (forty dollars). Every eight months, they may apply to be paid an additional two HOURS as a reward for continuing their participation. In that way, the per-capita supply of local currency is gradually and carefully increased. The newsletter testifies to acts of generosity and community prompted by the system. Decisions about the printing of currency (HOURS are printed on paper made partly from local reeds), manner of issue, and so forth are made at biweekly meetings of the Barter Potluck, a "wide open governing body" that's "more democratic and responsible than the Federal Reserve Board," according to the creator of HOURS, Paul Glover. The designs on Ithaca HOURS feature native flowers, local waterfalls, crafts, farms, and children. Glover and his peers feel that the millions of dollars of local trading, plus the community ties, generated by HOURS have contributed to what they call the "Grassroots National Product": "We regard Ithaca's HOURS as real money, backed by real people, real time, real skills, and real tools.

Dollars, by contrast, are funny money, backed no longer by gold or silver, but by less than nothing—$5.2 trillion of national debt."[22]

Other elements of community-based economics include nonprofit community development corporations, community development banks, revolving loan funds, barter or work exchanges, and rural and urban community land trusts. Ownership of affordable housing is facilitated by cooperative housing, in which the building is owned by a cooperative corporation, consisting of resident members who own shares according to the value of the unit they occupy. Another option is co-housing, in which apartments are built around shared space such as a large kitchen and dining area, guest rooms, workshops or sewing rooms, social places for children and teenagers, and a laundry room. Several cities have begun localizing their food supply by using farmers' markets and community-supported agriculture (CSA). The latter raises capital for farmers in the winter by selling "shares" in the produce that will be ready in summer and fall. Instead of getting 3 percent of the food dollar (as with corporate agribusiness), the farmer gets 100 percent; the shareholders get fresh produce (usually organic); and the community gets its greenbelt of nearby farms preserved because those family enterprises have been made financially viable. These options and many more are discussed in the growing body of literature on community-based economics by creative and pragmatic visionaries—some of the real heroes of our time—who are dedicated to the revitalization of *place*.[23]

Although such voices are rarely acknowledged by the media and other dominant institutions, once in a while one of them manages to focus a bit of attention on the real destruction being caused by the ideology of "free trade" in a globalized economy. In the introduction to a collection of insightful essays, *The Case against the Global Economy—and for a Turn to the Local* (1996), co-editor Jerry Mander cites an observation made in the *London Times* in 1994 by one of the book's contributors, Sir James Goldsmith: "What an astounding thing it is to watch a civilization destroy itself because it is unable to re-examine the validity, under totally new circumstances, of an economic ideology."[24] That ideology is served by a compatible political ideology—hence the term "political economy." Although more will be said in the final chapter about positive alternatives to the globalized economy, we must first consider the current flounderings of poor Prometheus in the political sphere.

～

The shape of modern political life was determined by the concept of sovereign power among modern nation-states that emerged from the Peace of Westphalia in 1648 and from the democratic values of the Enlightenment: liberty, equality, brotherhood [sic]. Today, however, both politics among nation-states and politics within nation-states are heavily influenced by the globalized corporate sector and the institutions that "guide" governments further into the sphere of "free trade." It is not widely recognized that many of the shocking political crises of the 1990s were preceded by economic tampering by the IMF, the World Bank, or other Western development agencies, which sparked insecurity among citizens and instability in their political economy. For example, a great deal of concern rippled through Slovenia and Croatia when word got out, in the 1980s, that the Yugoslav federal government owed billions of dollars for development loans that had gone to the poorer sections of the country, Serbia and Macedonia. The burden of repayment would fall upon the more prosperous regions, Slovenia and Croatia. Efforts by the latter to negotiate an adjusted role for themselves in repaying the huge loans were rebuffed by (Serbian) officials in control of the Yugoslav federal government. At that point, the small but long-standing independence movements in Slovenia and Croatia grew quickly. In addition, much development aid to the Yugoslav government was abruptly cut off once the Cold War ended. Another example of the political effects of modern development policy is the heartbreaking failure of the "people power" revolution in the Philippines to effect economic justice after deposing Ferdinand Marcos. That failure is closely linked with the "structural adjustments" that were forced on the new government.

When the long arm of the global economy causes a national government to issue and enforce policies that bring great hardship (although never to the Stratos elites), social upheaval or even armed rebellion may well result, as in the Mexican states that followed the lead of Chiapas. Even in the absence of draconian "adjustments," however, national governments face nearly overwhelming conditions in the new world order of GATT. Having lost control of the value of their currency during an earlier stage of globalization, governments now have little or no control over the fate of their economy; instead, they are left to react to the fallout. What, precisely, are they supposed to do about the majority of their populace that will not benefit from the new globalized economy, half of whom are considered utterly dispensable by it? What shall they do with the millions of rural people streaming into the huge slums of the mega-cities of the Three-Quarters World because modern policies have sacrificed the traditional local economies? What shall they do about the overdrawn water tables, the depleted fishing banks, the toxic soil and waterways, and the deforested drainage basins and flood plains? How shall they deal with the epidemics of infectious disease caused, in part, by the dislodging of microbes from tropical rainforests as the global market devours them?

The major challenge of the democratic political order in our time is to gain control over the runaway economic order of global capital so as to establish a new equilibrium within and among all nations and nation-states. Neither commerce nor trade is evil, but the abrogation by governments of moral responsibility for a viable Earth community, with humane conditions for all peoples now and in the future, is unconscionable. Like the corporate sector, the modern governmental structures throughout the world are operated by conscientious people in thrall to the ideologies of modernity. The so-called "realist consensus" that has long dominated international relations is simply the modern doctrine of the autonomous Lone Cowboy writ large: Nation-states are atomistic entities in the world that make all decisions based purely on self-interest and maximum advantage over other states.

Since ever-expanding production and trade is believed to be the way to attain ever-expanding well-being, all modern governance has served that goal—even though such policies today contribute to unemployment, poverty and homelessness, disease, violent crime, stressed and failing families, and ecological devastation. Regulation? Why, the market is already regulated, say the neoliberal proponents, by its dependence on abstract rules of conduct that protect life, liberty, and property, and by contracts. Moreover, just to strike a contemporary note, the laissez-faire theorists cite certain interpretations of chaos theory that "prove" that the economy is inherently unpredictable, so public policy should be abandoned. Fortunately, others applying insights from the new sciences to political economy, such as Peter Allen in the United Kingdom, point out that, even if a set of nonlinear equations is (temporarily) a "good" model of an economy, only under very special conditions will it exhibit chaotic motion. Governmental policy, he asserts, can be a perfectly legitimate actor in the system, able to respond to emergent phenomena at particular levels of "spatial/organizational structure."[25]

The ideology of neoliberal economics has even detached itself from the historical record, insisting to "emerging" markets and new democracies worldwide that democracy and laissez-faire corporate capitalism are actually conflated. Such propaganda overlooks the enormous role played by government in the post-World War II industrial-capitalist success stories (Germany, Japan, South Korea, Taiwan). In addition, Ricardo's principle of "comparative advantage" specifically assumed conditions in international trade that do not exist in the globalized economy of GATT. Nevertheless, governments of "developing" countries are strong-armed into adopting these fanciful policies, perhaps the largest scam the world has ever known. Squeezed between greed and need, the national governments succeed in satisfying neither.

The current awareness that the modern nation-state has become severely strained, or even ineffectual, has evoked a range of responses. Kenichi Ohmae, an enthusiast of the globalized corporate sector, proposes in *The End of the Nation-State: The Rise of Regional Economies* (1995) that we should simply drop the outmoded attachment to nation-states in favor of "natural economic zones"—areas that have economic cohesion as players in the global market, such as Hong Kong/Southern China, Tokyo and its outlying areas, and Research Triangle Park in North Carolina. For the Stratos, this makes immanent sense: Having knocked national laws out of the way with GATT, why not just replace the entire historical, cultural, and political structure of the public sphere with the contours of the global economy? This hair-raising proposal was offered partly as a response to a different option, Samuel P. Huntington's influential (some say "infamous") article in *Foreign Affairs* (Summer 1993)—later expanded to a book titled *The Clash of Civilizations and the Remaking of World Order* (1996)—in which he predicts that the fading power of nation-states will be replaced by the antagonisms among civilizational identities: Judeo-Christian, Chinese, Japanese, Islamic, and Hindu. Several other analysts of international politics thankfully envision more constructive possibilities. Richard Falk, for instance, has proposed intercivilizational *dialogue* on human rights and other issues, including not only the previously ignored Islamic perspective but also that of the indigenous peoples of the "Fourth World" (many of whom prefer to be called "First Nations").[26] He further believes that the modern nation-state, which previously acted in such ways as to deserve being restrained, now needs to be reconstituted and strengthened in ways that would enable it to provide effective protection for communities and regions against the destructive forces of the globalized economy.[27]

I tend to agree, but it seems likely that even the most well-intentioned proposals, of which there are many in the air today, would simply create new iterations of current problems unless we ground new policy in deep issues of existence—from which modernity has long since disconnected. We have ample evidence that tacking on various ameliorative mechanisms to structures of the modern political economy are resoundingly ineffectual. (An example is NAFTA's "side agreements," added to address human health and the environment: A report issued by the U.S. General Accounting Office in August 1996 concluded that pollution along the U.S.–Mexican border had worsened, in spite of millions of dollars spent, and could cost nearly $8 billion to correct over the next ten years.[28]) The purpose of governance is not to facilitate unqualified economic growth but to safeguard and enhance the commonweal, the well-being of its citizens.

An ecological-postmodern sense of that task would be grounded in the physicality of the Earth community. We exist through the bounty of the Earth's commons: the self-regulating balance of biomass and atmospheric gases that allows us to breathe; the massive circulation of water through rivers, oceans, and cloud condensation; the slow, steady creation of topsoil; the pollination of our crops by wild bees and other animals, each interacting with an array of wild and cultivated plants; and the cleansing, transporting actions of the winds. The land masses of Earth are organized into bioregions delineated by watersheds (drainage areas) of the river systems or other natural demarcations. Everyone lives in a bioregion and in the Earth's commons. Pollution and ecological degradation or breakdown occur in a bioregion or in the Earth's larger systems, not some vaguely theorized realm of "externalities." Nations inhabit, and evolve with, one or more bioregions. The health of communities and nations is dependent on the health of the bioregions. To consider this condition an unbearable affront was the tragic error of the modern worldview. To consider it an invitation to reciprocity, affection, and gratitude has been the response of countless nonmodern cultures—East and West, North and South. To *live in place* fully is the challenge that has spawned the "bioregional movement."[29]

Since the modern state is clearly entering some sort of transition, battered by both the global economy and the captive nations it has absorbed, it might well see this crisis as an opportunity to reconceive its reason for being—a unit of interdependent, not absolute, sovereignty dedicated to facilitating the well-being of its communities and its bioregions through a reconstituted sense of democracy. A second likely transition is the badly needed renegotiation of GATT and NAFTA. (A bill providing for the assessment and partial renegotiation of NAFTA was introduced in the U.S. Congress in November 1995.) The newly reconceived ecological-postmodern states could regulate trade in ways that protect and enhance the well-being of participating communities rather than exploiting and endangering them. The TNCs are guests in foreign countries and should be required to abide by the laws of the host nation.[30] A third likely transition is the widely called for-restructuring of the United Nations. A new global system of coordination could begin with the realities of the Earth: Nation-states would be encouraged to redraw their internal regions to match the contours of their watersheds, as New Zealand has done, in order to help us recover from the modern error of thinking we live on top of nature. Nation-states would send a representative to a macroregional council covering roughly the area of a continent, such as the North/Central Americas, and each of those councils would elect a representative to the Security Council of the United Nations. In that way, dominance by the Northern industrial powers would be replaced by a community of communities of communities.[31]

Among the first actions of the new United Nations, if NGOs and other grassroots organizations could prevail over the Stratos, would probably be the abolishment of the World Bank—with apologies to the world's poor for fifty years of devastating policies—and the strengthening of the public and private agencies that are already issuing micro-loans to small-scale, community-based entrepreneurs throughout the world.[32] Second, by freeing the captive nations so that they do not have to engage in independence wars, the new United Nations would nullify the cause of most current wars, which have high levels of civilian casualties, and most of the demand for the burgeoning small-arms trade. States would be forbidden to retaliate against internal nations that have taken a bona fide vote for independence, and a standing UN police force would intervene if a state waged war against a seceding nation. Once human rights for all minorities and other citizens are guaranteed in the newly independent nation's constitution—and in reality—the United Nations would help to facilitate new arrangements for regional trade, transport, and other coordination.[33] Third, to organize dialogue amid the extensive diversity (with many newly independent nations), the new United Nations would establish formal advisory channels of perspectives from the spiritual-cultural "civilizations," as well as designate spokespersons for the other species of the Earth community. A weave of geographical/ecological representation and spiritual/cultural representation would result. The modern perspective, with its secular "religion" of economism, core value of pure autonomy, and scientistic-managerial rationalism, would be one of the orientations in the mix but would no longer be the informing philosophy of the organization.

Even though I have focused here on three major transitions that are quite likely to occur in some form—a new role for nation-states, the renegotiation of GATT and NAFTA, and the restructuring of the United Nations—the ecological-postmodern directions I have proposed might seem unrealistic or "utopian" to many readers. My ideas are embedded in a political philosophy that has been emerging for the past twenty-five years—although, as I note in Chapter 4, its roots go back to seventeenth-century resistance to the enclosure laws and to the "new mechanical philosophy." The growth of grassroots movements around the world for environmental protection, democratic reform, community-based economics, human rights, spiritual renewal, nonviolent conflict resolution, and an end to militarism constitutes a substantive challenge to the modern ideologies of denial. For instance, seventy Green parties have emerged worldwide to further the efforts of these grassroots movements and to develop a coherent philosophy of sustainability. Believing that the economy should neither be owned by the state nor controlled by huge corporations, the Greens' beyond-left-and-right position is based on the decentralization of economic power. Unlike the economist parties, both liberal and conservative, the Greens advocate community-based economics only *in service to* the building and nourishing of healthy communities. Economics is not the central focus of the Greens' ecosocial vision; this is one of the ways in which it is *post*modern.

In many ways, the new political struggle is between "globalists" and "localists." Nearly every conservative and liberal party in the world today champions the globalized economy. The grassroots opposition, however, can be considered "localist" only if one understands that they favor international linking, both governmental and nongovernmental, that exists *in service to* the well-being of local communities. One example of such efforts is the Community Report Card, designed by the international

Women's Environment and Development Organization (WEDO) and now in use in several languages around the world.[34] The broadly defined "Green" political, philosophical, and spiritual opposition to rule by the Stratos and other champions of "maldevelopment" is not isolationist. National, regional, and global levels of coordination and cooperation are necessary to address the problems we face today, but the current structures of coordination operate as defenders of the status quo. For instance, the governmental representatives to the United Nations Conference on the Environment and Development (UNCED), held in Rio de Janeiro in 1992, insisted upon focusing on symptoms rather than causes of the problems: "deforestation" rather than the timber trade and pulp industry, "indebtedness" rather than the monetary system and maldevelopment policies, "unemployment" rather than the globalized corporate operations, and "population growth" rather than the forces blocking the sort of development that almost always brings down the birthrate (that is, education for women, small-scale economic opportunities for women, and healthcare for women and children).[35] In contrast, the statement issued by the NGO conference, held nearby, expressed the convictions of the community-based, ecosocial alternative, as the following excerpt indicates:

> The fundamental purpose of economic organization is to meet the community's basic needs, such as food, shelter, clothing, education, health, and the enjoyment of culture. . . . Beyond meeting basic physical needs, the quality of human life depends more on the development of social relationships, creativity and artistic expression, spirituality, and the opportunity to be a productive member of the community than on the ever increasing consumption of material goods . . . .Organizing economic life around decentralized, relatively self-reliant local economies that control and manage their own productive resources . . . is essential to sustainability. This strengthens attachment to place, encourages environmental stewardship, enhances local food security, and accommodates distinctive identities. Trade between such local economies, as between nations, should be just and balanced.

As for the Stratos and their compatriots in modern, industrialized and "developing" governments everywhere, it has become increasingly difficult, as various crises mount, for them to maintain with any credibility that they are the "realists" and the critics of unqualified economic growthism are "impractical" and "utopian." Already regional water shortages are causing disruptions and are predicted to become the cause of wars in the near future. Massive displacement of people from gargantuan "development" projects (such as dams that flood large areas), independence wars against the hegemony of the modern state, industrial pollution, economic "restructuring," and ecological collapse are swelling the ranks of permanent refugees worldwide to more than twenty-five million. In yet another schizophrenic response, the United States and other Northern governments continue to insist that unrestrained production, resource consumption, and centralization of ownership will bring global prosperity, while they cynically reprogram their spy satellites to identify sites of *ecological* collapse so they have advance notice of the inevitable "coming anarchy" that will most likely follow.[36] Warren Christopher, the U.S. Secretary of State, even declared a new policy direction in April 1996, making environmental concerns as central as human rights in U.S. diplomacy—as if the ecological crises worldwide were freestanding problems unrelated to the economic policies imposed by the North.[37] In the corporate sector, the banking and insurance industries have come to see the ecological analysis as being far more "realistic"—and painfully so, for them—than the ungrounded utopian outlook of growthism. These two industries, especially in Europe, have split from the position of the oil industry because they have realized they have trillions of dollars worth of insured property and long-term investments that will be destroyed by global climate change, which already is beginning to cause sharp increases in extreme weather of all sorts: droughts, cold snaps, heat waves, hurricanes, blizzards, and rising sea levels. Many of the corporations at risk are now initiating a massive shift of international investment away from fossil fuels and toward solar energy.[38]

In spite of such developments, most governments continue to defend their current policies and assure the public that more of the same will finally bring unimaginable progress and well-being. Moreover, they smugly exude the sense that their course of action is not only realistic but the only mature choice, while critics are dismissed as childlike and naive. Shortly after UNCED was held, a spokesperson for the Competitiveness Council (the corporate special-interest group that was ensconced in the Bush White House and chaired by Vice President Quayle) asserted on a national news program that UNCED was merely "a children's crusade" because it was dominated by "touchy-feely concerns with how to make the world better" and because it focused on government regulation and foreign aid rather than a supposedly more mature focus on the "fact" that market forces are the efficient way to protect the environment.[39]

Since those "grown-up" governments are less and less in control with regard to various destructive dynamics, however, grassroots groups have been experimenting with various ways to bring about more sustainable policy. In democracies with proportional representation, the Green party, for instance, has been rather influential at local, state, and federal levels, especially in Germany, Sweden, and, more recently, Italy. Elsewhere, other models for achieving sustainable policy have emerged in addition to party work. In Britain, the Real World Coalition of thirty-six organizations was formed in 1996 by three widely respected former leaders of the British Green Party (Jonathon Porritt, Sara Parkin, and Paul Ekins). Their *Real World Action Programme for Government* begins with the observation that British politics is not working because so many critical challenges continue to go unaddressed. The program proposes a range of policy reforms in twelve areas, highlighting a key reform in each. The Coalition campaigns for support of the *Real World Action Programme* during elections and monitors its implementation by the elected administration, with maximum attention generated by member organizations.[40] Like many other grassroots organizations in both the North and South, the Real World Coalition has discovered greater effectiveness by working outside of political parties.

In our own country, the democratic process—a grand achievement of the modern era—has become mutilated and suppressed by forces that grew out of modern values: rationalistic, scientistic management; the centrality of economism; and condescension toward the local and the domestic realm of concerns. In *Who Will Tell the People* (1992), William Grieder analyzes the disparaging attitude held by policymakers and experts with regard to the "broad political values" of the public:

> The real political contest, on issue after issue, is a struggle between competing value systems—the confident scientific rationalism of the government elites versus the deeply felt human values expressed by people who are not equipped to talk like experts and who, in fact, do not necessarily share the experts' conception of public morality. . . . The public's side of the

argument is described as "emotional" whereas those who govern are said to be making "rational" and "responsible" choices. In the masculine culture of management, "emotion" is assigned a position of weakness whereas "facts" are hard and potent. The reality, of course, is that the ability to define what is or isn't "rational" is itself laden with political self-interest, whether the definition comes from a corporate lobbyist or from a federal agency. . . . For elites, the politics of governing is seen as a continuing struggle to manage public "emotions" so that they do not overwhelm sound public policy. . . . The theme of unstable public emotions is a staple of newspaper editorials and learned conferences. . . . A favorite put-down of the unreasoning public, for instance, is the accusation that Americans wish to live in a "risk-free society"—a desire that is obviously utopian, too costly to achieve, and ignorant of scientific uncertainty.[41]

Yet the deeply felt—and extremely rational—concerns for body, nature, and place that arose from the public in 1995 in opposition to the "Republican Revolution's" proposed rollback of environmental laws was so strong that the usual rationale of sacrificing the real to the panacea of growthism was defeated.

Our political discourse is predicated on the modern political "fathers" knowing what is best for the benighted "minors," as Philip Slater demonstrates in *A Dream Deferred* (1991). Certainly the United States has treated other nations like children if they were considered insufficiently modern. Native Americans, African-Americans, immigrants, and women have all been treated like children by the cultural/political "fathers," who were white, of course. Technocracy, the globalized economy, and the "realist consensus" in international relations all fall within the realm of the political "fathers," who hardly bother to listen to the objections of such "children" as the technopeasants, the community-based activists, and the "nature lovers."

In a related analysis of political metaphors, *Moral Politics* (1996), George Lakoff, a professor of linguistics, traces the "strict father" model of morality and policy adhered to by conservatives in distinction from the "nurturant parent" model held by liberals. Conservatives in many countries believe that government programs corrupt people because aid interferes with the natural forces of competition, which force the development of self-reliance and competence. Lakoff notes, however, that in the United States there is a strange version of this orientation that is unknown among European conservatives: hatred of the government. This extreme version of the distrust of government has often been manipulated by the corporate sector to block passage of government regulation. For instance, the medical insurance industry, by running television and radio commercials that warned of the danger of one's family doctor being under the control of bumbling, power-hungry government bureaucrats, defeated not only the grassroots efforts to institute a single-payer healthcare system, but even even the market-oriented reforms proposed by the Clinton adminstration. (The lobbyists for HMOs and other medical insurers even fooled the American Medical Association; only the American College of Surgeons endorsed the single-payer option, which would remove the insurance industry from healthcare.) Once the threat of reform was defeated and the HMOs and insurers started "economizing" to bring down costs, doctors found themselves so thoroughly under the control of the corporate bureaucrats that some even began discussions about forming a physicians' labor union!

The reason that Americans have traditionally distrusted even democratic forms of governance more strongly than do other citizenry lies in our origins: America is about the escape from politics. Our nation was born as a pilgrims' refuge and made its wrenching break for freedom because Old World tyranny was unbearable. Most of the people who have come here over three hundred and fifty years were escaping economic oppression, but it was usually supported by authoritarian politics. Bruised and battered or simply constrained, immigrants arrived here with a desire to be left alone by government and allowed to seek prosperity. President John Adams reflected the American attitude that government was something to be set up and gotten out of the way when he explained that he felt compelled to engage in politics so that his sons could engage in commerce so that his grandsons could engage in art. We, unfortunately, have not regarded our great democratic experiment as an ongoing *process*, a continually improved-upon system of self-governance that calls for creative engagement by each generation.

The American quest for material security caused Europeans to dismiss us as philistines. In fact, we had a vibrant civic life, but it thrived in informal venues. de Tocqueville noted during his 1828 tour of the United States that we were singular as a citizenry in our propensity for forming clubs and organizations in order to address perceived needs in our communities. Until recent decades, most Americans came of age and lived out their lives in a rich social matrix shaped by communal pleasures and responsibilities. The historic accomplishment of the American political experiment was not only our well-balanced and resilient Constitution but also our grassroots solutions to the traditional Western tension between the individual and society: The structures of society were located not only in government or even in the "mediating institutions," such as churches and labor unions, but also in a plethora of self-organizing groups, clubs, and associations. Quilting bees, hobby clubs, barbershop quartets, Chautauqua events, and youth groups of all sorts provided a weave of relationships that nourished American democracy. Government may have been somewhat distant, but the commonweal was not. "Society," structured with countless cooperative efforts, was no longer construed as an entity that is agonistic to the individual; rather, it made a richly relational life possible.

As we are painfully aware, most of the vitality and the very structures of community life in the United States have been lost over the past twenty-five years. Nationally, membership in youth organizations is a fraction of what it was during my childhood, and the entire range of community organizations is drastically diminished. Isolation and insecurity plague Americans, who spend every evening in front of their television being seduced by wily commercials and vapid entertainment that promise relief of various sorts. The loneliness of feeling disconnected is compounded by the looming realization that the economy—being "downsized" through computerization and the exodus of jobs within the global market—may soon have no further use for you.

The breakdown of community has brought far more problems than personal malaise, of course. Juvenile crime is up. Civility in general is down. In most states, recently passed laws now allow citizens to carry concealed handguns. Politics, healthcare, and public education are all in severe crisis. In spite of the obvious connection among the massive job flight and downsizing encouraged by the global economy, the falling tax base, the cuts in public services, and the strains on communities, the Stratos of both major parties in this country have recently pushed for political decentralization *without economic decentralization*. What a coincidence: The corporate sector is centralizing ownership and control at a dizzying clip as the possibilities for government regulation are to be decentralized. Surely this is not the way to protect and enhance communities.

In the mainstream debate, both Republicans and New Democrats (corporate-friendly baby-boomers like President Clinton) have asserted that liberal democracy, the historic defender of the rights of the individual, has swung too far in that direction and must now reemphasize the rights of the community and society. Sometimes the new orientation is portrayed as the balancing of rights with responsibilities. Sometimes it is called "creating social capital," following the sociological theory of Robert Putnam.[42] Sometimes family and religion are recognized as "premodern" cultural components that are essential to modern society, as even Francis Fukuyama noted after he abandoned his prediction of a global "convergence" as the placid "end of history."[43] Sometimes a "communitarian" agenda, as developed by Amitai Etzioni and others, is promoted as the solution.[44] Nearly always, the emphasis in social prescriptions today is on regenerating "civil society."

These are all admirable goals, but—as I trust readers will recognize by now—they are firmly situated within the prejudices and limitations of modernity. Consequently, they advocate repair of that orientation but cannot correct or even identify the conceptual roots of the growing failures. They assume a dualistic struggle between "rights" versus "responsibilities." They use metaphors of economism: relationships as "capital." They look to premodern cultures only for their social structure, not their vital sense of embeddedness in nature. They seek "communitarian" solutions that stop short of addressing the destructive effects of the new globalized economy on communities. They seek, correctly, to revitalize our atrophied sense of civic life—but we need to go much further. To transform ourselves from being isolated, manipulated consumers glued to our television sets to being participatory guardians and shapers of our communities would be no mean feat,[45] yet we would still be scurrying around inside the glass box of modernity, still radically disconnected from our sustenance and our source, unless we replace the ideologies of denial and heal the wounds they have inflicted.

The call for social regeneration will probably grow even stronger in the near future, but why should we stop short of addressing the deep cause of so much of our alienation? Does it make any sense to speak of expanding our sense of civic, or political, engagement in ways that ignore all the recent discoveries cited in Chapter 1 about our profound physical, psychological, and cultural embeddedness in the processes and relationships of the natural world? Our inner lives have been hideously diminished by isolation from an *eco*social matrix, weighing us down with sadness and apathy. The antidote lies in recovering awareness of our context—*embracing the real*, which is the subject of the final chapter.

～

Tragically, the goal of hypermodern deliverance moves us in the opposite direction, replacing the biosphere with the technosphere as fully and quickly as possible in people's lives. Nowhere is this more apparent than in the last area in which we will consider the current state of the Promethean dream—education. I am defining education broadly to include not only the formal inculcation of knowledge and information that children and adolescents receive in classrooms but also the messages they receive about reality from the media and popular culture today.

As is well known to teachers and college instructors, an alarming proportion of young people today simply do not like to read. One reason is their shrunken vocabularies, down from 25,000 words to 10,000 words in less than fifty years for the average six- to fourteen-year-old child in the United States.[46] Many school children feel put upon if they are asked to read, so teachers increasingly "reach them" through the medium with which they are comfortable, videotapes. College instructors find that students simply refuse to read more than a small number of short books per course, as more would be "overwhelming." Textbooks have been "dumbed down," beginning in the elementary grades, according to limited "readability formulas" beyond which students cannot read without great frustration. Moreover, the practice of building vocabulary through weekly spelling tests in elementary school has been largely abandoned.

So many nonreaders are graduated from our high schools today that between a fifth and a quarter of the U.S. population is functionally illiterate, or partially so. Seventy-five percent of unemployed adults have difficulty reading and writing, and 80 percent of incarcerated adults are functionally illiterate.[47] Compared to a national illiteracy rate of 4.3 percent in 1930, it is difficult to see how the cheerleaders of Progress could wave their banners in this area. It seems that one of the noble dreams of Enlightenment democracy—universal literacy through free education for all people—succeeded after many decades of struggle in achieving a literate electorate only to descend rapidly after World War II from that pinnacle, which had looked so convincingly like an endless plateau. What, then, is a realistic expectation for the future? Perhaps it involves people sitting at home in front of a wall of sophisticated multimedia equipment that includes a powerful computer with which they instantaneously transmit messages around the world like the following: "Me like gud. Yu want?"

One of the main reasons so many young people today dislike reading is, of course, that they were mesmerized from an early age by moving images on a television screen. Because I have pleasant memories of watching "Kukla, Fran, and Ollie" and, alas, the more lowbrow "Howdy Doody" in the early 1950s, I saw no reason for concern when my daughter, born in 1971, took an interest in "Sesame Street" as a preschooler. I watched it with her and found it clever and engaging. Around that time the first criticisms of "Sesame Street" appeared, claiming that the program essentially trained children to watch television, not to read. "This show is brought to you by the letter E!" I thought, *What a bunch of grinches! How could anyone dislike "Sesame Street"? It's so cute!* Later on, though, I realized what the naysayers had been worried about.

In spite of being read to as a young child and developing various reading enthusiasms, such as Agatha Christie novels in fifth grade, my daughter at puberty got sucked into the mass culture and molded into a highly focused consumer of young-teen magazines, television shows, posters, and record albums featuring marketable teen-boy heartthrobs. Worst of all, *she stopped reading*, except for school work. I found this development deeply distressing because in the reader's communion with the mind of the author lies a richness of experience I could not bear for her to lose. In reading fiction, she would pace the dialogue, cast the characters, imagine the landscape, and enter into that magical world she had co-created. As a reader, she would deliberate over the author's insights at her own speed, or drop into a very private reverie, or be unimaginably moved by the fecund art of language and storytelling. *All this* traded down for the passive role of consumer of someone else's casting, pacing, imaging, landscapes, and manipulative soundtracks? A bleak fate indeed. A post-literate culture is not an egalitarian triumph but a wasteland, a grotesque amusement park for the functionally lobotomized.

As I had intermittently done in the past, I got rid of our television set and hoped for the best. It was a long time coming, but this child *saved* herself: After high school, she became a reader again! She even decided eventually to major in English and American literature at college.

(Other members of my family were not as thrilled as I with her decision: "Not another 'Unemployable English Major for Peace' in the family!")

What about the children born after her? I wonder if those born before, say, 1972 or so were the last American children to pass through their formative years before the full media onslaught of videogames, videotapes at school, quick-cut editing of rock videos and commercials, television for several hours per day, Walkmans, and computer software for preschoolers on up. Children whose entire existence has been saturated with these accoutrements reached college age during the 1990s. The effects of their electronic upbringing are considered by Sven Birkerts in *The Gutenberg Elegies: The Fate of Reading in an Electronic Age* (1994). In teaching a course in 1992 on nineteenth- and twentieth-century American short stories to a class that included many students from "relatively advantaged backgrounds," he found that they had difficulty slowing down enough—from the world of music, TV, and videos—to concentrate on prose of any density. They had problems with allusions and "pretentious" vocabulary or any that they considered archaic. They were uncomfortable with indirect or interior passages, and they were particularly put off by ironic tone because it flaunted superiority, making them feel they were missing something. Even bright students retreated into what Birkerts calls "glum illiteracy," telling him that a particular story "just bugged me." His experience is similar to that of many teachers I know.

On reflection, Birkerts delineated the gains and losses of a hyper-modern upbringing as follows:

> The gains of electronic postmodernity could be said to include, for individuals, (a) an increased awareness of the "big picture," a global perspective that admits the extraordinary complexity of interrelations; (b) an expanded neural capacity to accommodate a broad range of stimuli simultaneously; (c) a relativistic comprehension of situations that promotes the erosion of old biases and often expresses itself as tolerance; and (d) a matter-of-fact and unencumbered sort of readiness, a willingness to try new situations and arrangements.
>
> In the loss column, meanwhile, are (a) a fragmented sense of time and a loss of the so-called duration experience, that depth phenomenon we associate with reverie; (b) a reduced attention span and a general impatience with sustained inquiry; (c) a shattered faith in institutions and in the explanatory nar-

ratives that formerly gave shape to subjective experience; (d) a divorce from the past, from a vital sense of history as a cumulative or organic process; (e) an estrangement from geographic place and community; and (f) an absence of any strong vision of a personal or collective future.[48]

A flat, shallow play of rapidly changing sounds and images becomes the hypermodern child's field of consciousness. *That* is what those early critics of "Sesame Street" were on to, I came to understand: The letter E, dancing around the screen to upbeat music, was always going to be more engaging for the child than a dead E lying silent and motionless on the printed page. Here, as in other encounters with technology, the human capacity for adaptation can get us into trouble as we gradually mold our habits and consciousness to conform to the capabilities of the device. For childen who watch a great deal of television from an early age, the development of their brains' neural fields that is related to mental imaging is sometimes impaired. Traditionally, very young children are exposed to the "table talk" of family members, to grandparent's tales, and to bedtime stories—all of which evoke the child's visual imagination and, thereby, the growth of synaptic connections and neural networks. When a young child is fed a steady diet of visual images along with language, the brain adapts in the most efficient manner by finding the shortest connection between aural and visual stimuli, resulting in a massive elimination of neural development. Since subsequent stages of development of neural structure build on the earlier ones, the capacity for internal imaging and related learning can be permanently retarded. When this sort of technological damage is pronounced, children and adolescents cannot work well with metaphoric and symbolic systems of expression. They are also more prone to violence than their peers who have higher levels of skill in internal imaging. Fortunately, remedial therapies that build this skill have been found to increase learning and retention by up to 40 percent.[49] How many of the millions of damaged children will be reached by these therapies, however? What therapies can replace all the interactive time in families of earlier decades that is now given over to television programming of little value and hundreds of thousands of commercials?

The loss of intergenerational communication is also an effect of the other major influence on children's educational experience today: the growing use of computers in classrooms and homework. This use is on the rise in spite of evidence that it promotes passivity, dull creativity, and shyness and other problems in socialization.[50] The reason computer-based learning has attained such a dominant presence in teacher-training, and increasingly in the teaching of all grade levels, is far deeper than a "pragmatic" response to the requirements of employers. The kind of knowledge that is adaptable to computers and the type of interaction that is possible combine to deliver a potent amplification of the ideologies of modernity.

One of the most astute critics of computer-mediated learning, Chet Bowers, has focused attention on the largely unexamined ways in which computer use amplifies or reduces various cultural orientations. Foremost, it reinforces the modern sense of the individual as the basic social unit—an autonomous rational agent who is empowered by his or her ability to attain access to data and manipulate it. The tradition of communication from elders is replaced by the storage capacity of the CD-ROM and Hypertext, with which children are assured they will be able to create their *own* sense of the world. Computer-based technologies amplify the scientistic notion of thinking as data processing, and they amplify forms of knowledge that can be made explicit, digitalized, and communicated as context-free data and images. These technologies amplify the modern view of temporality that frames the individual's experience of time in terms of what is seen as relevant to an immediate problem or a personal sense of meaning, rather than the time cycles of the ecological and cosmological realm, of which nonmodern cultures are deeply aware. Computer use also amplifies a conduit view of language that is essential to the self-universalizing characteristics of modern consciousness. This view, like the metaphor "information superhighway," creates the illusion that what is being communicated between computers is culturally neutral—that is, objective, context-free data. Thus, computer-based education, emphasizes a decontextualized pattern of thinking, which increasingly reduces sensitivity to local contexts, cultural patterns, and ecosystems. It amplifies an exclusively human-centered, egocentric, and instrumental way of understanding moral relationships toward others and the rest of nature. Finally, computer-based technologies amplify the modern penchant for thinking about life in mechanistic terms, blurring the distinction, for instance, between "memory" and "data retrieval." Computers are hardly neutral tools for students but expressions of what Bowers calls "the particular messianic ethos of modernity."[51] The purpose of modern education is to further modern development.

The very characteristics cited above—and the "high-status forms of knowledge" that are compatible with them—are, of course, applauded by champions of modernity. An example is an article on computer-based education that appeared in *Scientific American* in September 1991. The author, Alan C. Kay, explains that even though "humans are predisposed by biology to live in the barbarism of the deep past," we can escape that fate through "an effort of will and through the use of our invented representations." He reminds readers that the Autonomous Individual of modern ideology is indeed a self-constituting being: ". . . each of us has to construct our own version of reality by main force. Literally, to make ourselves. And we are quite capable of devising new mental bricks, new ways of thinking, that can enormously expand the understanding we attain. The bricks we develop become new technologies for thinking." Focusing on new ideas is the way we can escape from "the old ways," which are, of course, embedded in religion, community, tradition, culture, the perspectives of elders, and a moral, reciprocal relationship with nature. Kay cites the ecological crisis as a suitable topic for children working on computers, since they would come to understand the interactions among people and animals. In Kay's article, as elsewhere in modern systems of knowledge, attention to "ecology" is tacked on by reducing the real to proportions that are managable within the assumptions of modernity. Bower notes,

> For Kay, and others conditioned to think that progress is guaranteed through continued technological innovation, there is no reason to limit the self by bringing our embeddedness in a larger mental ecology (as Bateson calls it) into the foreground or to complicate our view of language and thought by suggesting that the epistemology underlying the promise of the Information Age has closed off the multiple ways of knowing and communicating that may be essential to our long-term survival. The ecological crisis, for Kay, does not suggest the need to understand the moral and spiritual roots of the double bind that now characterizes modern society; rather it suggests the need for more computer simulations, more data, and more individually generated ideas. This failure to understand that the relationships and patterns that make up an ecology should involve, for humans, a sensitivity to the moral dimension of all relationships seems to be a tragic flaw in Kay's thinking. The

real crisis is not the lack of data or computer literacy, but the lack of moral and spiritual development that takes account of the interconnectedness of life.[52]

I fear that "a sensitivity to the moral dimension of relationships" is also being eroded by the gradual elimination of literature from the high school curriculum. A national survey conducted in February 1996 asked 1164 teachers which subjects they consider "absolutely essential." Seventy-two percent included "computer skills and media technology," while only 24 percent included "classic works from such writers as Shakespeare and Plato," and only 23 percent included "modern American writers such as Steinbeck and Hemingway." Only "sports and athletics" ranked lower than literature. Basic skills, good work habits, and the ability to manipulate data ranked high.[53] These are admirable as partial elements of an education, but to make them the principal goal is a pathetic reduction of a child's potential cosmological unfolding to the functional qualifications needed to render them well-trained workers in the hypermodern economy.

Many teachers have noticed a rapid decline in American adolescents' sense of moral reasoning during the current decade. Only five years ago, students often reported that they were well aware of a framework for moral reasoning but found it irrelevant. By the mid-nineties, many adolescents had no answer when asked what moral principles might apply to a particular circumstance. Can we really be so surprised, though, that alienation and apathy, random violence, and hate crimes are on the increase? When modernity's ideology of the Autonomous Individual, is the focal point of life as a student and then as a consumer in the hypermodern world, what result but a deep sense of disconnection could we reasonably expect? The interrelated realities of body, nature, and place, even on a purely physical level, render preposterous the idea of a purely autonomous organism—as if the Lone Cowboy had no interaction with air, water, and food, as if he were not connected in his very molecules with all entities born of the universe. Beyond the physical level, education should rightfully amplify, rather than sever, the unspoken sense of connectedness a young child feels with the world, just as the ecospiritual processes of socialization in a traditional native culture do.

With very few exceptions, theories of child development and education during the twentieth century have been thoroughly anthropocentric: the modern child coming of age in the "glass box" on top of nature. The most influential theory of them all is Freud's positing of *separation* as the essential process of healthy maturation. According to modern depth psychologists, children—or, more to the point, male children, since they were always assumed to be the human norm—made their way free of (maternal) relationship, passed through various stages of needs and experiences, and perhaps even delved into the "collective unconsciousness." What they did not do in this model, however, is step outdoors. An exception to the modern ideology of child development is the body-oriented, ecological, and relational approach of the Waldorf system of education, developed by the Christian eco-mystic Rudolf Steiner during the 1920s and still thriving.[54]

To reconsider child development and education in an ecological-postmodern orientation, we could hardly do better than consult *The Ecology of Imagination in Childhood* by Edith Cobb. Published in 1977, the year before she died, this luminous compilation of insights, drawn over twenty years, grew out of her experiences as an amateur naturalist, a mother and grandmother, and a student and longtime friend of Margaret Mead. Cobb came to see "a biosynthesis of perception (mind) and cosmos"—"a conjugation of mind and culture"—as the essential dynamic of child development. She saw that a child's cognitive processes are acts of integration of self and environment. A child moves not *away* from relationship to an autonomous state of the lone individual but, rather, moves *into* a cosmological exploration of the immediate environment and the perception of an ever-increasing complexity and inclusiveness in the structure of *gestalten*. The experience of childhood is an intersection of biology and cosmology, as body and universe are engaged in a harmoniously ongoing process. In perceiving the harmony of body and nature, the child perceives pre-verbally the logic of relationships, the beginning of physiological wisdom. Cobb suggested that the linear causal sequences emphasized in modern education should be complemented by "the reticulate approach to knowledge" derived from the intuitive levels that are closer to sensory experiences and the earth. Left to its own devices, scientific discourse depersonalizes relations with humans and nature. Cobb concluded that the ability to transcend "adaptive behavior that might be too narrowly confined" depends on cultivating "compassionate intelligence," a process of identification in which humility is the creative tool. In all this, Cobb warned that a child's development is regulated by the meanings of nature imparted by her or his culture.

Those cultural meanings must surely rush to catch up now with the assertions of body, nature, and place described in Chapter 1. The emergent postmechanistic sense of reality demands a rethinking of the nature of intelligence, moving from the Cartesian model of the detached spectator and manipulator to a sense of our place and responsibility in a dynamic web of ecosocial processes. In this model, connection and creativity are central. What would that mean for education? Far more than the usual call for school reform to produce more competitive workers in the global economy. That sort of reform has launched efforts by companies and foundations in Silicon Valley to get a computer on every school child's desk, a campaign they see as "patriotic." On the other hand, the current plethora of proposals for school reform also include efforts to ground education in ecological awareness in a deep and broad sense. The focus of such curriculum design is ecological *processes,* such as interdependence, sustainability, partnership, flexibility, diversity, and co-evolution. This approach is sometimes called "ecoliteracy," although it should not be confused with far more narrowly focused "environmental education."[55] A related approach involves bringing bioregional consciousness and "place-oriented education" into classrooms.[56]

As for ecological-postmodern options at the college level, enough has been said earlier in this book about economics, politics, psychology, and philosophy to give a rough idea of what those disciplines might be like— in a far more interdisciplinary curriculum, of course, than the modern model allows. New ways of conceiving research would also be central.[57] Before reading the contemporary philosophers of body, nature, and place mentioned in Chapter 1, philosophy students would, of course, immerse themselves in the foundational works of Goethe, Coleridge, Charles Sanders Peirce, William James, Henri Bergson, Alfred North Whitehead, and John Muir. In the field of history, much could be done to disabuse students of the received assumption that culture developed through the clever manipulations of some guys sitting around in that "glass box." For a consideration of how inventions first devised for ritual purposes (such as shoes, chairs, mats, rugs, forks, and calendars) were most likely evoked by the blood mysteries of the female body, for instance, students could read Judy Grahn's *Blood, Bread, and Roses: How Menstruation Created the World* (1993). To open their eyes to the cultural developments that derived from human interactions with other species, they might well read the late Paul Shepard's *The Others: How Animals Made Us Human* (1996). As for place, the results of treating it badly because a civilization felt superior to ecosystems are well documented in Clive Ponting's *A Green History of the World: The Environment and the Collapse of Great Civilizations* (1991). Even if these three assigned books were "balanced" with thirty anthropocentric, androcentric, Eurocentric, economistic history texts from the modern canon, the students, who have a very low tolerance at that age for "phoniness" or denial, would begin to see the ideological glass box as something of a tomb.

Regarding the state of education globally, two aspects of the Promethean reality are particularly relevant here. First, *seventy million children under age twelve* are not receiving any schooling because they must work full-time. As the "structural adjustments" forced on most governments in the Three-Quarters World reduce public services and sacrifice traditional employment structures, parents find that survival depends upon all family members bringing in a daily pittance. Second, the modern model of development and the mass consumer culture spread by the marketing efforts of the globalized TNCs inculcate a powerful message: Young people of the Three-Quarters World are pitifully backward and inferior if they do not manage to dress, eat, act, and live like the modern Westerners they see in advertising, movies, and even textbooks. The self-loathing that is implanted in nonmodern children is also felt by many adults, who are increasingly bombarded with visual messages about the sexy superiority of life in a modern consumer society.

The modern schooling brought into traditional cultures as part of the modern model of development can have devastating effects on children and their families. The process is astutely described in *Ancient Futures: Learning from Ladakh* (1991) by Helena Norberg-Hodge, who witnessed over the past twenty years the transformation of Ladakh (western Tibet, now part of the Indian state of Kashmir) from a society of self-sufficiency and cultural pride to one of broken connections and shame, especially among young men, over their nonmodern traditions. The modern schooling, which teaches children competitiveness and regimentation to prepare them for (scarce) modern jobs in the capital, renders local knowledge so low-status as to be unworthy of mention. The traditional Buddhist values of loving kindness and compassion do not seem to fit into the new world that absorbs the children. They study Homer and Tennyson and hope to acquire some of the Rambo toys and Barbie dolls that populate the bazaar. After close observation of the effects of modern "development" on scores of families, Norberg-Hodge concludes that it is a war against their identity, their sense of self, and their spirituality. All over the world, the spread of the globalized monoculture is forcefully eradicating ecosocial forms of culture that evolved *in place*. It is estimated that most of the world's six thousand languages will be extinct, or nearly so, by the end of the next century.[58]

~

In all three of the areas considered in this chapter—economics, politics, and education—technology has played a substantial role in creating the hypermodern condition. Technology is neither a force unto itself, dragging us along in its wake, nor merely an aggregate of neutral, value-free tools. The purpose and design of every new technology reflects our culture. In recent years, we have seen that technological innovation carries forth modern values into hypermodern forms. To judge them solely on the basis of a narrow, quantifiable sense of "efficiency" is to miss or to obfuscate their complex, systemic effects. Television, for instance, provides entertainment, but it also functions, in both its programming and its commercials, as the delivery system for modern values, as Jerry Mander has noted. It homogenizes values and desires while shutting out alternative visions. He observes,

> Television is uniquely suited to implant and continuously reinforce dominant ideologies. And, while it hones our minds, it also accelerates our nervous systems into a form that matches the technological reality that is upon us. Television effectively produces a new form of human being—less creative, less able to make subtle distinctions, speedier, and more interested in *things*—albeit better able to handle, appreciate, and approve of the new technological world.[59]

Those of us socialized in modern societies generally maintain an irrationally uncritical attitude toward new technologies. In keeping with modernity's radically experimental attitude toward life, we have been perfectly willing to allow our children and ourselves to be guinea pigs in whom various detrimental effects may or may not manifest. We place our trust in the new, of course, because modernity's faith in technological innovation as Progress is so pervasive. The public's enthusiasm for, or at least acceptance of, new technologies is facilitated by the marketing of selected features of new devices. In the Information Age, computers are touted as the great levelers, democratically delivering unlimited information to all individuals. True, individuals and grassroots organizations have used computer networks to their benefit—but not nearly as much as the entities benefiting from the enormous increase in centralized power. The huge data banks, the unnerving monitoring and surveillance capabilities, and the instantaneous movement of billions of dollars on behalf of financial speculators have had far greater effects than the delights of home computers.

Even a brief look at the effects of recently developed technologies on body, nature, and place (in addition to those already discussed) reveals that the ubiquitous technological triumphalism is yet another ideology of denial. As we celebrate modernity for its medical breakthroughs, we should also be aware that the fate of the *body* in the hypermodern future is to be engineered in ways that are more compatible with postbiological efficiency. For example, Grenada Biosciences of Texas has applied to the European Patent Office for a patent on genetically altered mammals; the patent application was carefully worded to include human females such as the possibility of a "pharm-woman" who would produce valuable pharmaceutical products in her breast milk.[60] In a related vein, it seems likely that the new capabilities for eugenics will go beyond sex selection and disease prevention to the designing of physical appearance and traits that increase one's "marketability." According to polls, young people are more amenable than older citizens in the United States to the sale of body organs, blood, eggs, and sperm; the hire of wombs as surrogate "incubator" mothers; and other market-oriented uses of biotechnology.[61]

The deleterious influence on *nature* of a range of technological interventions is by now widely recognized, at least in the most critical areas. What is astounding is that so many discoveries about very basic effects of widespread technologies have been made only recently. Not until 1996, for instance, did researchers determine that several pesticide chemicals (endosulfan, dieldrin, toxaphene, and chlordane), which are known individually to have only a slight effect on the gene that controls the amount of estrogen produced in humans, are 500 to 1000 times more potent as endocrine-disrupters when an individual is exposed to them in combination in the environment![62] (The level of estrogen has been linked to breast cancer and the malformation of male sex organs.) How is it that no one involved in toxicology research ever considered such a basic interactive possibility? Only blind faith in the modern models, among the public as well as the experts, could have blocked awareness of so many ecological realities for so long.

The effects of technology on *place* include paving it over, as is painfully clear to so many Americans who have fought unwise "development" in their communities. In addition, communities are now vulnerable to "cyberwar," computer-based disruption of power plants and telephone lines as well as the mass draining of bank accounts. (The FBI's code for such actions is to "darken a city," a computer skill that reportedly has led to the recruitment of hackers by "violent anti-government groups."[63]) More immediate casualties are the ecosocial affiliations with place that are displaced for people so engrossed in the "virtual community" of computer networks that those hypermodern relationships become more real and meaningful than interactions with family, neighbors, and others in their bioregion.

The fact that so many of the detrimental effects of various technologies have caught us by surprise should logically focus attention on *technology assessment*. As one might guess, however, this is not a development encouraged by those who reap profits from an uninterrupted stream of new technological products. One of the acts of the "Republican Revolution" in Congress was to close the Congressional Office of Technology Assessment in 1995. The even more alarming (to some) notion of public participation in determining technology policy has made more headway in several European countries than here. The Danish government's Technology Board, for instance, selects panels of citizens of varying backgrounds for conferences at which experts in, for example, genetic manipulation of animal breeding make presentations and are cross-examined by the citizens' panel. The government then publicizes the judgments of the panels through the news media, videotapes, leaflets, and local debates. Surveys show that the Danish public and politicians are better informed on issues addressed in this way than are citizens in other countries facing similar questions. In the United States, several proposals are afoot— and, unfortunately, underfoot—to broaden participation in decisions regarding technological development, such as requiring social- and political-impact statements, initiating voluntary social trials, and establishing community research-and-policy centers at universities.[64] Technologies are systems of social management and organization as well as production. Since they are inherently political, economic, social, environmental, and psychological phenomena, we can understand and address their full impact only if we mount a systemic analysis.

The gap between that level of public awareness and the actual "technological trance" operative in this most modern of societies was dramatically demonstrated in 1995. The "Unabomber" mailed the FBI a 30,000-word manifesto, which was later published in several newspapers around the country. The manifesto was a hodge-podge of criticisms of modern industrial society, much of which drew on common themes and insights from widely respected—and certainly nonviolent—critics of technology. From the time the FBI received the document, it made clear in press conferences that their investigation was focused on questioning scores of professors and high school teachers in cities linked with the Unabomber's mailings in order to try to ascertain where such ideas could possibly have come from! I was baffled that they were baffled. Moreover, I found it astounding that the national media accepted the FBI's puzzlement as unsurprising. Not a single reporter said, "Wait a minute: This school of thought is well established. It was pioneered by Lewis Mumford, Jacques Ellul, Rachel Carson, E. F. Schumacher, Herbert Marcuse, and others." So many authors have advanced the critique of technology in the past twenty years—Theodore Roszak, Ivan Illich, Neil Postman, Langdon Winner, Kirkpatrick Sale, Chellis Glendinning, Jerry Mander, Jeremy Rifkin, Susan Griffin, Joseph Weizenbaum, Andrew Kimbrell, Wendell Berry, Helena Norberg-Hodge, Jonathon Porritt, Gary Snyder, Irene Diamond, and others—that I have an entire bookcase of such works. Surely the mystery was not the source of critical thinking about modern industrial society but, rather, the Unabomber's personal motivation for twisting this tradition into violent deeds. I waited in vain to hear anyone investigating or reporting on the case say anything like this. Finally, I had to admit that this entire school of thought was apparently invisible to the modern American mainstream.

When the Unabomber's manifesto was published, media stories soon appeared on the surprising "resonance" readers were expressing with parts of the critique of technology—as if this were a new subject of thought. No one seemed to remember Mumford's warnings, thirty years earlier, of the "immense bribe" offered by the "Megamachine": the absorption of every human activity into the technological realm by seductive assurances of ever-increasing ease, power, and abundance. People who do entertain such concerns these days are often called "neoLuddites," a label proudly accepted by most of the writers listed above. The name refers to the Luddite uprisings in England in 1812–1813, wherein workers displaced by steam-driven looms and other "Machinery hurtful to the Commonality" smashed the new contraptions and stormed the factories. Immediately perceiving the destruction of their community that industrialism would bring, the people in the Yorkshire towns around the factories hid and protected the rebels. The government, however, passed a law that dramatically communicated the new values of the industrial era: Men who destroyed the new machinery would be tried for a capital crime and executed.[65] NeoLuddites, in contrast, strive nonviolently to awaken society from the technological trance. What is required of each new technology, they ask, to perpetuate itself? Whom does it empower? Does it foster diverse forms of knowledge? Does it de-authorize traditional forms of community? How much waste is generated by the technology? What are its secondary effects? What is its addictive potential? How does it affect our perception of our needs?

The ontological issues raised by these basic questions bring to mind Ernst Junger's observation at the end of World War I that technology is the real metaphysics of the twentieth century. Nowhere is that more apparent than in the contemporary celebrations of a posthuman, cyborg existence in which Technoman and Technoworld finally escape the constraints of body, nature, and place. The Renaissance dream of becoming terrestrial gods on earth—and beyond—is finally realized in the near-future extolled in such books as *Metaman: The Merging of Humans and Machines into a Global Superorganism* (1993) by Gregory Stock and *Out of Control: The Rise of Neo-Biological Civilization* (1994) by Kevin Kelly. Both of these books, as well as scores of similar works, assert that the advent of machine intelligence is creating an extension of the natural world, through which human existence is being redefined to our benefit. Software is now being "grown biologically" (evolved via random bits of code), leading to self-governance beyond the reach of humans. According to Kelly, the old, mechanistic, "top-down" type of control is being replaced with software that mimics nature. Eventually, myriad sensors will feed information into a huge web (of which the Internet is only one part), thereby creating a new "ecology." Life will be redefined as a continuum of different qualities. Kelly has formulated "The Nine Laws of God" by which adepts of the new technology can "incubate somethings from nothing" just as nature does.[66]

If one applies to these technologies the basic questions of assessment posed two paragraphs back, a colossal headache should result. A wrenching heartache is in order as well, for I do believe that the lure of the hypermodern dazzles only because our sense of being has been gutted by modernity. Because our ecological and cosmological self has been denied for so long, we do not comprehend what is being traded away.

Ten years ago, I attended an all-day presentation by two of our finest writers on the natural world, Barry Lopez and Richard Nelson. A love of language and nature—and a humility before both—permeated their comments, but one observation in particular lodged vividly in my memory. After speaking about the ways in which wild animals are so acutely aware of minute events in their considerable range of attention that their consciousness extends far beyond their fur into the sensate forest, Lopez observed that a bear taken out of its habitat and put into a zoo is still a form of mammalian life, but it's not a bear.

It's not a bear.

It's not a human if its felt connections with the unfolding story of the bioregion, the Earth community, and the cosmos are atrophied, denied, and replaced. *It's not a human* if it can no longer experience awe and wonder at the beauty and mystery of life, seeing nothing but resources and restraints. *It's not a human* if it is socialized to be oblivious to the unity of life, so lonely that it is vulnerable to all compensatory snares.

The only way we can recover a full sense of being is to develop awareness of the modern reduction and to cultivate a deeper participation in life. One of the whiz kids of Silicon Valley, called the "Sage of Cyberspace," said recently, "I think mankind is a species hell-bent on building artificial intelligence to overcome human loneliness."[67] How about "rebuilding" human intelligence? Loneliness is rare in most nonmodern cultures. Only poor Prometheus would mistake it for a species trait, as "natural" as a shriveled spirituality that craves relief.

DON'T CALL IT
ROMANTICISM!

W
E HAVE INVESTED SO MUCH FAITH in the ideologies of
modernity for so long that anyone who points out their fail-
ings and calls for a change of course seems to threaten our
common identity, our chosen destiny, and our covenant with progress.
Such critics are trivialized and placed firmly at the margins of serious
concern. They are called "unrealistic," "ill-informed," and "impractical"—in a word, "Romantic."

In common parlance, "Romantic" is a pejorative label connoting
a sentimental, immature perspective. It implies a lack of self-discipline, a
Dionysian indulgence. That association has been constructed from a mis-
interpretation of the German and British Romantic movements, some two
hundred years ago, as advocating "emotion" and "imagination" over rational thought. (What they actually meant by "imagination" and other
concepts will be addressed presently.) Critiques of modernity are seen as
recurrent outbursts of Romanticism that society must put up with, as little as possible, every twenty years or so. "Back-to-nature types," "spirituality buffs," "peaceniks"—all keep resurfacing, and all are regarded as
bothersome gnats by modern institutions. Science disdains as "Romantic"
anyone who fails to accept the scientific establishment as the sole propri-
etor of truth. Politics, left and right, shouts down as "Romantic" any
proposals so visionary as to reject core concepts of modernity like

economism, materialism, or an agonistic stance toward nature. As for the media, both public and corporate, they display an acutely loyal sense of which worldview is paying their salaries.

Since the popular media construct "the news" with deeply ingrained assumptions of modernity, they rarely have to mention the infrastructure of concepts behind it all. Imagine my surprise, then, to be leafing through the front section of the newspaper one Sunday in late April 1995 and catch sight of what seemed to be a brief lecture explicating the dynamics of the Scientific Revolution, the Enlightenment, and the Romantic movement. Wide-eyed, I read the paragraphs more closely. Following a brief mention of the Romantic works *Dr. Faustus* and *Frankenstein*, the reporter quoted a professor of history at the State University of New York in Albany: "Historically, there have been waves of frustration and resentment against rational and scientific thought. For example, the Enlightenment was followed by an age of romanticism, in which feeling was valued over rationality." The reporter also quoted a researcher at Polytechnic University in Brooklyn who said that nowadays "scratch most people and you'll get a Luddite." She went on: "The fear of knowledge is very deep in us. It's closely related to our fear of change—and it's eerily embodied in the movies."[1]

It was the usual depiction of science and rationalism as modernity's islands of sanity, surrounded by a sea of muddleheaded Romanticism, but why was this philosophical discourse featured in the news section where the most important events of the day are covered? I scanned backward through the article, which had begun on the front page, and discovered that the subject was the "Unabomber"! The influence of Romanticism was being linked with a vicious sociopath who had mailed sixteen letter bombs since 1978 to people associated with computer research or marketing, killing three people and injuring twenty-three.

Whether the bothersome persistence of "Romanticism" is blamed for outright violence or, as is more usually the case, for a range of indefensibly errant thought, the entire subterfuge is deserving of scrutiny. The first two objections that come to mind need not be elaborated here. That modernity's derisive portrayal of the Romantic movement is inaccurate will be discussed subsequently. Secondly, the pejorative use of "Romanticism" as a tactic to silence criticism of modernity is so commonplace that countless examples could be cited. My interest lies in bringing forth a third objection: An entire lineage of substantive resistance to modernity is blurred, diminished, and distorted by regarding it as mere recurrences of Romanticism. The various resistance movements do have a good deal of common ground with the Romantics, but what they all share is *a larger framework of values based on ecological and spiritual concerns.* The Romantics, like each of the other resistance movements, partook of that ecospiritual sensibility in a particular way.

Purely as a matter of historical accuracy, it makes no sense to label all movements resisting modernity as recurrences of Romanticism because some of them preceded the Romantic movement. True, the English Romantics mounted the first critique of modernity after the grand project of the Enlightenment, the French Revolution, had turned into the Terror, but earlier resistance had challenged earlier phases of modernity on ecospiritual grounds that would later re-emerge, in different form, with the Romantics. The "new mechanical philosophy," which had been framed in the sixteenth and seventeenth centuries by leaders of the Scientific Revolution, was squarely opposed by the "radical sects" during the English civil war (1641–1660). In contrast to the mechanistic worldview, with its minimalist sliver of spiritual content (Deism), the Levelers, Diggers, Muggletonians, Familists, Behmenists, Fifth Monarchy Men, Ranters, and Seekers were associated with the beliefs that God is present in everything in nature (panentheism), that matter is alive, that change occurs through internal dynamics other than a rearrangement of parts, and that any individual can have direct experience of the divine. Just as pejorative labels had been affixed to their respective movements, the entire religious orientation with which they were popularly associated was called "enthusiasm" and disdained as immoderation in religious beliefs. (To this day, more than three hundred fifty years later, the English maintain a horror of appearing enthusiastic.) During the 1640s and 1650s, many influential individuals supported the panentheist view, but after 1655 most of them converted to the "new mechanical philosophy," the winning side.

Another stream of ecospiritual resistance to the mechanistic, atomistic worldview of modernity preceded it by scores of thousands of years and continued alongside it: the cultures of native peoples. Agrarian communities in great number also stubbornly preserved ecospiritual sensibilities, including many pre-Christian practices and symbols, even though they were mocked by modern sophisticates. Although the resistance of both those groups was sometimes active, often with tragic consequences, they usually preferred to be left alone and watch modernity race by at its frenetic pace.

The mention of resistance movements that framed a critique and created alternatives no doubt brings to mind the celebrated rebels of modernity: Marx, Darwin, and Freud. After all, the movements they spawned certainly kicked over aspects of the status quo. Each of those movements, however, remained firmly situated within most of the overarching assumptions of the modern worldview. The resistance movements that were accorded recognition by modern sensibilities, even begrudgingly, were those that merely created new modernities via their "radical break": the mechanistic Darwinian perception of evolution, the Marxist version of economism, the Freudian emphasis on achieving separation from the female body, the Frankfurt School of critical theory that combined Marxist and Freudian thought, the machine aesthetic in design, and the International style in architecture. The most recent so-called "radical break," deconstructionist postmodernism, again continues some of the most problematic beliefs of modernity: discontinuity from nature, disembodied abstraction, solipsistic focus on human endeavors (this time as "language games" of power), hypersubjectivity without responsibility, contempt for spirituality, denial of any inherent unity in life as absolutely "fictive," and adherence to reductionism.

I wish to focus attention, instead, on movements that challenged modernity in a far more fundamental way. They neither limited their critique to the rearrangement of certain power relationships nor accepted the core discontinuities of the modern worldview. Although adherents of these movements are generally dismissed in modern schooling as quixotic losers who fell alongside the forward thrust of Progress, they recognized that reconnecting with nature and/or spirituality must be central to any real reshaping of social relations and institutions in the modern age.

With the following interpretive survey, I hope to move whatever slight appreciation already exists for these movements as a vaguely perceived "counter-stream" in Western history to a more sharply focused recognition that they were specifically countering *the ideologies of denial inherent in modernity* and were doing so from an ecological and/or spiritual orientation. Understood in that light, they constitute a heritage that is relevant to various efforts in our own time to challenge those very ideologies. Even as so many of the assumptions of modernity fade into disillusionment, the act of creating alternatives often seems a singular necessity, unrelated to anything that ever happened before. In fact, a substantive tradition stands behind the contemporary resurgence of body, nature, and place, which, if better understood, could be a source of inspiration. That lineage includes the Romantic movement, the Arts and Crafts movement, the cosmological and spiritual quests in schools of painting, the counter-modern Modernists, Gandhi's Constructive Program, and the counterculture. This chapter, then, focuses on the ways in which the ideas of that tradition were embodied, with the bulk of attention going to the major movements. It is a story of visionary responses to the crises that modernity dares not name and cannot solve.

THE ROMANTIC MOVEMENT
1775–1830

ALTHOUGH COMMONLY DISMISSED TODAY as a bunch of guys who got emotional about nature, the Romantics framed a critique of the ideologies of modernity soon after its last pillar was erected that has remained relevant, insightful, and utterly essential for two hundred years. We are still trying to come to grips with the problems identified by the Romantics. What is lost when a mechanistic worldview shapes not only modern science but also economics, politics, and education? How much of our humanity is never realized because modern socialization creates a disengaged consciousness that makes us feel alien to the Earth community? Is political change that is based on noble principles but unaccompanied by genuine spiritual renewal, such as the French Revolution, destined to create only new tyrannies, instability, and injustice?

The so-called "radical sects" during the English civil war (1641–1660) had protested an early phase of modernity—the extension of the "new mechanical philosophy" from the new science to religious beliefs and projections about the natural world. By the time of the Romantics, one hundred fifty years later, the mechanistic worldview had spread much further. Just as the new science framed by Descartes, Bacon, and Newton had discovered (or perceived) what seemed to be universal laws of matter and energy, so it was now claimed that economics and government were separate spheres that also operated in mechanistic ways according to universal, fixed laws. By the mid-eighteenth century, mechanistic thinking, along with rigid rationalism, had a firm grip not only on the new science, economic theory, and political theory—indeed, it had created them—but on the very sense of being, at least as it was perceived by the educated elite. It was against this first flush of a comprehensive modern worldview that the Romantics spoke out.

The Romantics opposed neither science nor rational thought. What they vociferously objected to was the unwarranted extension of principles applicable in Newtonian physics to our entire understanding of the nature of being. They struggled against the absorption of all reality into the scientistic abstractions of the "single vision," as Blake called the mechanistic worldview, in *Los the Terrible*:

> May God us keep
> From single vision, and Newton's sleep!

They rejected *instrumental* "reason" that was reduced to systems of abstraction, routine, and the denial of all relationships that could not be measured empirically. Reason that is disengaged and tightly regulated would starve other human faculties, they believed. Foremost, the Romantics asserted—sometimes with dramatic expressions of despair—that the modern worldview amounted to a self-destructive denial of our cosmological embeddedness, our dynamic participation in the sacred whole. This is the reason for Keats' indictment of mechanistic philosophy in *Lamia*:

> Do not all charms fly
> At the mere touch of cold philosophy?

The common association of the Romantics with enthusiasm for feelings is accurate only if one realizes that by "feelings" they meant what we would call "sensibilities" today. The Romantics believed that only someone with acutely attentive and receptive sensibilities was capable of deep thought, in contrast to the sort of reasoning performed by a bookkeeper. The key term used by the Romantics to denote the recovery of participatory, engaged consciousness was "imagination." This term referred not to the mere invention of ideas or images (a mental faculty Coleridge labeled "fancy") but to intellectual originality, daring perception, and visionary power. Coleridge contrasted the "brick and mortar" thinking of the mechanistic orientation with the synthesizing, "permeative," and "essentially vital" powers of *imagination*.

The role of perceptual breakthroughs in contemporary "revolutions," or paradigm shifts, in the postmodern sciences is now widely accepted, but the founding fathers of modern science had thought scientific reason ideally to be a state of mental passivity. Both Descartes and Bacon prided themselves on having devised a method of impersonal knowing that was impeccably objective because it was untainted by the dynamic faculties of mind, depending instead on a machinelike regulation of thought. Descartes regarded feelings as corruptions of pure perception, while Bacon viewed human powers of cognition as "a false mirror" that distorts and misperceives reality. As the mechanistic, rationalist worldview spread throughout European culture in the seventeenth and eighteenth centuries, the distrust of "imagination" was linked with disdain for spiritual "enthusiasm." The Romantics squarely embraced them both. As Coleridge wrote in a letter, "I have known some who have been rationally educated, as it is styled. They were marked by a microscopic acuteness, but when they looked at great things, all became blank and they saw nothing, and denied (very illogically) that anything could be seen . . . and called the want of imagination *judgment* and the never being moved to rapture *philosophy*."[2]

The Romantics also sought to resuscitate the relationship between humans and the rest of the natural world. Unlike Blake, who felt that one must pierce through the mechanistic "single vision" *and* the material world to arrive at the sublime heart of Christian spirituality, Wordsworth escaped the confines of "single vision" through communion *with* nature, "whence spiritual dignity originates." Wordsworth cultivated a receptive attitude toward the natural world, regarding his sensory perceptions, particularly seeing and hearing, with an open heart. Often they led him to an erotic swell of gratitude for the dynamic *presence* suffused throughout nature.

In contrast to the atomistic view of scientistic rationalism, the Romantics saw not mechanistic parts and cogs when they looked at nature but a sacred whole, an organic fullness of being. The Romantic philosophy of organicism was developed in England, mainly by Coleridge in his *Biographia Literaria* (1817) and his *Theory of Life* (1848). He was influenced in this effort by the German philosophers Schelling and (A. W.) Schlegel, the English "dynamic" physiologists (Hunter, Saumarez, and Abernethy), and, to a lesser extent, the organistic works of Plotinus, Giordano Bruno, Leibniz, and Jakob Boehme. Coleridge asserted that the absolutist pretensions of the mechanistic worldview—dissolving everything but "geometric abstractions" of figure and motion—should be appreciated as "a fiction of science," not because the observation of various mechanistic processes is false but because that focus yields only partial truth. In opposition to reductionism, he declared, "Depend on it, whatever is grand, whatever is truly organic and living, the whole is prior to the parts." Nature operates, Coleridge believed, through self-organizing processes of unfolding and becoming: "the organic form . . . develops itself from within." Within the sacred whole, change, subjectivity, and diversity are essential characteristics of the natural world. To flatten all this with utilitarian categories and the sort of scientific knowledge that posits humans in opposition to nature "strikes death," Coleridge insisted, to both the natural world and the human spirit.

A more engaged approach to science was also proposed by the most famous German Romantic poet, Goethe. In the last third of his life, he was lionized outside of Germany for his vision of the medieval legend of Dr. Faustus and earlier works. (The German critics apparently could not forgive Goethe his day job, a cushy appointment as a member of the Privy Council of the Duke of Saxe-Weimar, for they scorned him as a dilettante poet and scientist.) Goethe had long since distanced himself from the *Sturm und Drang* movement of his youth—in which adolescent males scandalized their families by declaring that they had become atheistic, republican "freethinkers"—and had come to prefer order and classical aesthetics. Yet his sustained effort to create a science built of subtle perceptions and participatory consciousness places him prominently in the Romantic project. Goethe challenged the arrogance of Newtonian science by asserting, "Everything factual is already theory." Sounding much like a postmodern philosopher of science today, he argued that experiments that manipulate nature merely prove the possibility of manipulation: the "manufacture" of certain types of results and a certain version of reality. Similarly, Goethe felt that hypotheses are too easily raised to the level of scientific dogma, which lulls the scientist to sleep. He also believed that scientists' excessive dependence on instruments increases our alienation from nature. Rejecting both mechanistic materialism and subjective idealism, Goethe based his natural philosophy on the concept of "passive attentiveness," the patient, receptive curiosity that yields a startling moment of insight. This method of gentle familiarity and blending, rather than aggressive invasion, is quite similar to the approach used by the Nobel Laureate Barbara McClintock, much more recently, in her discovery of "jumping genes" in maize plants.

Unlike most deconstructionist critics today, Goethe went beyond the assertion that modern science consists largely of constructed knowledge. He noted that *qualitative* experience is lost when a reductionist empiricism seeks only quantitative generalizations. In Newton's study of light and color, for instance, "the atomistic restriction and isolation" have banished the *feel* of vision, the *experience* of light and color. Goethe insisted on attention to the qualities of form, texture, color, and smell rather than mere measurements.

Anticipating by two hundred years the current emergence of non-mechanistic, post-Darwinian perceptions of evolution, Goethe observed that the way in which species "originate" in earlier species is through nature's processes of self-organizing organic shapings. Internal dynamics, as well as external pressures, were the means by which nature remained "ever changing, ever constant." Goethe perceived each form of being as "a tone, a modification, in a mighty harmony." In *The Metamorphosis of Plants* (1790), he framed a new area of science: morphology, the study of nature's "shaping and reshaping" through dynamic processes that are embedded in unity. For Goethe, nature was "She the Everlasting Oneness in the manyness divined."

Besides their opposition to the mechanistic worldview derived from modern science, the Romantics found equally objectionable the "uniformitarianism" of Enlightenment thought, which saw the world as consisting of simple, uniform components. Universal assumptions about the nature of the human and its suitability for rationalist social engineering were countered by the Romantic insistence that all individuals are unique and incomparable: Every individual is a revelation of the possibilities inherent in the human species. This emphasis yielded four areas of development in Romantic thought. The first—influenced strongly by Rousseau's pioneering break from the major assumptions of Enlightenment thought that prevailed in the late 1750s—was a diverse range of "emancipatory projects." Since individuals were now seen as inherently good, new forms of "natural education" emerged in which the creative unfolding of the child was central. This orientation later influenced Froebel in Germany, Pestalozzi in Switzerland, Montessori in Italy, and Dewey in the United States. Since nature was no longer to be tortured into grid-shaped gardens, a new design aesthetic of liberation emerged, replacing Renaissance regularity with curves, surprising turns, and "wild" areas. The emancipatory theme in Rousseau's *Emile* (1762) inspired the young Goethe and Schiller to write passionate tales of young men kicking over both traditional and rationalist restraints; later the works of Musset, Hugo, George Sand, and many others continued this literary stream.

Rousseau's most dramatic sphere of influence, however, was the political agitation that culminated in the French Revolution, which he did not live to see. His *Discourse on the Origin of Inequality* (1755) and *The Social Contract* (1762) indicted the corrupting influence of contemporary social institutions and called for a new order legitimated by the sovereignty of the people: the "general will," rather than rule by Enlightened despots. His works were cited frequently, not only by revolutionaries in France but by idealistic young people in neighboring countries. They believed, as the French Revolution approached, that a salvational liberation of all Europe was about to occur. Wordsworth recalled that feeling in *The Prelude*:

> Bliss was it in that dawn to be alive.
> But to be young was very Heaven!

A second effect of the Romantic emphasis on the unique characteristics of the individual was a high regard for subjectivity and expressivism. Unlike the "radical sects" before them and several of the ecospiritual movements that came after them, the Romantics were much less engaged with regenerating community than with celebrating artistic genius. The creative act was seen as heroic, the proof of an elevated level of existence. All this established an irresistible pull into narcissism for certain "creative types," in which individual expression trumped any relational or moral concerns. This sort of self-absorbed indulgence made the male Romantic ideal unappealing to several female writers of the day; their own Romantic works—which are finally being gathered in anthologies—are far more relational.[3] Sometimes, as in the case of Mary Shelley, they wrote critically of the enshrinement of the autocratic male creative genius. She let it be known that the joint inspiration for the creative but irresponsible scientist in her novel *Frankenstein* came from two famous male authors she knew well: her rationalist father, William Godwin, and her Romantic husband, Percy Bysshe Shelley.

The Romantic embrace of the particular, rather than a homogenized notion of "the simple," applied to cultures as well as individuals. Romantic spokesmen in several countries opposed the Enlightenment's "esprits simplistes" and emphasized, instead, the grand diversity of society. Herder asserted that the particular character of each nationality manifested itself in its *Volkgeist*, or folk-spirit. This unique character, apparent in a people's customs, institutions, art, and literature, was regarded by the Romantics as intrinsically valuable. In contrast to the Enlightenment projection of universal and immutable precepts, Herder argued in 1767 that the *Weltgeist*, or spirit of the world, is continually developing. He collected folk songs in several Slavic countries and encouraged a sense of cultural pride that spread throughout Europe. It should be noted that murderous national*ism* is sometimes traced to this Romantic enthusiasm for the particularity of culture, but the Romantics' organic vision honored diversity, not the dominion of any one branch over the entire tree of life, or even part of it.

Attention to the particular was also extended to the moment, the singular quality of one's fleeting perceptions of life. This focus was central not only in Romantic poetry but in music as well. Romantic composers shifted their focus from the shape of composition, which was central to classical works, to the qualities of sound. The particular *timbre* of various instruments, for instance, received close attention from such Romantics as Weber, Rossini, and Berlioz. The Romantic taste for creative experimentation manifested itself in Beethoven's late symphonies, Schubert's coloration, and Chopin's new tonalities, harmonies, and *rubato*. Entirely new genres, such as *Lieder* and "impromptus," were pioneered by Schubert's Romantic sensibilities.

Sensitivity to fleeting emotions and the eternal flux of life led to the Romantic sense of restlessness, which is evident in paintings by Gericault and Delacroix. In painting landscapes, Romantic artists eschewed the Enlightenment's notion of nature as an orderly background for decidedly rational human subjects; instead, they portrayed nature as wild, powerful, and unpredictably dynamic. Constable, Turner, and Friedrich all captured a sense of wonder at the grand drama of the natural world. The Romantics' appreciation of the High Middle Ages as an era of spiritual cultures was expressed by a group of German painters called the Nazarenes, who dedicated themselves to reviving the spiritual purity of pre-Renaissance art. (Later, the Arts and Crafts movement would admire the medieval period for different reasons, related to work and craftsmanship.)

Finally, the English Romantics' dashed hopes for the outcome of the French Revolution led them to see not only that a deep transformation of society would not be forthcoming from politics alone but also that a rapaciously destructive sort of transformation—industrialism—was gradually engulfing Britain no matter what political slogans were proclaimed. The "dark satanic mills" of the industrialized Midlands and the new view of workers as "machines" were deplored by several Romantic voices. Coleridge insisted on the interdependence of economic issues and social, moral, and religious concerns. Although the Continent was less industrialized, Schleiermacher observed that the notion of industrial progress as a salvational transformation was deeply flawed, as it depended on a restriction of the full capabilities of the worker. In France, Sismondi warned of the effects of overindustrialization and the amoral assumptions of the modern economic theory. Although the Romantics' dire pronouncements on industrialism did not get through to Marx, he was influenced in his early work by their critique of the new reduction of a human being to the worth of his labor as a commodity. Marx soon turned away from their deeply holistic analysis of alienation, however, to the more narrow confines of economism: The belief that all of society's problems stem from "the forces and relations of production," so the entire solution lies simply in restructuring economic dynamics.

For the purposes of this survey, three aspects of the fate of Romanticism are especially pertinent: how it died, how it lingered on in mutated versions, and how it was revived and distorted for base intentions much later on. In a very literal sense, the movement experienced an abrupt die-off after 1820—first with the deaths of Keats, Shelley, and Byron (1821–1824), followed by the deaths of Blake, Schubert, (Friedrich) Schlegel, Scott, Hazlitt, and Coleridge (1827–1834). Not only were most of the leading voices silenced, but British and European societies were gripped by then with the promise of increased well-being through industrialism. From the bully pulpit of nineteenth-century materialism, the concerns of the Romantics were relegated to the realm of the epiphenomenal. Such matters, in any case, would surely be resolved, it was thought, in the coming age of prosperity that was being made possible by economic expansion and technological innovation.

A last gasp of Romanticism emerged in France as the *"l'art pour l'art"* movement and in the Symbolist poetry of Rimbaud and others, which celebrated not merely sensory perception but the "total derangement of the senses." In Britain, the Romantics' high regard for acute sensitivities as crucial elements in spiritual and personal development became shrunken and domesticated to the level of Victorian "sensibilities"—especially concerning the emotive responses expected of ladies in the presence of, say, cabbage roses or pansies. A late, and often perverse, version of Romanticism in Germany was the philosophy of Nietzsche, who enthroned the creative hero as an *Ubermensch* and who felt that the natural cruelty of life, such as the exploitation of the working class by the aristocracy, should not be covered over with moralistic concern for what we might call the *Unterhund*.

A certain interpretation of that political posture was, of course, embraced several decades later by Hitler. But can it accurately be said, as one hears almost universally among (left) German intellectuals today, that Romanticism was a major *cause* of National Socialism? Surely the difference can be discerned between Herder's popular assertion that every nation has its intrinsically valuable *Volkgeist* and the Nazi assertion that the German *Volkgeist* is superior to all others on Earth. Self-aggrandizing, let alone murderous, nationalism was not part of the Romantics' respect for organic diversity.

Like the other movements in the lineage of ecospiritual resistance to modernity, the Romantics addressed many conditions that are still with us today. Unlike the others, though, they emerged from an era in which extreme artificiality was prized as proof of a highly developed people, or elite class. The rigid design of Enlightenment gardens, poetry, and social engineering relegated concern with "the natural" to the sphere of irrelevance and even crudeness. The Romantics, however, distrusted that sophisticated detachment. To them, it was essentially a cover, or denial, of profound loss. In response, they sought to spark a process of recovery, to claim the power, as Shelley put it, "to *imagine* what we know." In many respects, our situation today is again one of extreme artificiality, not because of eighteenth-century formalism but because so much of our children's learning, play, and socialization is now reduced to the realm of computers, videotapes, and television. To observe that something precious has been lost, covered over, and denied is regarded as dreadfully unsophisticated. No doubt exposing eighteenth-century taste is less daunting than opposing the twentieth-century technosphere, but the early Romantics, surrounded by a powerful worldview of smug detachment, launched a critique of great depth. They became extremely influential because they did not wade safely in shallow critiques but plunged directly into the deep waters that had been declared off-limits. Their triumph was partial and temporary, but their defense of the fullness of being lives on.

THE ARTS AND CRAFTS MOVEMENT
1875–1920

A RESISTANCE MOVEMENT that contains both a powerful critique and a dazzling burst of creativity might survive for decades beyond its time—but in sadly diminished form. Whether clinging to life in the struggling institutions that were born in its heyday or abruptly embraced by commercial interests in a trendy revival, the visionary depth of the movement is quietly relegated to the irrelevant past, considered too disruptive for the new terms of accommodation. What has been brought forward from the Arts and Crafts movement into upscale American magazines of the 1990s are reproductions and contemporary interpretations of "Mission Style" furniture and lamps. How odd to see them floating there on slick white paper, severed from the outpouring of pottery, fabrics, tiles, metalwork, jewelry, graphic design, and architecture, of which they were a part. Stripped of all intention and their populist crusade, they bear only mute witness to the rich philosophy from which they were constructed.

That philosophy—at once political, moral, and aesthetic—originated with the British Arts and Crafts movement, flowing initally from the extraordinary sensibilities of John Ruskin and William Morris. In exhibition catalogues today, the movement they inspired is usually pegged historically as a reaction against the ugly and shoddily mass-produced household goods of Britain's mid-Victorian period—that is, as a rejection of industrialism in the country that had been the first to experience the effects of the Industrial Revolution. That view, once again, lacks a recognition of the larger context of industrialism: modernity. The movement effected an engagement that was hardly one-dimensional. Above all, the Arts and Crafts movement mounted a moral challenge to the modern project. It did so with a stunning range of creativity and a solidly audacious grace.

IN BRITAIN

The Arts and Crafts movement had kinship with two earlier countermodern movements, although its own identity was distinct and far more widely influential in its time than its predecessors. The first influence was the Romantics' rebellion against modernity's new sense of the human as a Cartesian "machine" operating within the bounds of the "new mechanical philosophy." The Romantics had raised the alarm about the disintegration in modern society of much that is essential to the full human experience. Fifty years later, when the Arts and Crafts movement arose, the loss was even more extensive.

The other influence on the emergent Arts and Crafts movement will doubtless seem nearly incomprehensible to many modern readers, especially those raised in the New World. Having been schooled in the story of Europe's deliverance from the Dark Ages of medievalism to the dazzling possibilities of the rationalist Enlightenment, Newtonian science, Cartesian philosophy, and the laissez-faire economic theories of Adam Smith, we can hardly imagine looking backward across that deep divide for any relevant inspiration. Indeed, that was also the dominant cultural assumption in Britain, both before and after the remarkable love affair with the Middle Ages that gripped leading Victorian intellectuals during the mid-nineteenth century. For a few intensely charged decades, the modern doctrine of unquestioning faith in Progress was challenged by a vigorous appreciation of the era that had immediately preceded the modern age. The mid-Victorian embrace of the medieval world was, of course, selective and interpretive, but what guided their selection of admirable elements was hardly vacuous nostalgia. The medievalism that was so passionately taken up by the educated classes reveals concerns with the destructive aspects of modernity in their own time.

A fascination with the Arthurian legends of Britain's medieval past had begun with Sir Walter Scott's rediscovery of Malory's *Morte d'Arthur* in the late eighteenth century, but it was the publication in 1842 of Tennyson's "Sir Launcelot and Queen Guinevere," "Morte d'Arthur," and "Sir Galahad" that resulted in a Victorian obsession in artistic circles with Camelot. Another expression of Victorian medievalism in the 1840s was the Young England movement, led by Benjamin Disraeli and three other Conservative members of Parliament. Faced with increasingly vociferous reform movements demanding change in the cruel realities of the modern, industrialized economy, the Young England movement proposed an alternative extrapolated from relevant aspects of the Middle Ages: small-scale models of community (loosely based on the large, self-sufficient medieval monasteries); a return to the countryside; renewed respect for physical activity; principles of cooperative work and a less radical division between work and leisure; new societies based on equality of classes; and a sense of architecture as the measure of a civilization and the means by which a society connects itself with its past.

The force of medievalism in Victorian architecture, called the Gothic Revival, was a particularly critical influence on the British Arts and Crafts movement because so many of its leading designers trained as architects during the third quarter of the nineteenth century. The foremost proponent of the Gothic Revival was Augustus W. N. Pugin, an architect who converted to Catholicism at age 22 and shortly thereafter published a treatise titled *Contrasts; or, a Parallel between the Noble Edifices of the Fourteenth and Fifteenth Centuries, and Similar Buildings of the Present Day; Shewing the Present Decay of Taste* (1836). In it, he contrasted the philistine mishmash of modern buildings in Victorian London, many of them designed in accordance with rigid neoclassical dictates, with the graceful elegance of Gothic design, which depended on "the fitness of the design to the purpose for which it is intended." He appreciated the asymmetry of Gothic architecture as a response to need and condition, even identifying it with the moral order and stability of Christianity, as he asserted in *The True Principles of Pointed or Christian Architecture* (1846). Pugin emphasized that he advocated not a slavish replication of a particular style but the guidance of "True Principles" of the devotion, majesty, and repose of Christian (Gothic) art. An example of Pugin's sense of "the Gothic" as a way of life was his delight, on learning of his wife's first pregnancy, that they would soon have "a Gothic girl or a Gothic boy!"

For Protestants in Victorian Britain, a majority so firmly in control that they denied the vote to Catholics until 1829, the popish character of Pugin's crusade was distasteful. Even its embrace by the Tractarians and the Oxford movement, who advocated the reform of the Anglican Church through a revival of certain premodern rituals and traditions, was considered problematic. The way was cleared for widespread acceptance of the Gothic Revival in 1849 when it was reframed by an art critic, John Ruskin, whose parents had educated him for a career in the Anglican ministry but whose own passion as a student had been natural history. He argued that the moral force of Gothic architecture resides in the practice of natural theology, the belief that knowledge of God is revealed through attention to nature, the creation. The essential forms of the revival of Gothic design, he explained in *The Seven Lamps of Architecture* (1849), are to be found in leaves and plants, the structure of which was illuminated by contemporary science. Certain forms, he believed, are beautiful in ways that elude utilitarian explanations: They are traced "by the finger of God."

In "The Nature of Gothic" (from *The Stones of Venice*, 1853), Ruskin asserted that the Gothic soul embraces irregularity, imperfection, and change. He perceived in the Gothic heart "a magnificent enthusiasm, which feels as if it could never do enough to reach the fulness of its ideal; an unselfishness of sacrifice . . .; and, finally, a profound sympathy with the fulness and wealth of the material universe." Ruskin considered neoclassical architectural ornamentation to be "servile" to fixed convention, while Gothic ornament was "revolutionary" because Christian culture recognized the value of every soul and so gave freedom to the medieval workman's imagination to respond to the divine glory of the natural world. In contrast, any society—such as Ruskin's own—that thwarted the workman's free play of art, work, and spiritual expression was inherently unjust and immoral. He argued that the industrial "division of labor" was demeaning because it reduced workers to machinelike producers of components. He proposed that an environment of "healthy and ennobling labor" could be attained if a new ethos were to shift design and production to only those articles that are absolutely necessary, reflect creativity ("imagination"), serve "a practical or noble end," and are not mere copies or imitations.

As soon as Ruskin's pronouncements reached Oxford, they were read aloud in a booming, chanting voice by an idealistic university student, William Morris, who later would absorb and transform Ruskin's call for a moral aesthetic into the most famous designs of the Arts and Crafts movement, recognizable around the world for decades as evocative emblems of a social movement uniting art and labor in opposition to the destructiveness of the modern political economy. Near the end of his life, Morris paid tribute to Ruskin's influence by designing and publishing, at his own Kelmscott Press, an exquisite edition of *The Nature of Gothic*, which Morris called "one of the very few necessary and inevitable utterances of the century." Recalling its effect on himself and his circle at Oxford some forty years earlier, Morris wrote that *The Nature of Gothic* "seemed to point out a new road on which the world should travel." Morris and his friends at Oxford also read Ruskin's Edinburgh lectures defending the Pre-Raphaelite painters, who sought a spiritual purity they felt had been displaced by the Renaissance. Edward Burne-Jones, who was a lifelong friend of Morris's from college days and was later one of the most famous Pre-Raphaelite painters, recalled that they had been converted to the Pre-Raphaelite cause by Ruskin's words before they had ever seen the paintings in question.

Nine years after publication of *The Stones of Venice*, Ruskin framed his critique of modern economic theory: *Unto this Last* (1862). He launched a scathing attack on the effects of viewing people as the atomistic *homo economicus*, which is crucial in the reductionist projections of Adam Smith, David Ricardo, and John Stuart Mill. He scoffed at the scientistic presumption that economies are governed by natural laws that cannot be changed by human will, arguing that detaching "economic man" from the social context of actual individuals, and claiming that this supposedly isolated being makes all decisions on the basis of material gain, was simply bad science. He railed at the moral paucity of modern economic theory, which concludes that the sufferings of the working poor will be eased when they regulate their population and appreciate the fact that a bare subsistence income (the "Iron Law of Wages") is a rational aid toward that end. Similarly, he scorned the "natural law" decreeing that any attempt by governments or other institutions to improve conditions of impoverished individuals must not only fail but also damage the economy and thereby society.

Ruskin's critique was influenced somewhat by the writings of Thomas Carlyle, but his own urgent contribution was the demonstration that certain moral conditions are essential to the attainment of true wealth. Ruskin saw humankind as fundamentally moral and capable of unselfishness, honor, justice, and love. He believed that, because we can recognize justice, we know, for example, that an unjust wage is theft. Moreover, he argued, *value* resides not in use value or exchange value but in an entity's intrinsic power to support life. The richest man, he asserted, is one who has attained "the widest helpful influence over the lives of others." As with his writings on aesthetics, Ruskin saw in modern political economy the arrogance of the modern mind and its shrunken sensibilities.

Unto this Last was enormously successful—but not at first. The four sections of the book appeared originally in monthly issues of *Cornhill Magazine* from August to November 1860. It was savaged by defenders of modernity as "windy hysterics," "absolute nonsense," and "intolerable twaddle" and was mocked as the preaching of a "mad governess." The publisher of the magazine became alarmed and saw the essays anew as "deeply tainted with socialistic heresy," although the leading socialists of the day considered Ruskin too much of a religious Tory for their tastes. In book form, *Unto this Last* garnered a huge audience. By 1910, it had sold over 100,000 copies and had been translated into several languages, including an edition in Gujarati published by Gandhi. It directly inspired the new Labour Party, which entered Parliament for the first time in 1906, and provided the moral impetus for the countless reform laws that passed during the first half of the twentieth century. The Labourites, however, wanted to be taken seriously as contenders in the modern political arena, so they embraced *Unto this Last* solely as an economic treatise while ignoring Ruskin's larger condemnation of modernity's mutilation of spiritual life and the integrity of the creation. Leaders of the Labour Party liked to say that the works of Ruskin and Morris had been more important to their founding than those of Marx, but the former were politically pruned by the Labourites so as not to challenge modernity's radical break from nature. The notion of water, light, and soil as true wealth of priceless value was not declared in the platform of a British political party until some seventy-five years after the deaths of Morris, in 1896, and Ruskin, in 1900: the Green Party of the United Kingdom.

While the Victorian Labour politicians adopted those elements of *Unto this Last* that were useful to them, a fuller—and hence more radical—reception of Ruskin's ideas guided the growth of the Arts and Crafts movement in Britain and abroad. Its proponents believed that if the dignity and creativity of the worker were freed from the "slavery" of the industrial division of labor, this freedom would yield a new model of both production and consumption. Homes would gradually become furnished only with necessary articles born of "honest" design and honorable production. Both workers and consumers, both individuals and society, would be transformed by the creation and use of everyday objects featuring indigenous materials, honest (uncovered) construction, natural dyes, motifs inspired by nature, and newly invigorated vernacular styles from the country's past. The Arts and Crafts aesthetic was a clear rejection of ostentatious Victorian ornamentation and sham, the desperate emblems of a prosperity that honored nothing but itself.

Incorporating principles espoused by Pugin, Ruskin, and Morris, the Arts and Crafts movement strove for an organic unity among design, materials, production, and use. The ideal of collaboration among "fine art workmen" inspired the founding of guilds, firms, workshops, schools, intentional communities, associations, and cycles of influential exhibitions. All of them sought to close the chasm between the decorative, or "minor," arts and the fine arts (painting, sculpture, and architecture). The movement's fondness for strong vertical lines, presumably influenced by Gothic architecture, was expressed less in the exterior design of houses than in interior fixtures, paneling, and furniture. It shows up as well in Burne-Jones's long, languid figures, both male and female, who are almost architectural in their elegant poses and became emblematic of the term "Pre-Raphaelite" in paintings and stained glass windows.

The Great Exhibition (also known as the Crystal Palace Exhibition), held in London in 1851, is sometimes erroneously considered to be the event that triggered the beginning of the Arts and Crafts movement. True, it demonstrated, to the embarrassment of the British, the uninspired design and shoddy quality of their industrially produced goods, but that experience triggered various efforts to reform *industrial* design, which was not of interest to the movement. In fact, William Morris, who was taken to the exhibition by his parents as a boy of seventeen, manifested a prescient sulk and refused to go inside. The origin of the movement could better be located in Morris's Red House, ten miles east of London. Morris, recently married to the Pre-Raphaelite model Jane Burden, had commissioned the house from his friend Philip Webb and set about decorating the interior with his friends in 1859. They painted murals on the walls, foliage on the ceilings, and patterns on wooden chests. Morris designed a frieze of female heroines from Chaucer's *The Legend of Good Women*. He also initiated at Red House a new trend in English garden design, with a careful balance of lushness and decorum, of the mysterious and the familiar, of the evocative and the homely—with the garden considered a part of the house. Later, this style became known as the Arts and Crafts garden.

In 1861, Morris and six partners established a firm, whose name was eventually shortened to "Morris & Co.," to produce furniture. In time, it became the best known interior design firm and tastemaker in Victorian Britain, producing furniture, tapestries, embroidered panels, stained glass, tiles, wallpaper, carpets, and drapery and upholstery fabric. Following the ideal of designers being immersed in the realities of production, Morris learned to dye, print, weave, and embroider. His designs followed Pugin's principle that flat surfaces require the honest design of flat patterns, as opposed to the ubiquitous round cabbage roses and plump, sculpted leaves of Victorian carpets and wallpaper. Morris produced more than sixty designs for fabric and wallpaper, which influenced scores of other designers. To this day, he is considered by many art historians to be the finest creator of pattern in Britain since the Middle Ages.

The most striking characteristic of Morris's designs is a sensuous vitality derived from his deep love of nature. The density of his stylized ecosystems (in patterns such as "Arbutus" and "Willow Bough") reflect his firsthand knowledge of the fields and woodlands he had roamed as a boy. He also paid close attention to the flowers in his garden at Red House and elsewhere. Everything—vines, stems, leaves—seems to be embracing everything else in his best work, such as the patterns "Honeysuckle" and "Acanthus." The other strikingly evocative characteristic of his designs—although this is never mentioned in British commentaries—is the fact that they are sometimes organized around a gracefully erotic focal point, such as the patterns "Pimpernel," "Bluebell," and "Snakeshead." Morris believed that creative interpretation in home furnishings aided people in their contemplative periods, which, following Charles Fourier, he considered to be naturally arising states of mind that alternate with periods in which one desires to be active and working productively. Morris further believed that forcing anyone to be active during the contemplative phase, or vice versa, causes utter misery.

Morris's sense of design eschewed both mere naturalism and mere abstraction, including the geometric abstraction that was so popular when he began designing. He explained in *Some Hints on Pattern Designing*, "Ornamental pattern work, to be raised above the contempt of reasonable men, must possess three qualities: beauty, imagination, and order." A successful design, he felt, presents an imaginatively conventionalized depiction of nature that reminds one not only of that particular life-form but of all life that lies beyond it. Morris was attentive to "the material and spiritual sides of the craft" and asserted that the presence of any beauty in a piece of handicraft implied that the mind of its creator was "lifted somewhat above the commonplace" in an urge to communicate something to others that they may not have known or felt before.

I encountered William Morris's designs before I came to know of his writings about them, so my response was not influenced by his intentions. I found them arresting for their evocative power, which transported me beyond my atrophied modern sensibilities to *paying attention*, once again, to the lyricism and dynamic fecundity of the natural world. Ruskin's passionate yearning to reconnect finds form in the alluring ecosystems of Morris's designs. Surely they bear "the impress of human imagination" upon them, as Morris intended, but the particular imagination behind this work is fired by a deeply rooted love for the real. I must add that I have discovered, to my surprise, that some people cannot *see* Morris's designs. The more firmly modern a mentality, even if well educated in the arts, the more likely it is to dismiss Morris's work as irrelevant "nature stuff."

In his later life, Morris became a socialist, as did several of the other prominent Arts and Crafts designers, especially among the second generation. Unlike the others, however, Morris became recognized in only a few years as one of the leading socialists of Britain, producing an impressive stream of lectures, articles, stories, and poems on historical and contemporary struggles of the working class. In spite of his radical turn, Morris was approached in 1892 by a member of Gladstone's cabinet about the possibility of his name being put forward for Poet Laureate because of his popular early poems based on medieval themes and the Icelandic sagas. Morris flatly refused the honor, knowing full well that it was offered in recognition of anything but his recent verses, *Chants for Socialists.*

Morris agreed with the Marxist assertion that sufficient change would come only through violent revolution rather than the gradualism advocated by the Fabian socialists of his day. He came to see London as a "beastly congregation of smoke-dried swindlers and their slaves." His vision of London in the postrevolution utopia, however, could hardly have been further from the industrial dreams of "scientific Marxism." His charming novel *News from Nowhere* (1892) incorporates most of his proposals of the Tories' Young England movement of the 1840s—with the added dimension that all money has been eliminated. Morris wrote the story as a pointed rebuttal to Edward Bellamy's American utopian novel *Looking Backward* (1888), in which a rigid, centralized state has "rationalized" production to such an extent that goods arrive in homes directly from the factories via a huge tube! Far from wishing to eliminate work through mechanization—and very far from Marx's contempt for "the idiocy of rural life"—Morris created characters who derive fulfillment from the joy of freely given labor, usually in communal craft or agricultural work, and from their profound enjoyment of the natural world.

A second generation of Arts and Crafts designers—including Voysey, Mackmurdo, Baillie Scott, and Ashbee—continued and expanded the movement in England, which influenced the Celtic Revival in Ireland. During the 1890s, a new center of creativity also emerged at the Glasgow School of Art, where women had the rare opportunity to be trained in all aspects of both the fine and decorative arts. The "Glasgow Four" (who were two couples: Charles Rennie Mackintosh and Margaret Macdonald, plus her sister Frances Macdonald and Herbert MacNair) created designs that were influential in Europe and the United States via magazines and exhibitions. Their aesthetic featured mysterious symbolism, sensuous curves (in a Scottish version of Art Nouveau), and less reference to nature than the work of their English counterparts, who referred to the Glaswegian designers derisively as "the spook school." The plump Glasgow rose, sensuously poised on a long rigid stem, plus Mackintosh's stark white rooms and symmetrical decorative groupings of small white squares (derived from his interest in Japanese screens) beckoned the movement in formalist directions, especially when it was taken up in Vienna.

Nearly all of the second-generation Arts and Crafts designers moved toward increasingly stylized, streamlined depictions of nature. Their work is graphically interesting but not, at least in my experience, as deeply engaging as Morris's ecosystem patterns. French designers such as Verneuil and Seguy followed the same course, using plants, birds, and other animals in progressively stylized ways. Many of their designs were associated with Art Nouveau, which the English disdained: all those excessive tendrils evoking a dizzying sensuality!

To reflect upon the efforts and effects of the British Arts and Crafts movement, one could hardly find a more appropriate spot than Holy Trinity Church in London's Sloane Square, considered by many to be the "cathedral" of the movement. (The association may be somewhat misleading, as the pioneering Arts and Crafts designers were not a very churchy group; they did, however, receive many ecclesiastical commissions over the years.) Behind the altar rises a huge wall of rectangular stained-glass panels designed by Burne-Jones and made by Morris & Co. It is uncharacteristically disappointing, comprising a rigid grid (four rows down and twelve across) that looks as if God had laid out a giant game of solitaire with face-cards of the saints. On the left wall in a simple alcove with a low ceiling, however, is a long, horizontal panel of stained glass, designed by William Blake Richmond in the usual fluid style of Burne-Jones. It poignantly depicts, through various Biblical figures, the virtues held dear by the medieval world: Hope, Love, Justice, Wisdom, Fortitude, Patience, Faith, and Charity. More powerfully than any manifesto, this vibrant tableau—so resolute in line and form, so alluring in ways that defy words— declares the Arts and Crafts movement's rejection of the neoclassical virtue associated with modernity: the heroic individualism that slid easily into narcissistic utilitarianism.

"Modern civilization," as Morris put it, had corrupted work and life. Many people before had protested injustice, but the pioneering figures of the Arts and Crafts movement went far beyond an economic analysis. They dedicated themselves to countering the corrosive effects of modernity by focusing in immediate and accessible ways on work, home, art, nature, vernacular culture, and the unfolding of the person *in relationships*. In the words of Morris's and Burne-Jones's collegiate pledge to one another, they were dedicated to "holy warfare against the age." Yet they could not resolve the paradox that their revolutionary aims resulted in goods that only wealthy people could afford. Eventually their designs were appropriated for industrial production, which could be sold at cheaper prices. The London department store Liberty & Co., for example, was founded expressly for that purpose. Some say the energy of the British movement was largely spent by 1910. In any case, the aftermath of the Great War seemed to require something new: the streamlined, machine-inspired aesthetic of Art Deco.

It must be noted that one school of thought in the history of design, launched by Nicholas Pevsner's influential book *Pioneers of Modern Design: From William Morris to Walter Gropius* (1936), rather incredibly posits an unbroken line of influence from Morris—with his rejection of Victorian excess, in favor of clean lines in furniture—to the sterile high-modernist style of the Bauhaus. This interpretation ignores the radical change of course imposed by the director of the Bauhaus, Walter Gropius, around 1922: Morris's values and aesthetic went *into* the founding of the Bauhaus, but what came *out* at the other end was nearly the opposite of what Morris stood for. Morris's creative engagement with nature, use of indigenous materials, craft production, and vernacular style were considered hopelessly backward and premodern by the industrial designers who dominated the Bauhaus after 1922. Surprisingly, Pevsner's thesis still has a hold on many designers today, especially those who were educated during the forties, fifties, and sixties. When an impressive new biography of Morris was published in England in 1994, *William Morris: A Life for Our Times* by Fiona MacCarthy, some reviewers depicted Morris as an aspiring but failed Modernist who "looked backward" to create "sentimental" patterns based on nature![4] Engagement with nature is de facto "sentimental" and hence rather pitiable to proponents of modernity. This dismissive attitude surfaced again in 1996, when a debate over the importance of Morris broke out in the British press on the occasion of the centenary exhibition of his work at the Victoria and Albert Museum.[5] As I noted earlier, some people simply cannot *see* Morris's stylized ecosystem designs through the lens of modern ideology.

IN SCANDINAVIA AND ON THE CONTINENT

The Arts and Crafts ideals and aesthetic quickly spread to most countries of Europe, where they assumed national characteristics. All the adaptations had in common the fact that Europe was far less industrialized than Britain, so neither opposition to mass-produced goods nor alarm at the degradation of the industrial worker were central to the European branches of the movement. Nonetheless, from the 1870s on, the visionary works of Ruskin, Morris, and others evoked a creative response that reverberated for decades.

In Scandinavia and several countries of Central Europe, a movement now labeled by modern historians "national romanticism," or "romantic nationalism," embraced the Arts and Crafts ideals of craftsmanship, indigenous materials, and vernacular styles. This emphasis in art and design was a major expression of Scandinavia's search for national roots and identity in in the face of corrosive dynamics of modernity and political changes during the nineteenth century. Sweden had lost territory to Norway and Finland, and the latter was suffering through a tightening of control by czarist Russia. In Norway, and to a lesser extent in Sweden, the Viking Revival (also called the "dragon style" in design) merged interest in medieval culture and the artifacts from that era. Because of Finland's political situation, the cultural freedom to express national identity through design took on great significance. It was the theme of the hugely popular Finnish pavillion at the Paris *Exhibition Universelle* in 1900, which was designed by Eliel Saarinen and his partners. Their architectural office and residential community, Hvitträsk, embodied the Arts and Crafts ideals of unity in the total design of a room and a building, integrity in production, and creative use of the vernacular style. As on the continent, several of the leading Arts and Crafts proponents in Scandinavia believed that raising the standards of industrial design should be a primary goal of the movement.

In Hungary, "national romanticism" linked appreciation for folk art with the desire for independence from the Hapsburg Empire. As an expression of this political mood, the Gödöllö Artists' Colony was founded in Transylvania in 1903. There the ideals of Ruskin and Morris were applied not only to design but to helping the rural poor by providing them with cottage industry in craft production. At the same time, folk motifs were adapted to industrial design in a few factories.

In Germany and Austria the eventual fate of the Arts and Crafts movement would have horrified its British pioneers. Viennese artists and designers throughout the 1890s were intent on escaping from the ubiquitous historicism of the Ringstrasse Era, which had begun in 1857. They were also dedicated to the German concept of *Gesamtkunstwerk* (a total, unified design in works of art and architecture) and to the elevation of the decorative arts. One of the best known designers, Josef Hoffman, declared as late as 1903, "Our aim is to create an island of tranquility in our own country which, amid the joyful hum of arts and crafts, would be welcome to anyone who professes faith in Ruskin and Morris."

These public sentiments must surely be judged ironic in light of the orientation of the Wiener Werkstatte, which Hoffman had formed that year with Koloman Moser, a colleague from the Secessionist group of painters. The Werkstatte members' love of high-quality craftsmanship was disembedded from several core concerns of Ruskin and Morris: The Viennese designers desired continual escape from the past; they had no interest in "place" (vernacular styles and indigenous materials); their infrequent references to nature were primarily geometric abstractions; and they felt it was flatly impossible to "convert the masses" by challenging industrial means of production, so they focused solely on artistic freedom and pleasing their wealthy patrons. These preferences, of course, placed the Wiener Werkstatte squarely in the vanguard of Modernism. Their ideal was the totally autonomous modern artist unfettered by ancestors, tradition, or nature. Their fondness for spare, minimalist design—sometimes rigid, sometimes fluid—intensified after their close association with the Mackintoshes began at the close of the 1890s.

In Germany, modernity devoured the Arts and Crafts movement for a different reason: Industrialism had to be fed. Germany industrialized late and very rapidly. In the 1890s, several educational workshops for "art in craftswork" were established with the goal of improving industrial design. They were inspired by Ruskin's and Morris's call for simplicity, integrity, and fitness for purpose—but the German workshops rejected the critique of modern political economy and the moral imperative of individual expression through handmade work. Their aim was to improve German standards of mass production so that German industry could better compete with foreign manufacturers.

There was, to be sure, a minority position. A number of important German designers followed the British ideals more fully and founded artist colonies, such as the one at Darmstadt (funded by the Grand Duke Ernst Ludwig of Hesse), and schools, such as the one in Weimar (funded by the Grand Duke of Saxe-Weimar). Both views—the "utopia of the pulse versus that of the piston"—were represented in the Deutsche Werkbund, established in 1907 to effect an integration. Hermann Muthesius, who had written an admiring book on British design, insisted that Germany must forego the Arts and Crafts constraints and turn, instead, to forms created by "the children of the new age": the engineer and the industrialist. In opposition, Henry van de Velde expressed horror at the dismissal of unique creativity and argued that artistic freedom can never be united with the demands of industry. In spite of the verbal skirmishes, the Deutsche Werkbund produced a range of industrial designs—characterized by functionalism, efficiency, and suitability for machine production.

Although the outcome of the debate was inevitable, situated as it was in the midst of Germany's intensive drive to industrialize, the clash was played out one last time in the monumental struggle at the Bauhaus just after the Great War. With public funding from the Thuringer State Assembly, the Bauhaus opened in April 1919 on the site of the arts and crafts school in Weimar. Its founding director, Walter Gropius, was an architect who had been a member of the Deutsche Werkbund and was inspired by Ruskin and Morris—so inspired, in fact, that he chose for the name of the new school a derivative of *Bauhutte,* a medieval word that carried associations with artists' guilds and the communal society of the Middle Ages and with the contemporary interest in "national romanticism." Gropius's other stream of influence was the spiritual branch of prewar expressionist art in Germany, which sought a purity of abstraction beyond the material plane, as exemplified by Kandinsky, Taut, and others. The prewar expressionist turn from the physicalities of nature to the imagining of ethereal cosmologies would have disgusted Ruskin and Morris, of course, but it found fertile ground in German idealism. The belief that metaphysical transformation would deliver society from the devastating effects of modern materialism was trumpeted in Gropius's description of the Bauhaus as a "cathedral of the future," a place in which artists, craftsmen, and designers of all backgrounds would create "the new structure of the future . . . which will one day ride toward heaven from the hands of a million workers like the crystal symbol of a new faith."[6]

Unfortunately for Gropius, he failed to perceive that the trauma of the Great War had left many activists hostile toward metaphysical gestures and "cosmic wallpaper." Leftists, right-wingers, and Dadaists all attacked spiritual expressionism in 1919, focusing much of their anger on the Bauhaus. German Dadaists furthered the expansion of modernity by insisting that spiritual art be replaced by the "reality and clarity of engineers' drawings" (Georg Grosz) and by the realization that the machine is the new spirituality (Theo van Doesburg). In addition, a deep internal rift developed at the school as one of the professors, Johannes Itten, imposed the practices of an esoteric cult called "the Mazdaznan" on as many students as possible. Itten left the faculty in 1922, by which time Gropius was warning his colleagues against "wild romanticism" and excessive isolation. Adding to Gropius's problems, the State Assembly had begun grousing about public funding for Bauhaus faculty, who, they suspected, were probably socialists and, in some cases, unmistakably foreigners. To augment the school's budget, Gropius secured some industrial design commissions.

Crafts continued to be taught at the Bauhaus, but the new emphasis on art in service to industrial design carried the day. By the time the Bauhaus was closed in 1933 by the Nazi government (ironically, for being much too far from [the fascist version of] "romantic nationalism"), the name was associated internationally with minimalist, geometric modern furniture reflecting design values that are free of place, tradition, and nature. Few people would guess that the ultramodern Bauhaus had roots partially in the Arts and Crafts movement, an oversight that probably would be a great relief to Ruskin and Morris.

IN THE UNITED STATES

When it arrived on American soil, the Arts and Crafts movement acquired the tenor of a democratic project to spread virtuous living to all people by encouraging a taste for simple, well-designed furnishings as an escape from the nineteenth-century version of modern consumerism: the glut of Victorian bric-a-brac and decoration. Artificiality was eschewed in favor of the "real," the "authentic." As an alternative to the materialism of ostentatious Victorian decor, the honest surroundings of the "craftsman" aesthetic were associated with right living. Consequently, the American version of the Arts and Crafts movement focused more on what might be called a counter-modern "moral consumerism" than on rescuing the industrial worker from his alienation. Still, the British belief that handicraft can yield transformative benefits for the designer/maker, as well as the user, was maintained. Beginning in 1895, Arts and Crafts associations, schools, and workshops were established not only among the well-to-do but also in immigrant neighborhoods. Magazines of the day published architectural plans for craftsman bungalows that were affordable to working-class as well as middle-class families. To furnish them, furniture and other goods in the Arts and Crafts style were made widely available, as several designers compromised with partially mechanized production and became entrepreneurs.

Exposure to the leading British designers occurred through subscriptions to British journals, such as *The Studio*, and through international exhibitions in Philadephia (1876), Chicago (1893), Buffalo (1901), St. Louis (1904), and San Francisco (1915). Ruskin's book on the decorative arts, *The Two Paths*, was also read widely and was reprinted nineteen times in the United States. The leading magazine of the American movement, Gustav Stickley's *The Craftsman*, devoted its first issue to the design theory and social analysis of William Morris and the second issue to that of John Ruskin. The changing subtitle of that journal reflects the direction of the American movement as it separated from its British parentage: first, *In the Interests of Arts Allied to Labor*; then, *For the Simplification of Life*; and finally, *Better Art, Better Work, and a Better and More Reasonable Way of Living*. The fact that Stickley, along with his brothers, manufactured Arts and Crafts furnishings that were sold through his journal and through the Sears Roebuck catalogue no doubt steered his editorial decisions in commercial directions, but he also published thoughtful coverage of the movement throughout the country, which was attentive to the philosophical dimension. Other magazines were founded to spread the new domestic gospel in purely consumerist terms: *House and Garden*, *House Beautiful*, and *Ladies' Home Journal*. In helping to bring issues of "quality of life" into public consciousness, this idealistic movement ironically foreshadowed the ontological orientation so familiar to us today: "You are what you buy." The moral benefits of simple living were eventually shunted aside by the tactics of the emergent advertising industry.

Nonetheless, the American movement's aesthetic accomplishments—

including original developments that won the admiration of British and European designers—were evoked by a moral and spiritual quest to regain authenticity in the modern age. The Arts and Crafts preference for indigenous materials, vernacular culture, and creative depiction of nature expressed itself regionally in this country. There was little attention to printed fabric, carpets, or wallpaper but a great deal of work in pottery, metalwork, jewelry, furniture, lamps, book design, and architecture.

In the east, the first professor of fine arts at Harvard and a friend of Ruskin's, Charles Eliot Norton, wrote about the British movement and served as the first president of the Society of Arts and Crafts of Boston. The vernacular style in New England was the colonial, which was admired by Arts and Crafts designers for its frank exposure of construction elements and honest use of materials. Appalachian handweaving and immigrant crafts such as embroidery and lace-making were also seen in a new light, as were articles and patterns from Native American cultures, which were considered by many to be the epitome of the simple life.

In Chicago, the Prairie School of architecture placed the Arts and Crafts imperative for design unity firmly in the landscape. The movement's ideals of simplification and integration were invigorated by Louis Sullivan's visionary writings on an organic architecture suitable for a true democracy because it would cast off the shackles of neoclassicism, dominant since the beginning of the modern age, and would reunite culture with nature. Several of the architects in Sullivan's firm were involved in founding the Chicago Society of Arts and Crafts. A young draftsman in Sullivan's employ, who left in 1893 to establish his own firm, became the pre-eminent architect of the Prairie School: Frank Lloyd Wright.

Wright's belief that a building should "associate with the ground and become natural to the prairie site" resulted in strong horizontal lines on the exterior and free spaces in the interior that were not enclosed by the traditional structure of rooms as adjoining boxes. He did away with the foyer, which he considered undemocratic and un-American since it functioned as a screening area in which the social class of a visitor determined whether he or she would get any farther. His interiors maintained the Arts and Crafts fondness for the (Gothic) vertical in his banks of tall, narrow windows and in many of his chairs. Although Wright evolved a number of styles after his Prairie School years, he lectured on organic architecture throughout his long career and continued to incorporate innovative references to nature's textures, colors, and structures in his work.

He was increasingly viewed by his peers as an irrelevant eccentric, however, as architecture came to be dominated from the 1930s through the mid-1960s by the ultramodern International style, so named because the sterile boxes that housed modern skyscrapers and similar buildings carried no "constraining" references to place.

In California, the Arts and Crafts movement came into full bloom. In 1907, on a third visit to the United States, the influential British designer Charles R. Ashbee wrote that the best work in Arts and Crafts in America was being produced on the Pacific Coast. The reason for this, theorized Stickley in *The Craftsman*, was California's geographic distance from the "demoralizing influence of the classic formula of the art successes of other nations." He found in California a "truer democracy" than elsewhere because there was less separation between thinking and working—or between thinkers and workers—which, he reminded his readers, Ruskin had identified as a core failure of the modern age.

Nationally, many of the leading Arts and Crafts designers (such as Sullivan, Wright, and Tiffany) spoke of "higher truth," "the spiritual," and "unity," but in California this orientation was joined by an interest in Theosophy, in mystical Christian sects such as Swedenborgianism, and in Eastern religions. In and around San Francisco, a school of painting called the "California Tonalists" evoked a contemplative mood through their interpretations of nature using subtle light and muted colors. Japanese art also was admired, for many of the same virtues that Arts and Crafts designers saw in the Gothic—its asymmetry (thus its "naturalness" and flexibility), its association with craft production, and its spiritual relationship to nature. Several California architects—and Wright as well—appreciated Japanese design for its lyrical suggestion of nature and its expression of the essence of an experience.

The most sublime blending of the Arts and Crafts aesthetic with the influences of Japan is found in the paneled interiors designed by Charles Sumner Greene. His use of Japanese joinery, lyrical carved panels resembling the art on Japanese screens, and elegant furniture that is solid yet poignantly graceful all create a gestalt that is clearly "raised above the commonplace," as Morris would have put it. Ashbee judged Greene's Arts and Crafts furniture "the best in the country": "Like Lloyd Wright the spell of Japan is on him, he feels the beauty and makes magic out of the horizontal line, but there is in his work more tenderness, more subtlety, more self-effacement than in Wright's work. It is more refined and has more repose." The architectural firm established by Charles Sumner Greene and his brother, Henry Mather Greene, embraced Morris's dictate that one should determine what is truly necessary and then make it beautiful.

In touring the Gamble House in Pasadena, designed by Greene and Greene in 1908-09, one is shown through room after room appointed with Charles Sumner Greene's extraordinary furniture until arriving, as the last stop on the docent tour, in the shocking ambiance of Mr. Gamble's study, the only room in the house with Stickley's Mission furniture. By contrast, it is jarringly crude, heavy, and clunky. Yet Mission designs are the Arts and Crafts furniture that fill catalogues and magazines today. Surely the wrong body of work was revived.

Overall, the American branch of the Arts and Crafts movement was an energetic mix of the commercial and the profound. To counter the disintegrative forces of modernity, a rapidly industrializing country turned, if only briefly, to an aesthetic credo that promised to ground home and family in a simple, serene sanctuary in a philistine age. The human would be rooted, once again, in nature and place; the culture would be freed to draw deeply and unfold in wisdom. These sentiments faded from public consciousness after our victory in the Great War, replaced by an expansionist boosterism that gripped the twenties. Although pockets of the Arts and Crafts movement persevered, larger forces of upheaval and fragmentation were grudgingly accepted as the price of Progress.

The many intentional communities founded at the turn of the century to produce craftwork in keeping with the ideals of the Arts and Crafts movement were short-lived. A few of the commercial enterprises, such as the internationally recognized Rookwood Pottery in Cincinnati, lasted until the late 1920s, but the Modernist hour had struck, and the machine aesthetic was the rage. Even the most famous Arts and Crafts architects and designers received few commissions after 1920. Many of the crafts programs in public schools were maintained until the 1950s, but the largest legacy of the movement survives in the institutes of higher education that were born of the Arts and Crafts vision. Among these are the California College of Arts and Crafts in Oakland, the Cranbrook Institute near Detroit, Berea College in Kentucky, the Pratt Institute in Brooklyn, the Penland School of Crafts in North Carolina, the ceramics program at the State University of New York at Alfred, and the Newcomb Pottery in the Sophie Newcomb College for Women at Tulane University in New Orleans.

I am told that in some of the art schools mentioned above, interest in computer graphics has resoundingly pushed aside any attention to Ruskin and Morris. No attempt is made to establish continuity, however strained, with the school's founding vision. In that sense, the gradual process of turning away from Ruskin and Morris in those schools mirrored the course of the American Arts and Crafts movement itself, although the accommodation with industrial production was much swifter in the latter. Within ten years of the movement's immigration from Britain, several of the original American advocates were straining to convince themselves and others that industrial production could, after all, be understood as a form of craftwork. That position was eventually abandoned for a full surrender to the "pragmatic" embrace of mass production—and, for some, to a conservative stance of blaming business problems on supposedly lazy industrial workers! Morris's depiction of the "smoke-dried swindlers" who owned the dehumanizing factories was put out of mind.

The ideologies of modernity swept aside the Arts and Crafts movement, first with the dominance of machine production and later with the allure of the machine aesthetic. Yet the problems identified by the pioneers of the movement have not been solved. They have merely been "managed" by Progress in ways that compound the causes of uneasiness.

COUNTER-MODERN COSMOLOGICAL AND SPIRITUAL QUESTS IN SCHOOLS OF PAINTING 1890–1951

TOWARD THE END OF THE NINETEENTH CENTURY, a reaction arose in artistic circles against the distorting and destructive effects of materialism in the modern age. Although these cultural rebels sought spiritual renewal as a counterforce, they considered modern Christian institutions to be inadequate as standard-bearers in the struggle for several reasons. Since the Reformation and the Enlightenment, the various Christian denominations had strained to become more materialist and rationalist by emphasizing the *historical* Christ and marginalizing such teachings as their heritage of creation-centered medieval mystics. Additionally, studies in comparative religion and biblical exegesis were increasingly demonstrating Christianity to be merely one tribal expression of religious impulses. Finally, Darwin's alarming theory about the origins of life reduced Genesis to a deflated ontology, even as it gave scientific credence to modernity's own true faith: progressivism.

As an alternative to an enervated Christianity, hope was invested in esoteric teachings that claimed to reveal eternal and universal truths beyond the material plane. Adherents believed that a new social order—in fact, an entire new age—could be born of the recovery of those truths. They embraced such works on occult cosmology as the Hermetic texts and the writings of Robert Fludd, Jakob Boehme, and Emmanuel Swedenborg, but the most widely influential vehicle of occult teachings was a synthesis called Theosophy, which was created by Madame Helena Blavatsky.

Responding to both the fears and yearnings of the times, this eccentric Russian aristocrat shrewdly trumped Darwin by proclaiming a *spiritual science* that embeds the merely material expression of evolution of species within a much larger spiritual evolution. Progress writ large! Blavatsky's fanciful blending of various realizations from Buddhism and Hinduism, plus a number of geometric and numerological symbol systems, was presented as the harmonious incorporation of all the core wisdom traditions of the ancient world. Her synthesis was influenced by both scholarly studies in comparative religion that found common content in ancient mythologies (such as an essential dualism and a triune godhead) and popular works based on alleged access to ancient wisdom. The spread of Theosophical teachings to a wide audience was accomplished through translations of Blavatsky's two main explications, *Isis Unveiled* (1877) and *The Secret Doctrine* (1888), plus the establishment of scores of Masonic-like lodges across Europe and the United States.

Among those influenced were several famous artists who became fathers of abstract painting. Unlike the other counter-modern movements in this lineage, these esoteric artists regarded nature as a rather crude material manifestation masking the far more interesting subtle realities that invisibly inform all matter. Whereas Goethe, Shelley, Coleridge, and Ruskin valued botanical studies as a path of knowledge that could lead to communion with the sacred whole, the esoteric artists who emerged several decades later brushed aside nature almost entirely. Their interests lay in creating evocative expressions of that which is invisible to the "common man," thereby providing the catalyst for social evolution. The sense that this new art was replacing religion and was the source of a new social order prevailed in many circles until the aftermath of the Great War, when esoterica was seen as powerless against the machinations of mass slaughter.

Even without that devastating negation of their messianic promise, the esoteric painters' attempted transcendence of modernity was compromised by their attempts to fit their rebellion into modern contours: the conformity with scientism, the search for immutable laws, and the focus on the autonomous individual as discontinuous from nature but conversant with abstract principles. Still, theirs was an ardent quest to recover that which is lost through the modern reduction of the real to dumb matter in a dead universe.

SYMBOLIST PAINTING

By the late 1880s, the spreading fascination with the occult sparked a new direction among several young artists who felt that the Impressionists had drained meaning from painting by focusing solely on the play of light on material surfaces. The new painting was conceived not only as a recovery of spiritual meaning but as an expression of far more profound wisdom than previous religious art. Cosmic signs and symbols, ethereal figures, synesthesia, sacred geometry, vibration, and auras were all employed as a visual vocabulary of forces informing the material plane. Symbolism quickly attracted followers in France, Britain, Germany, Austria, Norway, Russia, the Netherlands, Switzerland, and Spain. They sought to bring the truths of the invisible world into the visible realm by creating new introspective forms of allegory, often with a melancholy cast. Well-known exemplars include Edvard Munch, Vincent Van Gogh, Paul Gauguin (in his Brittany period), the Glasgow Four, Gustav Klimt, Egon Schiele—and later, in the United States, Georgia O'Keefe and Arthur Dove.

Three of the Symbolist painters deeply influenced by Theosophy eventually moved further and further from figurative expression until they arrived in the initial stage of an entirely new tradition: abstract painting. Beginning in 1908, Frantisek Kupka's dynamic experiments with the human figure, Piet Mondrian's vibratory trees, and Wassily Kandinsky's dreamlike visions of the "spiritual atmosphere" in Moscow street scenes each drew their creator across the threshold into the invisible cosmos described in the esoteric texts.

EARLY ABSTRACT PAINTING

Kupka expressed cosmic rhythms of celestial bodies, "Newtonian disks," and fugues of forms. Mondrian employed increasingly abstract geometric planes—a pre-Cubist development in the Netherlands—in order to convey the occult's "clarity of thought" with a "clarity of technique." Although he passed through various stages of disenchantment with Theosophy, he remained steadfast throughout his life in his vision of the new art as a "slow path to the Spiritual" (contrasted with the fast track of formal spiritual practices). Eventually, he identified the progression of his paintings into increasingly stark geometric compositions with a decidedly modern version of spirituality: "the autonomous life of the human spirit becoming conscious" through the expressed abstraction of the inward and the purely universal.

Kandinsky also painted some geometric grids but only during his tenure at the Bauhaus, which took place after Gropius had switched its focus to modern industrial design in 1922. His most captivating work is the early abstract paintings done between 1911 and the outbreak of World War I, when he had to leave Munich and return to Russia. Although he sometimes retained a slight amount of figurative line, he increasingly used dynamic shapes and bold colors to allude to the *presence* of objects, which are usually embedded in swirling energy fields.

This highly original work was inspired by both Theosophy and Anthroposophy, a breakaway Christian version of esoteric teachings created by Rudolf Steiner. Kandinsky was also influenced by early discoveries of postmodern physics in which the apparent solidity of objects, and even their atoms, was shown to be an illusion. He later recalled, "The disintegration of the atom was to me like the disintegration of the whole world."[7] In 1913, Kandinsky (who had left an academic career in law at age thirty to study painting) published an explication of the theory informing his new art, *Concerning the Spiritual in Art*. In it, he linked "the modern sense of insecurity" to the inevitable obsolesence of ideas that is inherent in the progressivist view of life: Since past principles, science, and wisdom were eventually discarded as false, might not our contemporary knowledge meet the same fate? He attributed this groundlessness to the "harsh tyranny" of materialist philosophy: "Our minds, which are even now only just awakening after years of materialism, are infected with the despair of unbelief, of lack of purpose and ideal. The nightmare of materialism, which has turned the universe into an evil, useless game, is not yet past; it holds the awakening soul still in its grip. Only a feeble light glimmers like a tiny star in a vast gulf of darkness."[8]

Kandinsky felt that painters and composers were in the vanguard of a "spiritual revolution" that would lead to a new social order. He was particularly fascinated by the esoteric concept of synesthesia, the mixing of sense perceptions such as the shape of color or the color of sound. He believed there are two types of pictorial composition: melodic (simple) and symphonic (complex). He also asserted a necessary link between "color-harmony" and "form-harmony" and corresponding vibrations of the human soul.

When he returned to Moscow during the war, Kandinsky's association with Kazimir Malevich and other Constructivists drew him toward an interest in abstract geometric compositions, whose purity was believed to point most clearly to the "fourth dimension," the Constructivists' favorite metaphor for the transcendent consciousness necessary to perceive a new world. He brought that focus with him to the Bauhaus after the war, inserting a new vocabulary of geometric symbols into his continuing depiction of cosmic space as a metaphor for a utopian world. The paintings of his final decade, after he moved to Paris in 1934, continued his blending of geometric forms in cosmological compositions, with some introduction of biomorphic shapes favored by the Surrealists. When a new edition of *Concerning the Spiritual in Art* was published in 1947 and an exhibition of his paintings held in New York, Kandinsky's influence spread to the emergent school of painting called Abstract Expressionism.

DADA AND SURREALISM

The assumed rationalism so central to modernity was the target of two protest movements around the time of World War I. The nonsense word "Dada" was applied to the first of these in 1916 by an international group of artists at the Caberet Voltaire in Zurich. The movement soon spread to Germany and New York. Dadaists regarded the mounting carnage of the Great War as both the bankrupt ending to the Enlightenment's long-standing promise of the perfectability of the human through rational social engineering and as the failure of prewar, Symbolist painters to usher in a new age. Consequently, they sought to demote art as a fraudulent moral safety valve and to replace it with the "gratuitous," by which they meant paradoxical, spontaneous gestures that revealed the inconsistency and absurdity of the rationalist worldview. These developments had been anticipated by the "anti-art" events and creations of Marcel Duchamp and others in Paris, beginning in 1912. His "Readymades," in which everyday objects were isolated from their normal context and purpose, entailed a process of dissociation or displacement similar to the earlier efforts of the Symbolist poets to liberate hidden meanings of words and transport readers beyond the objective, material realm.

For the purposes of this survey, the most interesting Dadaist was Jean Arp, a poet and painter who created a new curved, organic morphology that drew many painters beyond the Cubist fascination with fragmented rectilinear structures. The closed curves of Arp's biomorphism reflected the profound unfolding of the real: "The starting point for my work is from the inexplicable, from the divine." He called his biomorphic sculptures, which he continued creating into the 1950s, "concretions"—entities that had grown, like "the earth and the stars, the matter of stone, the plant, the animal, man." Reflecting on the early days of Dada in Zurich, Arp wrote, "Dada was against the mechanization of the world. Our African evenings were simply a protest against the rationalization of man. . . . Even then I had a foreboding that men would devote themselves more and more furiously to the destruction of the earth."[9]

By the mid-twenties, several of the Dada artists had moved in the direction of a new, more programmatic movement, Surrealism, although a tension remained between the two orientations. The Surrealists felt that the Dadaists had only negation to offer, whereas they were dedicated to creating a new way of seeing. In 1924, their chief theoretical voice, André Breton, defined the new art as pure "psychic automatism" that expresses "the real functioning of the mind" by focusing on the "superior reality" of dreams. Rather than simply rejecting the rationalized, individualized self, as had the Dadaists, the Surrealists sought to move beyond the individual self to the larger world of nature—both inner and outer nature. Each of the painters invited into the group by Breton had developed a technique of automatism (unpremeditated painting) as a way to connect with the larger intelligence. Their goal was to capture the content of the present moment in such a way as to effect a rapprochement between the waking and dreaming states.

Their styles were widely diverse: Joan Miró, for instance, expressed the physical world as a dance of playful, energetic forms; Yves Tanguy's inner landscapes, in contrast, were often eerie, primordial vistas populated by life-forms that are quirky yet fluid and not unfriendly. Many in the movement followed the assertions of Freud, which were still influential in Breton's second manifesto, written in 1929, calling for new procedures that would return to Surrealism's "original scientific basis" for progress toward liberation through self-knowledge. This was to be done "free of the alibi of art." For some Surrealist painters, the way to knowledge of the larger self—that is, self-in-nature—was through imagery of hermeticism and mysticism, as in the work of Remedios Varo and Leonora Carrington in Mexico.

THE DYNATON GROUP

Three painters—Wolfgang Paalen, Gordon Onslow Ford, and Lee Mullican—came together in San Francisco in 1949 and sparked one another in a post-Surrealist exploration of cosmos, psyche, and art. Paalen and Onslow Ford had been among the second-generation Surrealists in Paris. In fact, Breton had anointed Onslow Ford, Matta Echaurren, and a few other young painters in the late 1930s as the "next wave" of Surrealism, honoring their revival of automatism as a creative method (in the tradition of Arp, Miró, and Tanguy) but newly linked with "more ambitious problems." By this, he meant their interest in postmodern physics and their rejection of illusionistic narratives (exemplified by Salvador Dali's work). The wave-particle theory framed by the Nobel-Prize-winning physicist Louis de Broglie, for instance, was the inspiration in the early 1940s for Paalen's expression of the quantum level of "the real" in his swirling images and spatial apparitions, which he called "Cosmogons."

In the years before the group came together in San Francisco, the two former Surrealists (Paalen and Onslow Ford) had become immersed in the art and cosmology of various Native American cultures when they moved to Mexico around 1940, independently of each other. Mullican had been raised in Oklahoma, an area rich with many native cultures. Consequently, their efforts to circumvent the ego of hyperindividualized modern man focused on transcendence *through* nature to communion with the microcosmic and macrocosmic worlds. The name Paalen chose for their group, *Dynaton*, is the Greek word for "the possible."

In independent exhibitions, as well as their one group show, in 1951, the Dynaton painters were inspired by the revelations of postmodern physics that reconciled the Western split between mind and matter, such as the Viennese physicist Ernst Mach's "psychophysics." Like the quantum theories of consciousness being put forth today, the Dynaton group's paintings expressed a unitive dimension of the psychic and the physical realms of matter/energy. Onslow Ford's exploration of "great spaces of the mind," an aesthetic orientation he calls "ecomorphology," continues its sixty-year unfolding to this day. Mullican, too, continues to create cosmological imagery infused by his intimate relationship with the natural world. Paalen died in 1959.

COUNTER-MODERN MODERNISM 1905–1939

M ODERNISM WAS A MOVEMENT WITHIN THE ARTS—literature, design, architecture, photography, and painting—that has endowed a legacy of much confusion, not only because of the range of contradictory values and perspectives clustered under the umbrella term "Modernist" but also because of its paradoxical relationship to the larger, embedding context called "modernity." "Modernity" refers to the era in which we still live—the overarching orientation that began with Renaissance humanism, the Reformation, the Scientific Revolution, and the Enlightenment. Nearly all the confusion and seemingly baffling ironies that characterize commentaries on the Modernist movement in the arts are clarified by recognizing two major streams within it: one carried forth the basic orientation of modernity in new dress, while the other was a protest movement *against* many of the tenets of the modern worldview. Both were named "Modernist" to mean merely "the new." The latter stream rejected the received worldview, but called it simply "the status quo," "traditional thinking," or "nineteenth-century triumphalism"—all of which referred, of course, to the most recent stage of modernity.

The most prominent face of pro-modern Modernism was the machine aesthetic, an ontological metaphor that ignited the imagination of artists, writers, designers, and architects in the 1920s and 1930s. The architect Le Corbusier called the house "a machine for living in"; the literary critic I. A. Richards believed a book to be a "machine to think with"; the film director Sergei Eisenstein proclaimed the theater a "machine for acting"; and the photographer Alfred Stieglitz saw the American skyscraper as a colossal "machine." Oddly, all of this was considered dramatically new, when, in fact, the machine metaphor had been widely embraced during the final foundational movement of modernity, the Enlightenment. This time around, the mechanistic sense of life was fleshed out in streamlined curves and stark, rigid expanses. As before, an energetic burst of antinature, humanist faith was believed to infuse this aesthetic with revelations of sublime truth through the discipline of mechanistic structure, function, objectivity, and standardization.

Most cultural historians find it shockingly incongruent that European architects of the "heroic period" of Modernism (the 1920s), who designed (static, domineering, macho) buildings on behalf of social utopianism, could later design (static, domineering, macho) buildings for the Nazis. It is also considered "ironic" that the (hyper-Modern) utopian designs were later adopted by powerful bureaucracies and huge corporations. All three, however, were economic and political options *within modernity* so all could share pro-modern Modernist aesthetics with ease. (It should be noted that the neoclassical gargantuan buildings erected by the Nazis violated classical proportions with impunity in favor of a Modernist functionalism; for instance, they would extend a row of pillars for an entire city block on a montrous building or use absurdly huge doors, all to reinforce the looming presence of the Reich.)

Counter-modern Modernism, in contrast, belongs in our survey of spiritual and/or ecological resistance because it sought to cut through ideologies of denial and to embrace the real, even when that entailed a disconcerting loss of comfortable assumptions about the nature of being. This Modernism is sometimes dated from 1905 because Einstein's general theory of relativity and the shocking discoveries in quantum physics during the next two decades displaced the Newtonian sense of reality as the mechanistic interaction of quite separate phenomena: mass, energy, space, and time. In a related development, the philosophers William James and Henri Bergson asserted that time was a matter of flow and duration rather than a series of discrete points.

The counter-modern Modernists rejected the Victorians' historicism, macrocosmic focus, and philosophical idealism concerning the progessive and systematized coherence of life. They focused, instead, on fragmented, discordant, and random experiences in life. They eschewed grand schemes of schematic explanation, preferring empirical explorations of the particular, with close attention to analyzing function. Since "social thinking" (based on the modern belief in economic expansion as a panacea for social ills) had failed to be effective, there was a shifting of focus to the individual and the inner life of the mind. This Modernism faded when its concerns with interiority were pushed aside by the worldwide Great Depression and the rise of fascism and Stalinism.

It might seem that counter-modern Modernism was a *via negativa,* a quest for truths of reality based on the discarding of concepts seen to be artificial. Not surprisingly, a sense of cultural pessimism and disintegration was common to this Modernist mood, but their vision encompassed a new integration, a new sense of complexity and unpredictable events in the seemingly mundane realm. The Modernist novels of James Joyce, Marcel Proust, and Virginia Woolf, for instance, are constructed with patterns upon patterns of thought about experience that convey a deeper grasp of reality than do nineteenth-century novels. As T. S. Eliot said of Modernist poetry in 1931, the aim of its concreteness and precision was "really to *unite* the disparate and the remote" and "to give them a fusion and a pattern with the word."[10]

That heroic effort now seems, from the vantage point of the 1990s, rather quaint in its belief that art holds the possibility of unity for a fragmented universe. The discoveries of postmodern science, plus the experiential base of various meditation practices, have demonstrated that life *is* a creative mix of fusion, pattern, and particularity. Matter/energy arises and passes away trillions of times per second from the common quantum soup. We shimmer in vibratory fields that are unimaginably vast. The atoms within us respond to nonlocal causality: up close and remote, all at once. "The real" captured by the artist-elites of counter-modern Modernism was that *part* of the real denied by the mood of modernity that immediately preceded them. Theirs was a correction of smug Victorian concepts, a crusade sprung from reactive energies. They rejected the Hegelian sense of a historical progressivism that had arrived in such dubious achievements as European imperialism, industrialized society, and positivist science. They detested the Victorian cult of sentiment—which, as we have seen, was a trivialization of the Romantics' call for a participatory consciousness of deep engagement with the natural world. These Modernists set out on their own quest for deep engagement with the real by embracing the fragmentary and the discordant in order to allude to the mysterious mesh that links all beings and events but is far more subtle than mechanistic ideologies.

A small portion of the counter-modern Modernists took a far bolder leap toward the grand communion, kicking over tea cups and drawing rooms and constricted struggles of the hyperintellectualized mind. D. H. Lawrence, in particular, sought to steer the Modernist exploration of sensibility in the direction of cosmological reengagement. The disappointments and frustrations experienced in modern love relationships—a common subject in Modernist novels—were, Lawrence felt, a result of the hideous shrinking of eros to the puny sphere of two individuals:

> Oh, what a catastrophe, what a maiming of love when it was made a personal, merely personal feeling, taken away from the rising and the setting of the sun, and cut off from the magic connection of the solstice and equinox! This is what is the matter with us, we are bleeding at the roots, because we are cut off from the earth and sun and stars, and love is a grinning mockery, because, poor blossom, we plucked it from its stem on the tree of Life, and expected it to keep on blooming in our civilized vase on the table.[11]

It seems quite possible that Lawrence hoped his own tortured sense of gender relations would be transformed, along with that of society, if only we modern humans could recover our cosmological presence and the "pagan mind" that grasps so much more than time-as-a-straight-line. In an essay explaining his final novel, "A Propos of *Lady Chatterley's Lover*" (1929), he urged us "to go back, a long way, before the idealist conceptions began, before Plato, before the tragic idea of life arose, to get on our feet again." Through the "daily ritual" of reconnecting, we could reverse the diminution into "bodilessness" and alienation. In this final statement, published posthumously, his vision of "togetherness of the body, the sex, the emotions, the passions with the earth and sun and stars" becomes a prayer for modern life: "We must get back into relationship, vivid and nourishing relation to the cosmos."

GANDHI'S CONSTRUCTIVE PROGRAM
1915–1948

A S THE EUROPEAN EMPIRES DISINTEGRATED in the wake of World War II, the governing of their former colonies fell to an elite stratum of colonial society who had been educated in Europe and schooled thoroughly in the ideologies of modernity. India was no exception, although it very well could have been if Gandhi's vision had prevailed.

With tragic consequences for India's future, he was marginalized, as

soon as independence was assured, by Nehru and the other Fabian socialists, who had learned in London to invest their faith in the modern
state. Like those young men, Gandhi had studied law in England, but his
formative experience there had occurred decades earlier, when a burst of
creative resistance to the modern political economy had been in the air.
Ruskin, Morris, Kropotkin, "Simple Lifers," Theosophists—all of these
thinkers were discussed and debated in the circles to which Gandhi grav-
itated during the years 1888–1891. When he left England for South Africa
with his law degree, he was deeply influenced by reading Ruskin's *Unto
this Last* and Tolstoy's *The Kingdom of God Is within You*. Once he returned to India and saw the degenerate conditions of village life under
the British, he began to conceive a grand project of renewal.

Although Gandhi served as a brilliant strategist for three decades in
the struggle for independence, he viewed postcolonial statehood as a mere
preliminary condition for the revival of India. As early as 1915, he began, with the founding of his first ashram, to train volunteers as agents of
village revitalization. Initially, they addressed the most pressing problems—sanitation, hygiene, healthcare, and elementary education—as
well as the practice of courtesy among children. One of Gandhi's projects in particular, the revival of the craft of hand-spinning cotton yarn and
weaving it into cloth (*khadi*), was enormously successful on several levels. It built confidence within the Indian independence movement since
cottage-industry production of *khadi* provided an alternative to buying
British cloth, previously the only option. The rebirth of the craft of making *khadi* also improved the standard of living for millions of extremely
poor villagers by providing additional clothing and income. For both villagers and activists, the heady experience of self-reliance and successful initiative prompted them to move beyond the usual dispirited fatalism of
conquered peoples. They began to seize their fate in ways that gradually
reduced the formidable British *raj* to the secondary role of *re*acting.

Gandhi's vision for a new India, after independence, was informed
by his long-standing critique of the modern mentality. He felt that a
hardness of heart, lack of imagination, and atrophy of sympathy were dehumanizing characteristics of the twentieth century. Their increase, he rea-
soned, followed from the modern assumption that the key to well-being
lies in the multiplication of industrial production and material gain, when
in fact, it spawns greed, callousness, and diminished human relations. To
avoid this trajectory for India, Gandhi proposed "enlightened anarchism,"

a model of decentralized political structure whereby the new state would be a confederation of regions. His focus was not the abstraction of the modern state or "the masses." His focus was *place*: the village or town, the district, and the surrounding region. Gandhi's vision of development was to make villages and towns largely self-sufficient in economics, government, culture, spiritual vitality, and primary and vocational education. Higher education and expanded trade would be available at the regional level. A good deal of ownership in each district would be held by community trusts.

In contrast to the starting point of modern political theory in *rights*, Gandhi acknowledged only those rights that flow from *responsibilities* well met. He sought to renew and enrich the premodern sense of reciprocity, with nature as well as fellow humans, for the benefit of all. The quality of justice would be reflected in the protection from exploitation and structural violence afforded to the least powerful members of society. Since Gandhi believed "the outward" has meaning only insofar as it aids development of "the inward," he envisioned his social structure as a framework of opportunities for spiritual growth.

All this was regarded as hopelessly anachronistic by the ambitious young men who gained control of the new Congress Party and then the new government of India. They believed their perspective to be supremely superior because it was far more modern. The old man's "Constructive Program" (the umbrella term for all projects related to Gandhi's vision of social renewal) was tolerated as an ornament affixed to his immeasurably valuable function as leader of millions of citizens in the independence movement. The Indian pols apparently viewed the situation as a public relations problem, adopting the symbol of the spinning wheel as the icon of the Congress Party. But the content of Gandhi's Constructive Program? Focus efforts on the village and district levels instead of the cities? Place a good deal of ownership into community trusts instead of nationalizing industries? Encourage women to play expanded roles in their communities? Educate childen with a spiritual sense of service to others and respectful interaction with nature? The political sophisticates, who modeled themselves after the British Labour Party, prided themselves on seeing what hundreds of thousands of participants in the Constructive Program could not—that it was backward, irrelevant, and embarrassingly *romantic*.

Because the father of Indian independence consciously applied and expanded the ideas of several counter-modern theorists of the West, it is not accurate to say that India simply "took the Western path after 1947," as one often hears. The new Indian nation-state took a *particular* Western path, the one paved with modern ideologies. Its leaders turned away from Gandhi's visionary renewal of traditional strengths of culture and place. Had they not done so, India today would probably be the most financially and socially secure Third World country. Its staggering population growth, to name only one major problem, most likely would never have manifested at such a rate, as studies have shown that women have few children if education, healthcare, and small-scale economic opportunities, such as cottage industry, are available to them. At least the "lite" socialist leadership of the Congress Party protected the public from exploitation by transnational corporations for forty years—until the forces of the global market finally crashed through India's borders a few years ago. The country is now on a hypermodern path, welcoming huge concentrations of transnational capital that is creating, among other projects, export plantations for tomatoes and other genetically engineered crops. Today India's minister of finance speaks proudly of "creating a second industrial revolution." As always, every Indian politician claims in nearly all speeches and interviews to be following in the footsteps of Gandhi.

THE COUNTERCULTURE
1966–1972

IRONICALLY, the counterculture of the sixties was dismissed as *romantic* even though its ignorance of the Romantics was almost total. Except for frequently heard references to William Blake, the fact that a much earlier wave of malcontents had mounted a similar rejection of the ideologies of modernity *and* had arrived at a number of extremely relevant alternatives went unnoticed. The organic sense of life proposed in Coleridge's philosophy was not discussed. Goethe's new mode of science, based on gentle attentiveness and communion, was not revived. Ceramics and handicrafts were produced prolifically without an inkling that Ruskin, Morris, or the American Arts and Crafts movement had ever existed. In rejecting the reductionism of rationalism, the counterculture was so deeply anti-intellectual that it forfeited access to its own history.

As with earlier versions of ecospiritual resistance to modern ideologies of denial, the *alienation* of the modern person was the central concern. Unlike previous movements, however, the counterculture focused on liberating the body from the grip of modernity. Pointed shoes, girdles, cinched waists, bras, neckties, suits, teased hair, and crewcuts were eschewed so that the body could be decorated and honored with flowers, beads, and lively, flowing fabrics. Organic foods, herbal medicines, and handmade goods were preferred to their industrially produced counterparts.

The counterculture's embrace of the body is most prominently linked in the public's memory with free love, the beginnings of the "sexual revolution." Social critics have determined that the "flower children" were reacting against the "repression" of the fifties. That, of course, is a modern explanation, based on Freudian precepts. Previous decades had known sexual mores equally as strict, but the decisive element in the coming-of-age experiences of the counterculture in the late fifties and early sixties was the fact that gender and sexual relations were then shaped by a *postwar* sensibility. The "battle of the sexes" was not a dynamic of the workplace— the surge of "new women" into the professions in the twenties had been cut short by the Depression, and the Rosie-the-Riveters had all been turned out of their wartime jobs after 1945—but of intimate relationships. The huge reinsertion of World War II veterans into civilian culture— as conquering heroes—brought certain military values home. On a superficial level, G.I. haircuts were favored by boys and adolescent males throughout the fifties. On a profound level, sexual relations became a zone infused with tension and aggression. Teenage girls *guarded* their "rep," while teenage boys strategized victories that often were not tender. Sex was deployed in a staging ground where there were winners and losers.

From that gestalt of extreme alienation the counterculture separated itself and restored sexual union as a bodily sacrament and a joyful mystery. Candles, incense, and erotic communion gave a spiritual cast to this subculture, as did consciousness-expanding drugs and music, but the counterculture was dubbed the "love generation" for a larger reason. *Homo economicus*, the competitive producer, the isolated consumer, the entire atomistic society of broken communities—all of these lonely facets of modern life were countered by an openhearted intention to *connect*. Why *not* love everyone instead of interacting from the opposite stance? Trust, peace, love, and nonviolence all radiated outward from the recovery of the erotic.

They did not, it is true, radiate much beyond the fringe of the counterculture: The "straight" culture was tweaked via Dada-esque gestures or condemned with self-righteous disdain, and the New Left was often viewed as humorless captives of a macho economism. Yet the achievement inside the subculture of a functionally *relational* society in which hundreds of thousands of men and women lived according to an ethos of sharing and caring, of simplicity and acceptance, was a marked contrast to the acquisitive, aggressive nature of modern "success." Although gender roles remained largely traditional, with women baking bread and men building houses, the abiding values of the counterculture were those usually considered "feminine," relational, and ecological. From that perspective, the hypermasculine mood of the postwar years seemed bizarre and dehumanizing.

As in the case of earlier resistance efforts, several values championed by proponents of the counterculture outlived the movement itself but did so in the form of radically compromised adaptations. Had the counterculture studied its predecessors, it might have foreseen not a revolutionary dawning of the Age of Aquarius but a repetition of the fate of the earlier counter-modern movements: The most profound resurgence of the real in each movement was so powerful as to survive into the following decades but only on terms of radical accommodation. The Romantics' attention to "imagination" (participatory consciousness) mutated into the Victorian cult of feelings and delicate sensibilities for young women. The Arts and Crafts movement's designs for handmade products, born of indigenous materials and the craftsman's integrity, were taken up by industrial production and mass-marketing. And the concentric circles of erotic communion in the counterculture? The recovered erotic was manifested *without community or the ethos of caring* in the atomistic modern society of the seventies as "swingers'" orgies, serial relationships barren of love, predatory sex with teenage girls (the beginning of the dramatic increase in the number of unwed, adolescent mothers), and the narcissistic "Me Decade."

Other, less central values survived with less radical degradation. Attention to "the natural" expanded into society at large and grew into the ecology movement and the preference for organic food and herbal medicine, which is still on the increase today. The same may be said of the renewed attention to the spiritual dimension of life. On the other hand, the rejection of rigidly rationalist schooling led, not to a widespread reform of public education on the model of successful systems of relational, ecological learning such as the Waldorf Schools, but to an anti-intellectual "dumbing-down" of textbooks and standards that had stultifying effects. Other factors, such as a decrease in attention spans and a concurrent increase in the use of television and video games, also contributed to the diminished levels of knowledge. By the eighties, surveys found, alarmingly, that many young American adults did not know basic history or geography.

For all the excesses of the counterculture, which are to be expected from a youth movement, its extraordinary optimism—the belief that life was on the verge of becoming profoundly better for everyone, and that *anything* could happen—was its most remarkable characteristic. Why, then, were "the sixties" eventually so hard on most participants, especially those who were deeply committed? Perhaps dreams so daring and discontinuous from the status quo contain a sacrificial dimension: They alter the dreamers forever, shaping the contours of their minds with the memory of ecstatic communion and the dull ache of its inestimable loss.

Were all these struggles and ecospiritual resistance efforts in vain? As their more "agreeable" principles and creations were modified and absorbed by the modern mainstream, had they not become fodder for a periodically flagging triumphalism they abhorred? Once the marrow of their fresh ideas was sucked out and reprocessed, they were trivialized as eccentric footnotes in the history of the modern era. Or they may have been actively resisted and crushed—and met the same fate.

In recent years, however, the corrective impulses inherent in resistance to modern ideologies of denial have earned the respect of at least a few cultural historians. One example is the study of American opposition to modernity from 1880 to 1920 by T. J. Jackson Lears, *No Place of Grace*. That particular expression of "antimodernism," he found, sustained a note of protest against a complacent faith in progress and a narrow positivist conception of the real, but it also furthered a shift to a therapeutic ideal of self-fulfillment that contributed to the emergent culture of consumption. The resistance was tamed, but it was well founded in the pathos of modern denial. In immersing himself in original sources from that period, Lears repeatedly encountered the centrality of a spiritual yearning: "The dominance of the religious motive, of the longing to locate some larger purpose in a baffling universe, helps to explain the personal, idio-syncratic qualities of much antimodern protest. God lives, Blake wrote, in the details. The details of American antimodernism disclose its most enduring significance, as a *cri de coeur* against the evasions and self-congratulations of the oncoming twentieth century."[12]

Today that *cri de coeur* is rising again, not as a helpless cry of despair but as a resonance emanating from deep within the body politic. It has depth because it grapples with elemental issues and draws on a rich heritage of corrective efforts. Cynics like to cite Lewis Mumford's observation that that heritage often had the effect of cushioning the hard edges of mechanized, regimented life in the modern era, thereby making it more acceptable. Mumford judged the larger effect of the resistance efforts, however, to be their "opening the way for a more organic culture" and offering "a fresh vision for the entire cosmic process." Their major legacy, he strongly felt, was the sorely needed worldview that has been belatedly bestowed with the name "ecology."[13]

EMBRACING THE REAL

A CALL FOR NEW MYTHS IS IN THE AIR—which fills me with trepidation. One often hears, at least in certain circles, that a new mythic vision for the future is needed, one that would replace the triumphalist Myth of Progress and the Myth of Salvation-through-Free-Trade while inspiring confidence and optimism. Perhaps— but the creation of new myths is troubling for several reasons. First, who are the sources of mythmaking in our modern consumerist culture? Hollywood and Madison Avenue. Unless one feels that viewing *Star Wars* constitutes a profound religious experience, pinning our hopes on the simplistic and exceedingly commercial American dream-machine seems unwarranted. Second, the deconstructionist influence that has spilled over from academia into several quarters of society has drained the validity and meaning from all storytelling, belief systems, and discourses of knowledge, which are now seen as *mere mythologizing*, the invention and imposition of a particular narrative frame of reference. An advertising slogan, the Declaration of Independence, the Gospel according to Mark, a scientific research report—all are considered *mere narrative*, just another social construction. Because of this influence, many people today, especially young adults, would ignore "yet another empty myth." Third, even before the deconstructionist sense of narrative as ironic posturing arose (that is, was *socially constructed*), the modern usage of "myth" had become so debased that it has long been synonymous with untruth or ignorance, lingering misunderstandings that should be dismissed. The term was rarely applied to the extraordinarily powerful mythic projection in which all modern societies are embedded: history as a progressive trajectory, getting better all the time.

Far from being vacuous storytelling, myth in its true sense is a communion with the deepest truths of existence. It articulates a relational field of cosmological energy, a sphere of participation that includes the narrator and listeners (or the reader) along with the forms of universe life that appear in the story. Origins, fruition, waning, and loss—the cycles of arising and passing away—are punctuated with unexpected dramatic turns. All of this is contained in the sacred space unfurled by the telling of the myth.

We live within the most extraordinary mythic drama imaginable. Fifteen billion years ago, our universe was born in a vast and mysterious eruption of being. Out of the fireball came all the elementary particles of the cosmos, including those that later formed our home galaxy, the Milky Way, and our planetary home, the Earth. All the land, the waters, the animals, the plants, our bodies, the moon, the stars—everything in our life experience—is kin to us, the result of a cosmic birth during which the gravitational power of the event held the newborn particles in a miraculously deft embrace. Some 4.6 billion years ago, gravity's allure drew together a range of elements 8 light minutes from a blazing star—our sun—and layered them by weight into a sphere, with iron at the core. The elements sought their own positions in the layers that formed, creating among themselves all the minerals in Earth's body. On the smaller celestial bodies nearby (such as Mercury, Mars, and our moon), the electromagnetic interaction overpowered gravity's pull; on the larger ones (such as Jupiter, Neptune, and Uranus), the opposite relationship developed. Only on Earth were the two in balance.

On Earth's crust, molecules continually broke up and recombined into new and larger molecules. Lightning created the possibility of amino and nucleic acids by providing intense heat framed by severe cold. Molecules that assembled themselves from amino acids became protein, while others formed of nucleic acids and sugars became ribonucleic acid (RNA) and deoxyribonucleic acid (DNA). The long chains of RNA, DNA, and protein molecules found themselves drawn into various partnerships, creating a dynamic bioplasm of bacteria in warm mud and shallow seawater. From Earth's store of potential, the great mediator chlorophyll later developed, enhancing our planet's relationship with the sun through the wonder of photosynthesis. A rambunctious bursting forth of Gaian life stretched over hundreds of millions of years and continues today with new speciation and the unpredictable movements of Earth's body. Tectonic plates drifted away from Pangaea, mountains pushed upward, and rivers cut gorges. Animals emerged, differentiating themselves into species by the millions. Humans evolved from furry cousins, discovering the pleasures and perils of self-conscious life.

As the universe acts, through trillions of micro-events each second, certain possibilities arise. On the Earth, rotating in spun pirouettes while it glides gracefully around the sun, the *cosmologic* continues to weave novelty and continuity into a web of life processes. Every manifestation of universe life in the Earth community emerges into being in its own way, but none does so in isolation. Animate or inanimate, our relatives are all around us, lighting the night sky, rushing through a river bed, thrusting upward through Earth's crust. Life-forms self-organize, thrive, and dissipate in spans of a microsecond or longer arcs of billions of years.

The story of the universe is a mythic drama of creativity, allurement, relation, and grace. Our species brings to it the capacity for self-reflexive awareness and responsible acts. Reflecting on our dynamic context, from the subatomic to the cosmological, we notice the essential role of creative *process*, constitutive *relationship*, and the *unitive ground of being*. Our great spiritual traditions, speaking in thousands of languages, have set their sacred stories of ultimate mystery within the grand epic of orbiting planets, changing seasons, eclipses, moon tides, and meteor showers. In the midst of all this action, in the unspeakable beauty of the Garden Planet, the story of every person unfolds, nestled within the embedding stories of family, clan, community, bioregion, region, nation, continent, planet, and cosmos.

This is a situation that "needs new myths"? Surely not. What we need is attentive engagement, cultivated awareness, and a taste for wisdom. We have had some highly problematic plot development to be sure, but the dramatic challenge before us looms as powerfully as ever: Will each of our stories unfold with the fullest potential of their particularity, complexity, and communion, or will they fail the universe by holding back and becoming less than they could?

A first step in recovering our connection with the larger reality is to realize that humans are surrounded not by a collection of objects but a community of subjects. In late 1995 astronomers discovered *50 billion more galaxies* than they had known of previously. This cosmological event was widely reported in the news media, in the wake of which I heard three paradigmatic responses. The first was from a modern mentality: *So what?* The second was from a famous literary scholar of the deconstructionist-postmodern persuasion who felt despondent about our fate as a satellite of a "banal and decentered star," upstaged by the magnitude of the new discovery. I found this reaction terribly sad and utterly hilarious, so I consulted the most insightful cosmologist I know. I asked Brian Swimme, "What's the meaning of the discovery of 50 billion 'new' galaxies in the universe?" Without an instant's hesitation, he declared exuberantly, "We can never be lonely again! We have all these relations we didn't know about!" Ah, yes.

As the deconstructionists remind us, all human knowledge is situated in particular social constructions. As nonmodern cultures have never lost sight of, however, all human endeavors are situated in *eco*social, or *cosmic*-social, construction: the dynamic processes of the larger reality without which there would be no body, nature, or place, let alone "social construction." To see our story in fuller, richer terms is essential to correcting the destructive course of the modern age.

Story, by its very nature, is the most powerful way of communicating. If we sit through a one-hour lecture that contains a two-minute story, it is the latter we remember weeks and months later. Among people working to bring about an ecological-postmodern transformation, story is often employed to good effect. An example is *Hope for the Seeds*, a book published by the Columban order of Catholic priests, who work with the peoples of Mindanao in the Philippines and elsewhere. In what the author calls a "comic book format," colorful illustrations fill each page, except for one or two sentences of text. The book opens with a brief account of the birth of the universe and then tells a native story about the mango tree, involving the first woman and man in Mindanao, Diwata and Mahusay, who taught their children to respect the ways of the plants and animals with whom they shared the island. The book tells of the native peoples' way of life in the lush lowlands and the hills. It then turns to the contemporary devastation of their "web of life": clear-cut, eroded hills; chemically degraded soil; and shrinking catches of fish amid ruined coral reefs and mangrove forests. The book asks how "a new and healing relationship with the living world" can be found and answers with "a tribal legend, based on a solar eclipse, that challenges us to care for the earth." It is the story of the first T'Boli princess, Boi Henwu, whose pet python was about to eat the sun so that she could fall asleep. The people roused the protector spirit of the sun, Nga Bal, by singing, dancing, and playing their instruments. The sun was saved. The book notes that, according to this story, people have the power to keep the sun shining.

The text continues, "Today the peoples of the Philippines need such a story because the life-giving power of the sun is being blocked not by the moon but by the exploitation of the earth." The book explains that the ecological devastation is caused by "export-oriented corporations, industries, plantations, and agribusinesses." It notes, referring to the Philippine Catholic Bishops' pastoral letter on ecology in 1988, *What Is Happening to Our Beautiful Land?*: "The Bishops see signs of hope wherever people oppose the plunder of the Philippines and work to restore the life of its dying earth." Lively illustrations tell the story of successful grassroots campaigns against the Chico dam project, the Bataan nuclear plant, and illegal logging in various areas. The drawings also celebrate the many ecological restoration efforts. The text closes by connecting both types of activism to the ecospiritual wisdom of the native story told at the beginning of the book: "Today individuals and organizations who are working to save the life-systems of the Philippines are fulfilling the promise made by the children of Mahusay and Diwata." An appendix contains both the Bishops' pastoral letter and an afterword, "Grounding Our Hope: Prophetic and Shamanic Healing for the Life of the Philippine Oasis," which weaves together the Christian and native perspectives on the Earth community.[1]

Another story in defense of body, nature, and place was composed by Helena Norberg-Hodge's Ladakh Project to change the public perception of the modern model of development being imposed by the Indian government on western Tibet (Ladakh), which is now part of the Indian state Kashmir. This story was created as a play, *Ladakh, Look Before You Leap*, because theater is a popular form of entertainment and is also a medium through which Buddhist moral precepts are taught. The central character is a young man who has been sent to college in Lahore and is now back at his family home in Ladakh, which he finds unbearably nonmodern. He refuses to eat the traditional food and wears only hip Western clothes and sunglasses to express his cosmopolitan sophistication. He smokes cigarettes and speeds around on his motorbike with his friends.

One day, his grandfather becomes ill, so the young man is sent to bring the doctor. Since the doctor is Western-educated and has recently returned from the United States, the young man is thrilled to be able to ask him all about life in such a modern country. As the doctor tends the grandfather, the young man peppers him with questions. The doctor replies that polyester shirts, such as the one the young man is wearing, are worn only by poor people, while the wealthy prefer only natural-fiber, handwoven clothes like those made by his father and grandfather. (In Ladakh, the men traditionally do the weaving, the women cook, and both sexes work in the fields.) Moreover, the doctor continues, well-to-do people in America eat only stone-ground whole-grain bread like his mother and grandmother make, but the poor eat the industrial, soft white bread that is now trucked in and sold in the bazaar—the sort preferred by the young man and his friends. As for housing, the doctor adds, wealthy people (in dry climates like Ladakh's) live in custom-designed molded-adobe houses like his family's, while the poor live in cement-block units like the ones the Indian army has constructed near the bazaar that the young man so admires. The boy is taken aback, the grandfather recovers, and the audience is delighted, having seen the modern model of development through an ecological-postmodern lens. In tandem with this awareness, the Ladakh Project has introduced an ecologically sound and nondisruptive model of development, including Trombe walls for solar heating and small solar-heated ovens.[2]

These are small stories situated within a larger one. Such stories link our health, mental as well as physical, to the larger health, the integrity of the cosmological unfolding in all societies and all persons. I would like to add another story, one situated in the heart of our own hypermodern country. It presents the positive vision that the reader has been promised in earlier chapters and also pays tribute to the lineage of creative resistance that preceded us, by engaging with a representative figure from that heritage. The genre I have chosen is the tale of a time-traveller, a device used often by William Morris to tell stories of the distant past (such as the English peasants' revolt of 1381 in *A Dream of John Ball*), the recent past (such as the Paris Commune of 1871 in *The Pilgrims of Hope*), and the desired future (such as the England of 1952 in *News from Nowhere*). My model, specifically, is *News from Nowhere* (1892), "nowhere" or "no place" being the translation of the Greek *utopia*.

Morris's utopian novel opens as the narrator, William Guest, is returning home one early winter night after a political meeting to his "shabby" neighborhood in the Hammersmith district of London. He walks down to the edge of the Thames, so fully enjoying the wind, the moon through the branches of an elm, and the swirling water that he almost forgets he is in an extremely polluted city. He enters his home and passes a fitful night. In the morning he awakens to a bright, warm day in June and finds, to his surprise, that the Thames is sparkling clean. He gradually realizes that he is in a future time and that England has undergone an astounding ecosocial transformation. He is shown around by various inhabitants, who explain their society to him. At the end of the story, the narrator and three acquaintances have rowed up the Thames for three days in order to help with a wheat harvest. A woman in the party leads William Guest to her home, a lovely old stone house with a slate roof and many gables (here Morris described his own beloved Kelmscott Manor), and then they all go over to the church for a community supper. Gazing at the festivities from the threshold of the church, the narrator speaks to a male acquaintance but realizes with shock that he can no longer be seen or heard. He awakes in his own bed in "dingy Hammersmith," recalling that his friends' last looks at him had seemed to urge him to go back and act on what he had seen: "Go on living while you may, striving, with whatsoever pain and labour needs must be, to build up little by little the new day of fellowship, and rest, and happiness."

Here, then, is a simple tale of gratitude and transformation, a story of the future that honors the past and suggests a course of action for the present.

NEWS CLIPS FROM SCIOTOPIA

FROM MY FAVORITE SPOT ON THE BANK, I could hear the children I'd been watching across the river, but I could barely make out the colors of their clothes any longer. The soft light of dusk was thinning, leaving trees and buildings blackened against the evening sky. Before they were really needed, sensors had turned on the streetlights along the banks and on the bridges, puncturing the twilight suspension between the light and dark worlds with a hundred shocking stars. Their reflection on the water mixed with the fading light, as the voices of the children grew louder in the near dark.

My gaze was pulled back to the river's edge at the bottom of the slope where I was sitting. I had seen something move, heard the splash of oars, and now made out, to my great surprise, the shape of a rowboat—even though private boats were not allowed on this stretch of the river because of the water-buses. I watched as the boat, propelled by a solitary oarsman, turned into the shore almost directly in front of me. The rower, a man, got out and pulled the boat up onto the shore. He looked around and spotted me, then began walking up the slope, calling out to me as he approached, asking if I spoke English.

"We like to think so," I called back.

"Well, then, where am I?" His English accent was unmistakable now. His voice was booming and somewhat self-amused, as if he were laughing at his fate.

"On the banks of the Scioto."

"How far is that from the Thames?"

He had nearly reached me and was passing through a pool of light from a nearby lamppost.

"I guess about two thousand miles, southwest."

As he got closer, I could see that he was rather short and somewhat stocky, with a full head of grey hair and an untrimmed grey beard and mustache. He was wearing dark trousers and a blue serge shirt with a yoke across the front. When I finally saw his face, the muscles surrounding my solar plexus contracted fiercely with the shock of recognition. The long straight nose. Those hazel eyes, both dreamy and world-weary. A noble face, long fixed in photographs, was suddenly before me. It felt as if I would remain frozen forever on that spot.

"Why are you staring at me? I'm . . . ."

"I know who you are—I think. Would your favorite hamlet on the plains of the upper Thames valley be . . . Kelmscott?"

He registered great surprise, then let out a belly laugh.

"You're at it again, aren't you?" I continued. "Time-travelling, . . . 'Willy-am.'" I used the English pronunciation to make him feel more comfortable.

"Am I? What is the date then?"

"June 27, 2024."

"And this Sci. . . ?"

"Scioto. If you keep heading downstream, it will take you to the Ohio and then the Mississippi and then the Gulf of Mexico. Or—you could stay here a bit. Beautiful, isn't it?" I asked with a sweep of my arm toward the lights on the water.

"Yes. Yes, it is. An excellent river. May I sit down?"

I nodded, and he eased himself down onto the grass, examing the texture with his hands. "What is this?"

I smiled. "We got rid of those English lawns long ago. They took too much water. This is a blend of native grasses and clover. It works fine."

"And . . . did you 'get rid of' England as well?"

"Tsk, tsk. Still bitter over losing the colonies. Actually, some time after you died, you people lost your entire empire—which, as a socialist, is news I should think you would applaud."

"Absolutely. And Britain itself?"

"The Fabians—the 'gas-and-water socialists,' as you called them—did rather well with the new Labour Party as a vehicle. Labour adopted a few bits out of Ruskin's work and yours—but basically bought the whole industrial model. Still, they did a lot for working people—even got socialized medicine in the late 1940s. But it all was pretty much gutted in the 1980s when capital put the squeeze on."

"The plot never thickens."

"No kidding. Your prime minister actually reverted to Hobbes! Insisted there's no such thing as society, only unconnected individuals—organized, à la Adam Smith, by the mechanisms of the market."

"They could still run that tripe a hundred years on?"

"Well, they made their move—over here, too—because they saw the end in sight for their opposition."

"Not those wretched Fabians, surely."

"No, no. Bigger players. Much bigger. Marx's prediction of the 'inevitable' violent overthrow of capitalism was finally played out, in the last place you would ever imagine."

"Scotland?"

"No. Russia. Practically a feudal society."

"Splendid!" He clapped his hands so loudly that I recoiled for an instant.

"No, not splendid. The opposite of splendid. Remember that simple little phrase in Marx, 'the dictatorship of the proletariat,' just a temporary reign of the vanguard until the state withered away?"

He nodded.

"Well, it was developed by Lenin, Stalin, Mao Tse-tung, Ceausescu,

Pol Pot, and countless others into the leftist version of the totalitarian nightmare. Mass murders. A police state. *No* opposition allowed. And a life of privilege for the party elite."

Blood rushed to his face as he pounded the ground and leapt up. "No! I don't believe it! It couldn't have gone that way!"

"Believe it. Besides, even if it hadn't, the Marxist vision of 'scientific socialism' was practically the opposite of what you had in mind: love of nature, love of the vernacular, love of contemplative design. I'm telling you, William, you would not have fit in with the *actual* communism."

He paced back and forth, muttering things I could barely make out. I said nothing.

"So what happened?" he called out as he passed by me.

"Turns out that a highly centralized command economy is very inefficient. They couldn't even unload fishing boats till the word came from Moscow. Of course, if they could have hung on another ten years, they probably could have pulled it off with vast computerized monitoring, as a lot of transnational corporations were doing by the 1990s."

"Computers?" he called out.

"Aaargh! Too hard to explain. A system of devices for communication and calculating . . . and surveillance. Anyway, Russian communism—the Soviet Union—was approaching bankruptcy by the early 1980s because of their economy plus, all the money they'd spent on an arms race with the West. The capitalist governments knew this, through their intelligence operations, but they pretended to their citizens that the situation was the opposite: terribly threatening and cause for a huge federal expenditure for new weapons systems. Our president and his vice president, who succeeded him, nearly quadrupled the national debt in twelve years while lining the pockets of the defense contractors. We're still stuck with huge interest payments on it. Meanwhile, that president, in the early 1980s, tightened the screws on organized labor. It had gotten weak and, after the threat of communism finally disappeared, by the 1990s, workers *really* got squeezed. Talk about time-travelling! It was getting downright Dickensian for lots of people."

"And?" he shouted.

"'Contradictions' indeed became extreme, but not exactly the ones Marx identified. Pollution, massification, the corporate corruption of democracy. People got fed up. They wanted a market economy but not that kind."

I patted the ground. "William, come sit down. Things got better. Really."

He sat down but stared straight ahead at the river.

"They even moved in your direction, sort of."

"I scarcely see how that could have been possible," he said sourly.

"Nor did most people back then. A number of things happened in the late 1990s, though, that seemed to create a new context. I guess one of the main events that boosted new thinking in a big way was the awarding of the Nobel Prize for economics in 1998 jointly to Herman Daly in the U.S. and Paul Ekins in the U.K. (The Nobel Prizes were first awarded shortly after your death, to honor important work.) The selection committee finally awoke from their dogmatic slumber and got a reality check somehow. Year after year, they'd been decorating the 'Chicago school of economics,' literally one department, the source of unimaginably destructive neoliberal cant that had spread worldwide. Anyway, when they finally shifted their recognition to *sustainable*, ecologically sane economics, it gave lots of governments in the Three-Quarters World—and here, too—the ideological support they needed to make some moves toward community-based economics and ecologically sustainable policy. The Nobel Prizes don't effect change, but they convey a significant measure of appreciation that often has rippling effects."

"Ekins, you say."

"He did pioneering work in figuring out the nuts and bolts of sustainability. He also published studies of grassroots movements worldwide. And Daly . . . why, he was the father of ecological economics altogether."

"A sound selection then."

"It was long overdue, but they were merely the first of several ecosocial Nobel Laureates. *And* that same year, the Nobel Prize for peace went to UNPO."

"*Un peau?*"

"No, an acronym: Unrepresented Nations and Peoples Organization. They sought legal recognition for ancient nations that had been absorbed by modern states—all the native nations around the world, plus the Basques, Kurds, Tibetans, the Celtic nations, and so on. They helped negotiate peaceful settlements to several independence wars. Some ancient nations just wanted greater autonomy within the state. UNPO helped with those struggles, too."

"The Celts left the United Kingdom?"

"Not all of them. Poor Ireland finally ran the blighters out about twenty-five years after you died. The Scots and the Welsh stayed in the U.K. but with much greater autonomy after the year 2000. Same with Brittany vis à vis France. Cornwall and Man didn't make much of a fuss over any of it. But all six of them formed a Celtic Commonwealth, mostly for cultural exchanges."

"Now, that I'd like to behold."

"Ah. Your two Welsh grandfathers."

"How on earth did you know that?"

"Biographers, William. Unfortunately for you, your work was so influential that you now have no secrets from posterity. Anyway, the Celtic union was typical of the alignments, old and new, that took shape around that time. The European Union, which was mostly an economic scheme, was already well underway then, but after UNPO got the Nobel Prize, much more attention was paid to saving Europe's minority languages and cultures from being streamlined into some hideous monoculture. UNPO's elevation really advanced the emerging politics that recognized the sovereignty of nations as well as modern states. Combined with the honoring of sustainable, community-based economics that year, it just seemed as if the 'Greening' of the political economy in lots of countries took off, after decades of struggling to become established. Actual Green *parties* were only a small proportion of the ecosocial grassroots phenomena, but over here the U.S. Green party, in coalition with other groups, intensified their grassroots efforts to have an impact on the presidential election in the year 2000. They'd already won hundreds of seats at the state and local levels, but they decided to run *a team* for the presidency and the cabinet to let the voters see clearly what they would be getting."

"The same as they always get: manipulated and used."

I remembered then that his utopian society in *News from Nowhere* had converted the Houses of Parliament into a dung market! Everything worked smoothly with no government.

"Well, yes—and it had gotten much worse than you could imagine, but the first stage of serious campaign-finance reform was in place by then, and more came later. We've pretty much separated concentrated money from elections and legislation."

"My eye! *You* must be dreaming if you believe that."

"At any rate, with spending caps plus the elimination of big donations, the minority parties had more of a chance. The Greens were doing so well in the polls the month before the election that the Democrats finally admitted they couldn't beat the Republican-Reform coalition unless they linked up."

"How could that cruel charade called voting have any real effect?"

"It had a tremendous effect. I'll never forget that press conference in October 2000. I think everyone in the country was watching it—on our televisions, another device. It transmitted pictures and sounds from that room in Washington. Anyway, there sat Silent Al, a defender of the environment—and even ecospirituality—who'd lost his voice on those matters for eight years as Vice President. He was flanked by six members of the Green-team ticket, whom he vowed to put into his cabinet: Ralph Nader as Attorney General, Dolores Huerta ('mother' of the United Farm Workers union) as Secretary of Labor, Paul Hawken as Secretary of Commerce, Winona LaDuke as Secretary of the Interior, Jim Hightower as Secretary of Agriculture, and Christiane Northrup (past president of the American Holistic Medical Association) as Secretary of Health and Human Services. *And that team won.*"

"To what effect?"

"Not a utopia, granted—but tremendous strides were made in community-based economics and development, community-supported agriculture, and the health of bodies and bioregions. Not *because* government started getting more and more Green. That was only a reflection of what was already happening. Things are very different now, William, but it's clear you'll have to see for yourself. Let's take a walk."

We walked up the slope and onto the esplanade. I waved to some neighbors across the street who were walking in the direction of our building. As William scanned the row of two-story apartment buildings and townhouses that lined the frontage street for several blocks, I held my breath, remembering what a blustery critic he was of architecture he considered graceless and uninspired, such as the "modern" mishmash that had taken over much of Victorian London.

"Rather good," he finally pronounced.

"You'd be surprised at what's in the walls: bales of straw or blocks of rammed earth. Both turned out to be very good for insulation. Our summers are quite hot now, so all our buildings are designed for maximum natural ventilation, often with water-filled cooling towers that air passes over. You'll notice them as we walk around, but they fit in well. A lot of these buildings are co-housing: private apartments with communal kitchens and so on. They're built in a rectangle around a large inner yard and garden. You'll see lots of small patches of gardens, too—in front of most of the buildings, in window boxes, as climbing roses and vines growing up the walls. We're not purists about native species, but nearly everyone plants some natives, especially the ones that had become endangered. These trees lining the streets are mostly walnut and the larger varieties of apple trees."

"No horse-and-carriages or those filthy steam-engine monstrosities, I'll wager."

"No private vehicles at all in the center of the city, except for lots of bicycles. We have quiet trains, shuttle buses, delivery vans, and golf carts for the elderly and disabled—all run by polymer fuel cells, usually hydrogen. The engines give off only water. In fact, they feed a small amount of electricity *into* the power grid if they're connected after their daily service. The car-less core has been expanded year by year, as more neighborhoods have wanted it. Some of the close-in neighborhoods were actually made possible by going car-free. Suddenly there were building sites galore where there had been scores of parking lots, gas stations, service garages, and parking structures.

"Obviously, it was a huge challenge for our urban planners and architects, especially since so many other aspects of life were in transition around then. We never could have come so far so fast if the local university hadn't jumped in in a big way, weaning itself from its usual corporate and agribusiness orientation. They set up a community research and planning center in 2001, which is still going strong. The first year was spent gathering information since so many ecological solutions had already been figured out by then but were not widely in use—like waste-treatment greenhouses that produce clean water from sewage in five days. Then we had a year of discussions all over the city, then a year of decision-making. Then came fifteen years of construction, conversion, retrofitting, and planting. It's still going on, of course, but not with that kind of intensive burst."

I led William down a side street, past more two-story apartment buildings, congregate and assisted-care housing for elders, shops, offices, workshops, and small parks.

"Most of the neighborhood businesses you see are cooperatives. They have a much lower rate of failure than other start-up ventures. That building is an incubator for new businesses. They can stay there for their first couple of years at low rent and get advice, services, the use of equipment, and so on."

William had stopped in front of a furniture-making workshop and was peering through the plate-glass. "Why, look over there! It's a variation of the Morris chair."

"But of course. A very comfortable design. I'm sure that one's not made of English oak, though. Most of our wood comes from tree farms nearby—New Zealand species that mature in only three years, plus some selective harvesting from forests. Our paper comes from kenaf plants, also grown on local farms. That's the crop that replaced tobacco throughout Kentucky, Virginia, and North Carolina."

"Don't your farmers raise any food?"

"Tons. And most of them were able to decouple from the agribusiness megamachine because one of the first things we did was to get our institutions to buy locally produced food, furniture, paper, and so on. That was even more important than setting up the farmers' markets around the city and the wholesale-buying networks in the neighborhoods."

We crossed a park and walked through a ring of benches where people were enjoying the summer evening. In the center was a large circular maze of gravel paths with low-growing flowers in between them.

"Recognize that? Stand on a bench and look down at it."

William walked over to an unoccupied bench and ascended. He knew the maze pattern instantly. "It's the labyrinth on the floor at Chartres!"

"The very same. One of the girls' clubs at the high school did it for a design project. You'll see these gravel paths of rounded pebbles in lots of the pocket parks and communal yards. Walking on them barefoot massages all the end-points of the energy channels in your body. It's Chinese medicine, the preventive sort. The girls wanted to combine it with a contemplative exercise—so walking the Chartres labyrinth is an inner and *inner* toning."

"The Gothic lives! I'm greatly relieved," he said, stepping down.

"The labyrinth's a very ancient symbol. I'm particularly proud of this construction because it reflects so much of the heart of our new education: love of quiet reflection, care for the body, continuity with cultural and spiritual history, and creativity in and with nature. I'm in curriculum design. That's my work. These girls had gone all the way through our new educational system, which is based on relationship. Students learn that everything in the universe is related, literally kin, because everything they can see and touch is composed of elements that came into being with the primeval fireball. The youngest children focus on relationships in the family. The next year they learn about relationships among plants, animals, and elements in the schoolyard. The next year it's the neighborhood around the school, then our quadrant of the city, then the city, then the bioregion, then our unglaciated part of the state, then the entire state, then the Ohio River watershed, then the eastern Great Lakes region, then the Midwest, then the nation, then the continent, then the hemisphere, then the planet, then the solar system, then the universe. They learn, all along, that each of these levels, or perspectives, is an expression of the cosmological whole. Mathematics, literature, social studies, and science offer them different ways to think about dynamic relationships within the whole. In short, they're thoroughly embedded!"

I saw that William had removed one boot and was starting to take off the other. "Oh, but I'm trying to get us to the community center before it closes. There's still an hour or so left, but there's a lot I want to show you. It takes sort of a long time to walk the labyrinth with full absorption. Would you mind?"

We continued across the park to the side door of a large building, which, I explained was a school by day.

"Now, William, there's a sizeable possibility that someone might recognize you here. Probably not the young people. They read *News from Nowhere* and some of your other work in a high school anthology— *and* they write an essay on the question of whether our local currency is a better idea than your utopian abolition of money, by the way—but there are no photos of authors in that book. Some of the older people, however, might well recognize you from photos in exhibits and books. We'll just try our luck."

We stepped inside the door, and I showed him the weekly schedule of various meetings and activities on the wall: ecological restoration projects, community boards, community business networks, buying cooperatives, summer camping groups, mother-daughter groups, father-son groups, massage classes, garden clubs, choral and instrumental music groups, book discussion groups, adopt-a-grandparent groups with children, and classes of all sorts. I explained that functions like these were also going on in churches and other civic spaces.

We stopped at the first door and looked in. In three of the corners, the children's desks had been converted to adult chairs by flipping them over and lowering a padded seat. I looked at the placard outside the door: "Pre-marital Counseling."

"This is our answer to the tragically high divorce rate twenty-five years ago. It was terrible on the children. Some right-wingers back then tried to lock the exit doors on bad marriages by making divorce much harder to get. What came out of our discussions on community revitalization was a consensus for intervention on a couple's way *into* marriage. We've made it a municipal requirement that couples have six sessions with a counseling team of wise elders (one male and one female) over age fifty-five. They're familiar with lots of marriages by then and, of course, they go through a training program. So, with their life experience plus the training, they skillfully draw out a couple's expectations and attitudes. For instance, the prospective bride and groom is each asked to name behavior in various circumstances that would be unacceptable or hurtful to them. Most likely, their answers are totally different from each other's, right? That leads to a chat about the differences in male and female sensibilities. Expectations about children is a big topic, too. The counselors make no ruling, but a number of couples discover they're mismatched in crucial ways. The others proceed with their marriages and, according to statistics, live at least more happily ever after than in earlier decades. Of course, young people also get intergenerational guidance through group discussions in the mother-daughter and father-son clubs. It works a lot better than tossing kids out into the world to figure out everything on their own."

I saw that William was gazing across the room at the night beyond the windows. Perhaps this was a painful subject, what with his own unhappy marriage to Jane. And Ruskin's, too! What tortured personal lives those two giants suffered. Freud was wrong, surely, about a mechanistic sublimation, a rechanneling of sexual tension and blocked release. After all, sexual release is available solo. Rather, Ruskin and Morris threw themselves into so much work, I feel, to escape the deep sadness. They kept their minds distracted from the emotional pain by changing the course of the nineteenth century! But who's to say that these great—if quirky—souls would not have accomplished just as much if they'd had happy love lives. To think about their enormous suffering had always saddened me.

"Let's move on, William. Over here there's a massage class for parents and children. They learn relaxation and energizing techniques. Of course, some of this is covered in school in body arts—movement, dance, meditation in which they direct their attention to various parts of the body, and intentionality. That's the key, it was found, in traditional methods of healing all over the world: The intentional mental focusing of energy helps a great deal with both healing and staying healthy."

Out of the corner of my eye I saw someone fast approaching and turned to see my friend Pamela.

"Marie! How are you? Who's your friend?"

William turned from the doorway, and I started to introduce him. "This is . . ."

"Oh, my lord! You look just like photos of William Morris! Excuse me, but you do!"

I stared at William as if to check her observation while my mind raced.

"And a good thing it is," I replied quickly, "because he's preparing a one-man show about Morris. He just came down from Kent. He was trying out some of the material on the drama students at Kent State. He's always been good at English accents. It's great that you recognized him. He's put on a few pounds and let his beard grow scraggly for the part."

William started to give me a hard look but suddenly let out a booming laugh. "She's right. I've grown into the role."

"I'm Pamela. What's your name?"

"It'll help him stay in character," I interjected, "if you just call him 'Willy-am.' Helps his concentration."

"All right—*William*. You know, I just came down from the community theater group. Why don't you come upstairs and do part of your act? They'd love to see it."

I smiled broadly. "That *would* be fun. Wouldn't you say, William?"

"The truth is," he told Pamela, "I'm still working on it. My act never seems to be finished."

"*I* know," I proposed, "you could get in character and read some of the passages from Morris's lectures that are in the anthology. I'll get a copy from the library. The ones about art and design and nature would be good because some of the younger people in the theater group went through our curriculum. Every child learns to design all sorts of things—paintings, fabric, gardens, stories, poems, group structures, conflict resolution. Theoretically, they learn to love to create well-designed solutions."

"Art done by and for the people! Art, the divine solace of human labour, the romance of each day's hard practice of the difficult art of living!" William exclaimed.

"Very good! You do know your Morris!" Pamela responded, applauding.

William blushed a bit, so I turned his shoulders toward the staircase and herded us all in that direction. I suggested to Pamela that she go on ahead and announce the unscheduled performance while we stopped in the library.

"You are given to devious ways," William said with a wan smile.

"A visit from you without hearing you give a speech? It would be . . . lacking, would it not?"

He took from me the book I'd picked out, *Pioneers of Ecological Postmodernism.* "Where, then, are the passages you'll have this monkey perform?"

I found the pages I had in mind and stood silently while he looked them over.

"Not half bad," he said. "This fellow has his head on straight."

We crossed the hall to a large room where there were about twenty-five people, whose faces lit up when they saw William. Heads nodded in agreement. Apparently Pamela had emphasized the actor's remarkable resemblance to his character, whom she described, I'm sure, for those who know only the name *William Morris.* I took a seat toward the back of the group, as he announced that the excerpts he would read were from two lectures, one delivered to the Trades Guild of Learning in 1877 and one to the Working Men's College in 1881. He had taken reading glasses from his shirt pocket and now gave forth in a round, sonorous voice that often intensified with a rough-and-tumble burst of passionate conviction.

> Everything made by man's hand has a form, which must be either beautiful or ugly; beautiful if it is in accord with Nature, and helps her; ugly if it is dischordant with Nature, and thwarts her; it cannot be indifferent; we, for our parts, are busy or sluggish, eager or unhappy, and our eyes are apt to get dulled to this eventfulness of form in those things which we are always looking at. Now it is one of the chief uses of decoration, the chief part of its alliance with nature, that it has to sharpen our dulled senses in this matter: for this end are those wonders of intricate patterns interwoven, those strange forms invented, which men have so long delighted in: forms and intricacies

that do not necessarily imitate nature, but in which the hand of the craftsman is guided to work in the way that she does, till the web, the cup, or the knife, look as natural, nay as lovely, as the green field, the river bank, or the mountain flint.

You may be sure that any decoration is futile, and has fallen into at least the first stage of degradation, when it does not remind you of something beyond itself.

What we want to clothe our walls with is 1) something that is possible for us to get; 2) something that is beautiful; 3) something which will not drive us either into unrest or into callousness; 4) something which reminds us of life beyond itself, and which has the impress of human imagination strong on it; and 5) something which can be done by a great many people without too much difficulty and with pleasure.

Every work of man which has beauty in it must have some meaning . . . the presence of beauty in a piece of handicraft implies that the mind of the man who made it was more or less excited at the time, was lifted above the commonplace; that he had something to communicate to his fellows which they did not know or feel before, and which they would never have known or felt if he had not been there to force them to it . . . .

Without order neither the beauty nor the imagination could be made visible; it is the bond of their life, and as good as creates them, if they are to be of any use to people in general. Let us see, therefore, with what instruments it works, how it brings together the material and spiritual sides of the craft. I have already said something of the way in which it deals with the materials which nature gives it, and how, as it were, it both builds a wall against vagueness and opens a door therein for the imagination to come in by. Now, this is done by means of treatment which is called, as one may say technically, the conventionalizing of nature. That is to say, order invents beautiful and natural forms, which, appealing to a reasonable and imaginative person, will remind him not only of the part of nature which, to his mind at least, they represent, but also much that lies beyond that part.

Unless you know plenty about the natural form you are conventionalizing, you will not only find it impossible to give people a satisfactory impression of what is in your own mind about it, but you will also be so hampered by your own ignorance, that you will not be able to make your conventionalized form ornamental. . . . It follows from this that your convention must be your own, and not be borrowed from other times and peoples; or at least you must make it your own by thoroughly understanding both the nature and the art you are dealing with.

Without the decorative arts, our rest would be vacant and uninteresting, our labor mere endurance, mere wearing away of body and mind.

Decorative, noble, *popular* art will make our streets as beautiful as the woods, as elevating as the mountain-sides: it will be a pleasure and a rest, and not a weight upon the spirits to come from the open country into a town; every man's house will be fair and decent, soothing to his mind and helpful to his work: all the works of man that we live amongst and handle will be in harmony with nature, will be reasonable and beautiful: yet all will be simple and inspiriting, not childish nor enervating; for as nothing of beauty and splendor that man's hand may compass shall be wanting from our public buildings, so in no private dwelling will there be any signs of waste, pomp or insolence, and every man will have his share of the *best*.

As he read, William had occasionally shifted from side to side but had also planted himself in such a way as to make his whole person seem open to the audience. He held the book in his left hand and let the other fidget a bit, as if an overflow of energy sought to be doing the very design work he was describing. He closed the book and looked out at us, an audience applauding both his slightly eccentric delivery as well as his character's vision of design.

It's just as well he doesn't know how bad it got between then and now, I thought. Design was anything *but* organic—first the Modernist sterility, then the aggressive disjunctions of postmodern pastiche, then the long way back to biomorphism only because the herd started moving that way in the 1990s, not because of any deep convictions.

I realized I had better hustle him out of there before he was asked about his acting career. We said good-bye to Pamela and the others and took the book back to the library. This time, William's eyes fell upon a framed panel near the door inscribed with graceful calligraphy:

> But let the children walk with nature, let them see the beautiful blendings and communions of death and life, their joyous inseparable unity, as taught in woods and meadows, plains and mountains and streams of our blessed star, and they will learn that death is stingless indeed, and as beautiful as life, and that the grave has no victory, for it never fights. All is divine harmony.
>
> —John Muir, 1916

"One of ours," I said. "Actually, he was born in Scotland—but he was raised in Wisconsin, walked to Florida once, and ended up spending most of his life in the Sierra Nevada range, especially the Yosemite Valley. Said there wasn't an honest man in all of San Francisco, but he went down there when necessary so he probably knew about the Arts and Crafts boom in the area at that time—which means he probably knew about you."

We went downstairs, where I showed him the mural the school children had made with acorn caps, walnut shells, and dried materials. It was a map of the two major rivers in our immediate watershed, their convergence, and the various creeks that flow into them. On either side were a dozen crayon drawings of native plants and birds.

"All the children recognize the map of our watershed. It's as familiar as the shape of our state. They learn their Earth address as well: between one of these tributaries, east or west of the Scioto or the Olentangy Rivers, in the northern half of the Ohio River basin, on the North American plate. They also learn the history of the land, the story of its life."

William was studying the drawings of the plants and murmuring something I couldn't make out. Just then I heard chairs being moved around in the rooms as some of the groups were about to disperse, so I guided him out the side door opposite from where we had entered before I had to introduce him to more friends and acquaintances.

Outside he was intrigued with the huge overhead trellis that wrapped around two sides of the school, from which large shade trees spread out into the park. I explained that the thinning of the ozone layer and increased levels of radiation made it necessary to keep the children under shelters or slathered with sunblock and always wearing sunhats and sunglasses. The vines growing over the trellis stayed on top, rather than hanging down, because a glazed fiberglas sheet was laid over it to block the ultraviolet rays.

He was curious about two shallow arches, six inches deep and seven feet high, that were built side by side and were made of the same wood as the overhead trellis. They led only into the brick wall and were inscribed with *Abandon All Hope, Ye Who Enter Here.*

"Oh, those are our Bill Gates," I explained. "The faculty designed them as an irreverent monument to computerized education—which was actually used in elementary schools back in the 1990s!"

I decided we should leave my neighborhood, so we went back to the river and walked across the Broad Street bridge into the downtown area. Strolling toward the tall buildings must have reminded William of economic forces because he pressed me for a fuller accounting.

"No, you're right," I agreed. "Not everyone is employed in neighborhood collectives. Far from it. There are a million people in our metropolitan area. There's a lot of manufacturing in the retrofitted factories on the west side and new ones that have gone up elsewhere. They ship products mostly to the adjacent states. What's different now—besides more ecologically responsible production processes—is that there's lots more local ownership and profit-sharing."

"I'll never believe that happened voluntarily. The profit-grinders think the workers exist for the purpose of slavery, always kept sweating and anxious for their livelihood. The owners don't even think of it as oppression!"

"It wasn't voluntary, but it was self-induced—in a way. It's just that corporate domination got so excessive that people finally got *really* fed up. A boycott of the mega-corporations' products forced them to sell off at least half of their accumulated production facilities, and the workers were given the opportunity to buy them with local or regional financing. Also, all sorts of local services had been bought up by giant national corporations: movie theaters, grocery stores, funeral homes, waste disposal companies, newspapers, beauty salons, and *lots* of retail stores. The centralization of ownership had reached astounding levels by the mid-1990s, leaving all communities vulnerable."

"At about the same time, huge numbers of people—both labor and middle management—were turned out of their jobs because manufacturing was moved to countries with very cheap labor. Plus, those computers I mentioned were replacing people. Anyway, all those unemployed people, many with lots of education and business experience, finally realized that the mega-machine was never going to give them back their jobs, so they shifted their focus to community-based possibilities. A number of astute business people back then saw the backlash against distant, concentrated ownership coming. They built up local companies in a regional market and were positioned to enjoy lots of sales when the boycotts of the corporate giants finally spread.

Of course, what really assured the kind of fiscal behavior the public wanted from business was the 1999 revision of the tax code. To qualify for the lower tax rate, corporations must now spend an amount equal to a certain percentage of their payroll on employee training or education, and an amount equal to another percentage has to be invested in their pension funds. They have to pay half of the healthcare coverage for each worker; the rest is paid through a special tax. They must offer profit-sharing, have good safety and environmental records, and avoid any grotesque disparity in salaries between the lowest and highest paid employees. In some companies, the top officials were paid a hundred times the wages of the workers!

With computerization and all, there just weren't enough jobs, though, so everyone now works a thirty-hour or twenty-hour week for wages and then pitches in with all the community service work that needs to be done."

"So—my distinction between useful work versus useless toil might have received a hearing."

"No doubt. Plus, something else you were concerned about had finally reached the saturation point. Remember those early advertising signs that were being installed in the countryside? It got so that corporate logos and names were absolutely *everywhere* we looked, so community regeneration got tied into the move to decommercialize our surroundings. Boycotts of children's clothing that had corporate logos—which turned kids into walking advertisements—were among the early successful efforts. The whole city used to look very different when corporate advertising and sponsorship were plastered all over everything. Even public institutions, especially schools, were succumbing by the late 1990s because the tax base had been devastated by the elimination of jobs and the new community-based alternatives were not yet in place. The new tax code brought in somewhat more revenue but in much wiser ways: taxes on the use of scarce or nonrenewable resources, taxes on activities we want to discourage, and value-added sales tax on most purchases except necessities. These were balanced by a low tax on income—none, in fact, for the lower brackets."

We walked up the Broad Street slope on the east side of the river to the intersection with High Street.

"We're now at the crossroads of the city. These electric trains run all the way out to the suburbs, where they link up with intercity trains that travel in all four directions. Since our city has this division into quadrants formed by Broad and High, we decided to use that as a decentralizing structure. Each quadrant is linked up internally via boards and networks, from its inner-city core all the way out to the suburbs. Each quadrant has its own public school system, which participates in joint programs with its suburban schools. Same with the churches, synagogues, mosques, temples, and other local institutions. A lot of relationships have been established over the years among the neighborhoods in each quadrant. Gradually more racially and ethnically mixed residential patterns have emerged. Also, investment has come in from the suburbs to accelerate the rebuilding and retrofitting of urban homes and businesses. Oh, and something else: Each quadrant is responsible for our city's relationship with one of our four sister cities around the world and hosts one of our citywide seasonal festivals every year."

"It sounds appealing, but what's that monstrosity over there?" William asked, gesturing toward our neoclassical state capitol (which is actually not bad).

"Before I take you over there, you need a drink to soften your attitude about government. Let's go into this cider house. They have local applejack, hard cider, soft cider, and local beers—and it's dimly lit so maybe no one will recognize you."

Inside, I waved to one of the collective members I knew and got us settled quickly into a booth. A young man came over to take our order. He was the son of a friend of mine, now in his second year at the community college. We ordered two hard ciders.

"That boy," I explained after he'd gone, "is still in school because of a curriculum project I worked on. We got all the businesses, large and small, to agree to give hiring preference, for all their jobs that don't require a college degree, to graduates of the apprenticeship program at the community college. The students spend ten hours a week as apprentices in a business and the rest of their school time in classes on grassroots democracy, political economy, technology assessment, advanced ecological awareness of the Scioto watershed, world affairs, comparative religion, local anthropology, mediation skills, the arts, technological skills, and so forth. Our waiter has an uncle in the collective that owns this place and also produces a line of ciders and beer. He's hoping to get into the collective when there's an opening, but meanwhile he's an apprentice in the restaurant business."

The waiter, a burly young man with a ruddy complexion, returned with two glasses of dark cider on a small tray. "Here you go, Marie—two large glasses of wolverine blood straight up!"

"Patrick! That's revolting!"

"Oh. Sorry," he said, laughing. "That's what my buddy and I call the dark blend. It gives you lots of stamina, if you know what I mean."

"Wolverine?" William asked blankly.

I shot him a wide-eyed look of alarm that told him not to pursue his inquiry. Then I looked up at Patrick and explained, "My friend has a wry sense of humor. He refuses to acknowledge the existence of the Wolverines."

Patrick smiled and nodded, then returned to the bar.

"The Wolverines are mascots of the football team that's our university's big rival. Around here, *everyone* knows that, unless you're a space alien. The whole city identifies with the annual game. The half-time ritual is sort of a high mass of our civic religion, alas. We didn't dare disturb any of that with our transformative efforts— just worked around it—except that we got the groundskeepers to use a blend of native grasses. Also, we got the stadium to sell only locally produced food."

William allowed that the cider was quite passable. In fact, he had a second glass and a sandwich. When I paid for it all with a Buck, our Buckeye Hours local currency, and explained grassroots capital, he waxed enthusiastic—although he wanted to redesign the Bucks.

We went outside, crossed the street, and headed for the statehouse lawn. Since he had no fondness for the neoclassical columns on the capitol, their proliferation around the grounds was working him into a lather.

"It's because of the depletion of the ozone layer," I told him. "During the warm months, a lot of festivals are held here, so they hang tent-tops between those pillars."

We climbed the front stairs to the capitol's oversized doors. "It's locked now, of course, but this is what I want to show you . . . this chart over here—of the legislative chambers inside. See that diagonal break dividing the desks? On one side sit the state senators whose districts are in the unglaciated part of the state—that's the entire eastern and southern third of the state, foothills of the Appalachians with big rock formations, rolling hills, and second- and third-growth forests. On the other side are all the districts that were flattened by the Wisconsin glacier long ago. Within that main division, the senators are grouped according to the watersheds of our main rivers. Same arrangement over here in the House. This way, the physical realities and character of each area are brought to bear on the deliberations. And these photos up here? They're our Governor Team."

"Nothing new about that. It's the old Roman triumvirate."

"Except that each member represents a certain age group so we get a full spread: someone who's between twenty-five and forty to bring the initiative of youth, someone between sixty and seventy-five for the wisdom of age, and someone between forty and sixty to represent the confused middle! Our Mayoral Team is apportioned the same way. Each quadrant of the city elects its own team of three, and these twelve people compose the city council. They work closely with the neighborhood boards, of course. Lots of women throughout, William—an essential element of good government!"

"All this may serve some useful function at the local and state levels—if you've actually succeeded in eliminating the influence of the rich, of which I remain skeptical—but it's the national and international levels where war is constantly waged. Silent but deadly economic wars or else the bloodier sort that boost the home economy by tricking the workers into making sacrifices to produce arms in a hurry so that the armament bosses can get rich faster."

We sat down on the top step and watched the fireflies (which we call "lightning bugs," I noted) blink their tiny yellow lanterns in a seeming syncopation of sparks across the lawn.

"You're right. After you died, things kept unfolding in those same ways for about a hundred years, with horrifying escalations. Apparently the economic war of the 'developed' countries against the others had to reach an extreme stage—the effects of a global trade protocol called GATT—before a new system was worked out."

"Through more bloody uprisings, perchance?"

"In some places. But active nonviolence was successfully adopted against such great odds in so many situations in the late 1980s and early 1990s that it became the main vehicle of social change. It was used to overthrow brutal dictatorships in the Philippines, Chile, and Haiti and to topple the whole Soviet empire in Eastern Europe. Back then, nonviolent activism put a lot of heat on the Chinese government and the Burmese junta for human rights violations. Also, a whole range of nonviolent actions—boycotts, rallies, petitions, strikes, tax refusal, and other civil disobedience—were part of the resolution of the Palestinian situation and the abolition of apartheid in South Africa. After all that, nonviolent activism was widely seen as the *only* way to succeed since citizens can never outgun the state, with its vast armed forces. In addition, it became increasingly clear that violence begets violence, over and over again. To initiate or fuel it is almost tantamount to placing a curse on one's future and one's future generations. So—once all the independence wars were settled, the shift in the political economy was achieved almost entirely through nonviolent campaigns in scores of countries."

"Do you mean that the assassin's bomb was no longer hurled at all? From my experience with those among the anarchists in London who were so bent on violent means that they thought nothing of destroying any socialist organization that wouldn't go along with them, I would say the violence itself becomes more dear than the cause."

"Entirely true. It's a way of being that's so consuming that only the leaders *within* those movements can stop it. That's what happened, actually, with terrorist bombings in the 1990s that were claiming the lives of civilians over here and were sometimes carried out by young male Islamicists with backing from various organizations and two or three governments. The Islamic world didn't condone such violence and felt that the slaughter of innocents was a violation of the Koran—but they were terribly weary of being looked down upon and considered an anomaly in the international order. They comprised 25 percent of the world's population then, but an Islamic country had never had a permanent seat on the United Nations Security Council, for instance. That changed when the UN (an international coalition of governments, William) was restructured around the year 2000 as a community of communities of communities: a

geographical structure of nations, regions, and continents that was woven with the major cultural and spiritual perspectives: native peoples, Buddhist, Islamic, Jewish, Christian, Hindu, and secular humanist. Once the
Islamic world had a seat at the table as respected equals—who, by the
way, were quite interested in community-based economics as a counterforce to the globalized, industrial model—their leadership in many countries *really* let it be known through internal channels that the terrorist
violence had to stop, as it ran counter to the core values of Islam. They did
some internal policing, as well."

"I cannot imagine that even that successful resolution brought an end
to international violence. Surely the capitalist governments continued to
behave as they always have."

"They did. The state socialist governments had taken what they
wanted by force, too. By the mid-1990s, a new paramilitary presence
was added to the mix: the huge security forces employed by the transnational corporations to protect their property and their GATT-given rights.
All that was reined in when GATT was rewritten. Combined with the
new international structure at the UN, things have gone pretty well, although there are still recurring trouble spots."

"There always will be as long as capital is driving everything."

"Money *and power.* If the power is the democratic will of a people,
though, both economic and military war can be avoided. Today, war is
widely considered to be an idiotic failure, not an 'ennobling' proof of
manhood. We try to instill in our young people a sense of their responsibilities as citizens of their city, bioregion, state, nation, and world. There
are several organizations around here that focus on one of those levels,
but nothing makes as much of an impression, we've found, as personal
experience of other cultures. We urge our young people to spend at least
six weeks, usually the summer after high school, living and working in another country—or at least a part of the U.S. far different from here. A
number of the churches and colleges have exchange programs in Central America."

William's expression clouded. "I hope you don't insist upon it. It
wouldn't be right for everyone, you know."

I realized at once that he was thinking of his elder daughter, Jenny,
who was stricken with epilepsy, which ran in his family. An excellent student, she was taken out of secondary school after experiencing her first
grand mal seizure and later developed meningitis. Morris himself may

have had some sort of neurological irregularity, causing his sudden outbursts and sometimes awkward movements. His friends observed that he was never more content than when his hands and mind were fixed upon executing one of the dozens of crafts he mastered—several of which he revolutionized.

"No, of course not," I agreed. "It's entirely voluntary and up to the family and the child." I put my hand lightly on his forearm as I spoke. This was done out of genuine sympathy but also, I admit, to satisfy my curiosity as to whether he would register disapproval, as English people of his class often do, at being touched in conversation. He didn't even flinch. Well done, William!

We descended the stairs, and I showed him the native plantings from different parts of the state before we retraced our steps toward the river. He kept pressing me on the lot of the poor in our society. I told him that there were still relatively poor neighborhoods, but they were no longer plagued with despair over high unemployment, broken institutions, and anomic behavior that endlessly violated anyone who could be preyed upon. Our revitalization efforts in those neighborhoods had focused not merely on jobs but on the kinds of economic enterprises that built community ties and sponsored youth projects and ecological restoration work. Once people, especially the young men, started feeling useful, necessary, and responsible to other people in the community, the crime rate dropped, as did the level of teenage pregnancies initiated by older "predator" males, a social problem William found shocking. Our garden city bloomed in those neighborhoods, as well, as pride of ownership grew through the co-housing collectives, I told him.

When we reached the middle of the bridge, we stopped between two of the concrete planters overflowing with summer flowers and leaned against the railing to watch river currents flow through pools of light. We were silent for a long while, taking in the peaceful insistence of moving water and reflecting on the course of our evening. It was past midnight now. A few cyclists peddled over the bridge and, behind us, the Broad Street electric train swished by quietly.

At length, William said, "I thought . . . there would be more. After all this time."

"More of an *Earthly Paradise*?" I asked, referring to his most famous poem.

"I suppose so."

"We're simple folk, William. We opted for the art of the possible. Besides, you cannot imagine how *im*possible much of what we've accomplished seemed back in the 1990s. Jobs were being exported, computerized, and otherwise eliminated in huge numbers. People were scared—and with good reason. Violence and social disintegration seemed to be intractable. Environmental protection was still being fought tooth and nail by the corporate sector, who pretended it was simply a plot by liberals! Poverty and upheaval were on the rise throughout the Three-Quarters World, causing huge migrations of displaced people. To all that, governments responded with intensified levels of the very policies that had encouraged the crises. There was an extremely powerful momentum to stay the suicidal course.

"Just to find another way, William, just to create some sound alternatives, was enormously difficult. It finally happened because of the grassroots support and then *demand*. But it was dicey. It might well have gone the other way if enough people hadn't taken matters into their own hands and started making their own towns and regions less vulnerable and more secure—economically, ecologically, socially. From the perspective of your own utopian vision, I know this all falls short, but—really now—don't you think your abolishing government, money, *and* schools was a bit . . . ?"

He stiffened and assured me that *News from Nowhere* had been rather influential.

Oh, dear. I'd offended him. Instantly, Dorothy Parker's observation arose in my mind: *Writers want only three things in life: praise, praise, and more praise.* Still true a hundred years later!

"Of course it was, William! Your utopian story was savored for decades—and then was taken up all over again, as part of your newly appreciated *oeuvre* thirty years ago. I only meant . . . Well, I *am* in the education biz, you know," I said laughingly. "I believe that school can help to evoke the unfolding of the person and enrich one's sense of grounding. It can be a far different experience than the terrible time you had at Marlborough."

William turned his gaze from the water and smiled warmly at me. "Don't take me to be an old curmudgeon, Marie. I can see that your society has accomplished a great deal. In my circles, we, too, set about remaking the fabric of modern society, but the temptation to settle for palliation carried the day—the Fabians, New Labour, state socialism, and all that," he said wearily. "My undying hope, for it lived beyond me in my pages, was for an *essential* change in society: the equality of wealth and the end of privilege, the emergence of a new art, work with dignity, well-designed public institutions that satisfy the craving for splendor and completeness, an end to defiling the natural beauty of the earth, and private life for all that is decent and, apart from natural accident, happy."

I was too moved to respond at first, for his last remark brought to mind the association in all his utopian fables between social liberation, happy relationships for all, and sexual attunement. The time-traveller in *News from Nowhere* isn't quite able to experience it, though, for he finds that he has become invisible a short time after a "comely" woman leads him into her lovely old stone home. Over and over again—in poems, plays, fables, and tales, even up to the time of his death at sixty-two—his stories revolve around a stalwart young-ish man who is unnerved and saddened by his wife's long-term affairs. In the new society, in Morris's Green-socialist utopias, all would be happiness.

"William," I began, "we've tried here to eliminate a lot of the sources of *un*happiness: economic insecurity, undemocratic governance, alienation from the natural world and from each other, spiritual barrenness, and the commercialization of practically everything. After much discussion, we decided on a focus for the first twenty-five years of our new orientation: *Reconnect!* We've done a lot of building, both physical and cultural. I and others are now lobbying to have the focus for our next twenty-five years be *Deepen!* We haven't neglected the cosmological, spiritual, and psychological for the material projects, but we could go much further with awareness of that sort. (Of course, I should tell you that some people are lobbying for *Disconnect!* The Lone Cowboy ethos in this country dies hard.)

"What I mean to say is that happiness will never result from even the most perfect social structure. It comes from cultivating awe, joy, respect, wisdom, and compassion for all our relations in the Earth community. People hurt each other, William, because they lack awareness, deep awareness, that every person is a miracle of the universe. Our society here is slowly and haltingly discovering what that could mean. We still have tensions between different groups in the city. We still have exasperation between the sexes at times. I feel t....t women still need to go further in finding our true voices of embodied experience, though that situation has definitely improved. Childhood is less wounding now because we've done so much public education on what it takes to raise a healthy, happy child—and, of course, children love all the parental involvement with the schools since the work-week had to be shortened. I know much more can be done, but we first had to figure out how to recover from modernity's annihilation of inner life. You located that possibility in the emergence of a new art. That's why so many of your patterns evoke deep communion. They're sacramental—'the impress of human imagination' mingled with the exuberance of our bountiful earth. *Ave! Ave!*"

He considered this for a moment, then smiled. *"'Art lives on, life is brief.'"*

We continued to the other side of the river and turned left onto the esplanade. When we passed the spot where he had come ashore, we saw that his rowboat had disappeared, as would he. We strolled in the light of a three-quarter moon for five more blocks, stopping in front of a co-housing apartment building covered with honeysuckle and white clematis vines.

"This is where I live, William. I'd like to show you something. Will you come inside?"

We walked quietly upstairs to my two large rooms facing the river. I unlocked the door and asked him to wait outside while I turned on the lamps on the desk and the table. Then I took his hand and led him in. His eyes fell first upon the wall hanging I had made from an eight-foot length of his "Honeysuckle" chintz, printed in sage, peach, and cream. On another wall was a reproduction of his "Woodpecker" tapestry. The sofa was covered in his "Dove and Rose" fabric in sage and cream. He looked down and laughed to see he was standing on a reproduction of one of his Hammersmith carpets.

"I suppose this is why your rowboat pulled up in front of *me*."

"I suppose this is why all this work poured out of me, then. To give comfort, to inspire, to share what I knew beyond words—but who would ever have thought it would go on and on, even, finally, into the times I had wished for so intently?"

I went to a bookshelf and took down paperback facsimiles of his Kelmscott Press editions of Chaucer, Ruskin, Keats, Shelley, and his own sweet last fables: "Morris for the masses," I said, handing them to him. He seemed intrigued. If he was disappointed to see his extraordinary page designs without the companionship of their vellum covers and specially woven silk ties, he did not let on.

"When I was in Britain right after college, in the mid-1990s, I visited several of the extant homes and rooms you'd designed. I was on a scholarship from the Forum for the Future to study Green curriculum design, but I was also drawn to cultural history. I took trains all over, checking out the second-generation Arts and Crafts work, too, from Hill House to Chipping Campden. Nothing moved me like yours, though. It was an extraordinary period of discovery for me, a communion that shaped me, somehow, from then on."

He may have been a little embarrassed, for he changed the subject by rushing over to the chairs around my table. He pulled one out and held it up, marveling at the lines.

"It's a copy I had made of the living room chairs Charles Sumner Greene designed for the Gamble House in 1909. He was influenced by you, surely, but also, as you can see, by the grace of Japanese design. Nearly everything he did is sublime. I wanted to live with some of it. Come over here now. There's something else I want you to see."

I opened the door to the bedroom and ushered him in, showing him my bedspread and drapes in his "Willow" pattern.

"That's supposed to be wallpaper!" he exclaimed.

"I know, but Sanderson & Company took liberties later on. It looks nice, don't you think?"

He softened a bit but suddenly looked decidedly ill at ease. "I rather think I will soon—very soon—become invisible, since the woman in this time-travel story has now taken me to her home. That is how the tale ends."

"*Comely*. This 'comely' woman has led you home," I reminded him.

"Ah. Yes. Of course. A *comely* woman has led me here," he recited, smiling nervously.

"You aren't going to disappear yet, William. *I'm* writing the story this time, and we have all the time we need. Come back out here," I said, returning to the living room, "and sit down on the sofa with me for a moment, will you?"

He sat down and turned over the corner of the carpet to see what the machine-made version looked like. I waited until he sat up and looked my way, still somewhat apprehensive.

"As you have seen, our children learn massage and other body arts from an early age. We adults had to catch up by taking classes, but nearly everyone now knows three or four different systems of bodywork. I've become partial to the Chinese. It's so efficacious, simply by using gentle pressure on the acupuncture points. When the bodymind suffers deep sadness, William, it's held in our tissue, in the cellular memory. And when people go through life—even a great one—without being touched enough, the bodymind is deprived. And if, now and then, inherited neurological tendencies grip one's being, he may feel askew. But your bodymind has deep reservoirs of energy, which will rise to flow like rivers through your fourteen channels . . . if only the dams and blockage are cleared. Merely by soft pressure, merely a healing touch. May I do this for you . . . after all you've done for us?"

Already the tension had gone out of his face. His eyes looked kind but tired, deeply tired. He said he wouldn't mind a little rest and lay down on the sofa. I stood for a moment fixing the sight in my memory: Morris on Morris. Now *there* was a creation. Then I knelt beside him and put my left hand behind his neck. I asked him to close his eyes and placed my other hand below his rib cage. I waited until his *chi* pulse felt equal to my right and left fingers. Then I moved my right hand to his knee and waited again to feel the balance. In this way I moved from point to point, increasingly assured that William would return to the ages *eased*.

And so, Dear Reader, with the midsummer night's breeze rising off the river, bringing us the fragrance of flowering vines, we communed . . . with body, nature, and place.

MODERNITY IS TO US
AS WATER TO A FISH

MODERN PEOPLE are highly self-conscious, aware that they must adopt various ways of thinking and behaving in each of the unrelated spheres of modern life. Yet modernity itself seems astonishingly un-self-conscious. The entire interlocking structure of beliefs, assumptions, and ideologies constituting the modern worldview and the modern condition function as if they were merely the natural result of human progress. Although the relatively few people who have gone to college and studied sociology can rattle off a dozen characteristics and ideologies of modernity without effort, as can inhabitants of certain intellectual circles, modern society, for the most part, does not examine and reflect upon its assumptions. Its creative energies are focused elsewhere: on moving *forward*. This focus, too, feels like nothing other than a natural response to an inertial force.

I find the invisibility of modernity to be both fascinating and disconcerting, for the water around us modern "fish" is becoming increasingly cloudy. I had been intrigued by modernity when I was in college. Typically for someone molded by modern schooling, I gave little thought to the ways in which modernity might be limiting as well as expanding the possibilities for my generation. Not being a sociology major, I was not exposed to the analytical critiques of modernity, from Max Weber on. Instead, I discovered cultural history as I studied the various periods of

British and American literature. I became intrigued with determining the point at which society had moved out of the "benighted" past and had achieved modern sensibilities. Who were the first moderns? In truly sophomoric fashion, I began with the assumption that people in previous decades had no doubt aspired to being modern but could hardly be considered so, as they knew nothing of the advanced states of development I observed around me in 1965. Eventually, I learned that the Modernist poets and novelists of the 1920s and 1930s had declared a radical break from the fixed certainties of the modern era that had been accepted prior to World War I, that the Victorians before them had embraced a modern faith in industrial progress (fed by rapacious imperialism), that the Romantics before them had boldly thwarted convention in ways that many people today consider modern, that modern constitutions were born of the Enlightenment during the eighteenth century, that the Scientific Revolution during the sixteenth and seventeenth centuries established the essential truth-mode for the modern era, and that the struggle between the "ancients" and the "moderns" had been one of the central dynamics of the Renaissance. To my surprise, my search had delivered me to the *quattrocentro*. I could have traced the trail back much further, as I learned later, had I known how to follow the leads.

In the years following college, I did not think about modernity. This was somewhat ironic since my generation was immediately caught up in an international protest against the restrictions of modernity: the counterculture of the 1960s. Because of the antirationalist and anti-intellectual character of that eruption, the comprehensive scope of its critique was not generally articulated as a historical response to the modern era. There were exceptions, of course—such as the insightful commentaries by the cultural historian Theodore Roszak—but, more generally, the critique was simply expressed through music, dress, and short-lived efforts to recover community.

Not until the late 1970s, a decade after my collegiate fascination with modernity, did I become aware that a lot of other people had begun thinking about it, too. The term "postmodern" was in the air, charged with connotations of a muscular deconstruction of all "fictive unities" and "metanarratives"—all belief systems, all bodies of knowledge, and all faiths (scientific and otherwise). These "metanarratives" were declared to be totally arbitrary "language games" or subtly diffused power plays. The pastiche of fragmentation, juxtaposed shards, and objects free of context was widely believed to portray the naked truth, once false cohesions were deconstructed. In short, the organicism so dear to the sixties was just another lie to this new wave. The deconstructionist aesthetic soon made its way into art, architecture, and commercial design. Bookish sort that I am, I first noticed it while browsing in bookstores. Suddenly book jackets featured jarring clashes of mismatched typefaces in garish colors. True, the rigid, authoritarian style of much conventional book design had been supplanted, but—to my eyes, at least—the change hardly seemed an improvement. In fact, it seemed violent and wildly ungrounded. How could self-righteous belligerence and an aggressive denial of relational context be antidotes to modernity when they themselves were inherent in its problematic success?

As sociologists have noted, its success derives from a belief system that constitutes our normative view of life on Earth during the modern age. Its framework, as rigid as steel girders, is constructed from the following (im)materials. (An abbreviated citing of this list appears in Chapter 2.)

The human is considered essentially an economic being, homo economicus. *The proper arrangement of economic endeavors is believed to bring about contentment in all other spheres of life—which, after all, are believed to evolve primarily in relation to economic realities. That which is worthy of greatest attention is material substance, manufacture, and accumulation. (The* materialism *of modern societies is an odd version, however, as the actual material condition of the soil, water, and air is generally ignored.)*

Mass-production industrialism *is the best way to attain ever-increasing levels of well-being through consumption. Industrialism reflects faith in a rapacious mode of production to bring an age of abundance and contentment. Such faith is linked with* progressivism, *the belief that the human condition progresses toward increasingly optimal states as the past is continually improved upon.*

Objectivism *is the belief that there is a rational structure to reality, independent of the perspectives of any particular cultures or persons, and that correct reason mirrors this rational structure. Concepts exist by themselves, objectively, and categories are defined simply by necessary and sufficient conditions that specify the properties shared by all and only members of the category.*

A related concept, also essential to modernity, is rationalism: *Knowledge, belief, and the basis for action is properly derived solely from reason, the exercise of cognitive practices. "Pure reason" is valuable precisely because it is "untainted" by emotions, sensate knowledge, social constructions, and noncognitive awareness. The structure of rationality, that is, is believed to transcend bodily and cultural experience.*

According to the modern, mechanistic worldview, *the physical world is composed of matter and energy, which operate in various constellations of cause-and-effect, according to "laws" of nature. Occurrences of creative unfolding and complex interactive responses in nature have no place in this perspective. Understanding physical entities, no matter how complex, is achieved by breaking them down into smaller and smaller parts. Such* reductionism *seeks the smallest unit of composition and yields no knowledge about the interaction of parts of a system or the creative behavior of the system as a whole.*

Modernity also embraces scientism, *the belief that all fields of inquiry can attain objective knowledge by modeling their practices after the investigative methods of science. Scientistic prejudices extend throughout modern systems of knowledge and numerous institutions.*

Efficiency is increased in modern societies because social practices, work, education, language, and expectations become standardized, *that is, made uniform to a large extent. Customs and traditional knowledge particular to a community or region are considered quirky, backward, and anachronistic. Efficiency is further improved by* bureaucratization, *the structuring of human interactions in regimented, hierarchical, and inflexible modes, by which controlled and controlling amounts of information can be gathered by modern institutions. A related momentum within processes of modernization is that of* centralization, *prized for the increased control and standardization it brings.*

Modern interactions with nature are generally informed by anthropocentrism, *the belief that the human species is the central phenomenon of the natural world. This idea, and related ones, are executed with* instrumental reason, *modes of thinking used to achieve desired ends rather than to determine values. (In the school of philosophy called "pragmatism," "instrumentalism" refers to the validity of ideas, as guides to action, resting upon the success of the action.)*

Modern culture defines itself as a triumphant force progressing in opposition to nature. *Premodern and nonmodern societies are seen as having been "held back" by unproductive perceptions of holism and by conceptualizations of human culture as an extension of nature with reciprocal duties. Consequently,* contempt for indigenous peoples *is widespread in modern so-*

cieties. The drive to exploit "resources" on native peoples' land does not fully explain the modern obsession, both capitalist and communist, with dismantling tribal cultures.

Modern life is compartmentalized, *that is, considered to exist in discrete spheres or compartments, such as family life, work, social life, and so on. Learning, especially at the university level, is strictly divided into departments, which have little interaction. One of the "compartments," spiritual and religious life, is devalued in modernity because modern history celebrates the* escape from religion *and other "superstitions" via the new rationalism. To survive in the modern era, institutionalized religions have downplayed spiritual connectedness with the creation; instead, they focus on rationalist applications of morals and ethics. This "advance" resulted in the devastating* shrinkage of the cosmological context, *the sacred whole, to the scale of humans.*

Modern cultures are sometimes called "hypermasculine" *because traits considered masculine, such as the persona of rationalism, are valued more than those considered feminine, such as empathy. Patriarchal socialization also favors competition and a dominance-or-submission dichotomy as the structure of relationships, both personal and impersonal.*

The effects of this worldview on our consciousness are paradoxically quite opposite from the absolutist certainty of the modern ideologies above. An existential *un*certainty haunts the modern psyche. This is so, according to a particularly insightful sociological study by Peter Berger, Brigette Berger, and Hansfried Kellner, because modern life is shaped by functional rationalism (the imposition of rational controls over the material world, social customs, and the self), componentiality (the conception of reality as comprising clearly separable components), multirelationality (dealing with an enormous variety of relations), makeability (a problem-solving approach to reality, which is apprehended as "makeable"), pluralization (the vastly intensified demands on human consciousness to shift among multiple realities or "life-worlds"), and progressivism (an "upward and onward" view of the world). In *The Homeless Mind: Modernization and Consciousness*, Berger, Berger, and Kellner propose that people living in modern societies are afflicted with a permanent identity crisis. Modern identity is open-ended, transitory, and liable to ongoing change, whereas a particular subjective realm of identity is the individual's main foothold in reality. The authors note that modern identity is "peculiarly individuated," such that the right to plan and fashion one's life as freely as possible is taken to be a basic right, elaborately legitimated by a variety of modern ideologies. Religion, which formerly provided a cognitive and normative structure that made it possible for people to "feel at home" in the universe, is privatized in modern societies and, like other compensations of the private sphere, is experienced as fragile, possibly artificial, and essentially unreliable. Consequently, the task of each individual's creating a do-it-yourself universe in order to grasp at meaning is fraught with frustration. We of the modern world are homeless in the cosmos.

The groundlessness yielded by modernity's promise of unfettered freedom and pure potentiality increases as the technosphere enlarges. Modern social systems are disembedded because social relations are lifted out of local contexts of interaction and restructured across "indefinite spans of space-time," according to the British sociologist Anthony Giddens in *The Consequences of Modernity*. As social life "rolls away" from the fixities of tradition, living in the modern world feels increasingly like being aboard a careening juggernaut. Giddens is correct, I believe, in identifying many disembedded, disembodied aspects of contemporary life not as "postmodern," as is often claimed by deconstructionists, but as intensified and expanded dynamics of modernity, which he calls "radical modernity."

Our age is *hypermodern*, not so much because the tarnished ideologies of the modern worldview are still believed to be salvational, but because the *conditions* of modernity are now driven by the dynamics of the technosphere and the globalized economy. "Cyberspace" is hardly *post*modern. What could be more disembodied, disembedded, and decontextualized? Surely the computer age is *most*modern, to use a term suggested by David Ray Griffin.

Still, the effort to identify various postmodern developments intensified in the 1980s, during which two quite different clusters emerged. The deconstructionist variety (also called "constructionism," "constructivism," and "poststructuralism") got a grip on much of academia, particularly in the liberal arts and social sciences. In every discipline, the constructionists sought to demonstrate, often very aggressively, that all knowledge is determined ("socially constructed") in service to various power relations and that there is *nothing but* social construction in human experience. In contrast to this formalist critique of modernity, which focuses on the politicized forms and structures, the other cluster of post-modern thought focused on problems with the *content* of modernity, that is, the modern worldview. The second cluster lacks a widely accepted umbrella term, but is sometimes called "constructive," "reconstructive," or "restructive" postmodernism. In any case, this loosely constituted school of thought was vastly outnumbered by the deconstructionists—until that orientation began to lose adherents during the early 1990s. (A critique of the assumptions of deconstructionism is included in *States of Grace*.)

A truly *post*modern alternative would counter the modern ideological flight from body, nature, and place. It would be a grounded, deeply ecological, and spiritual postmodernism. My own contribution to such a possibility, *ecological postmodernism*, is presented in Chapter 2 and elsewhere in this book. It is closely related to the "restructive" orientation, which includes works by David Ray Grifffin, Charles Jencks, Richard Falk, and many others mentioned in the first three chapters. Ecological thinking, even when properly understood to encompass far more than a narrow sense of environmentalism, will not prevail unless it is fused with a clear understanding of the dynamics of modernity *and* an awareness of kindred *post*modern alternatives that are now gaining strength.

That clear understanding of modernity is made more difficult than it should be by the confusing labels. "Postmodernism," as I have noted, has at least two major connotations (although it is generally taken to mean "deconstructionism"). Further confusion ensues over meanings of "modern," "modernity," and "modernism." One would expect an overarching orientation like *modernity*, stretching from 1460 to the present, to have an "ism" attached to it—that is, an ideological belief system. The term "modernism" comes to mind as the likely candidate—but that term has a specific and limited meaning within cultural history, especially in the arts and literature. In these fields, it refers to the protest movement that extended from roughly 1905 (earlier in France) to 1939. The *Modernist movement* challenged the smug certainties of the nineteenth-century forms of the larger, embedding cultural context called *modernity*, which they thought of only as the "status quo" or the "conventional ways." When people use the term "modernism" today, then, one cannot know at first whether they mean it to be the adjectival form of "modernity" or are referring to the aesthetic protest movement in the early decades of this century. (In what I hope is a contribution to clarity, I present in Chapter 4 my sense of two quite different streams within the Modernist movement in the arts: a *pro-modern Modernism*, the machine aesthetic, and a *counter-modern Modernism*, the fascination with flux and fragmentation but also with subtle interrelatedness and the cosmological.)

In addition to all this, "modern" has sometimes been used in a positive sense to mean "the new" even by writers, such as Ruskin, who dedicated their entire life work to challenging the overarching orientation we call "modernity," or the modern era,—that is, the secular, mechanistic worldview that was cumulatively established by Renaissance humanism, the Reformation, the Scientific Revolution, and the Enlightenment. Ruskin's connotation in *Modern Painters* is simply "the new," specifically the new aesthetic. This use of the word can be traced back to the third century!

Another obstacle to critical discussions of modernity is the emotional resistance, or even hostility, exhibited by people if their identity is deeply embedded in the modern worldview. They hear a critique of specific failed aspects of modernity as a wildly unrealistic rejection of everything we know today—and everything they are. Naturally, this interpretation calls forth a defensive response on their part. Besides, modern socialization insists that progress has delivered us to a time far better than any other and that we will continue to be propelled away from harm and hardship if only we will stay the course. Consequently, alternatives are seen as risky and frightening.

Those who champion modernity like to remind malcontents that premodern life was full of superstition, persecution, and various irrational cruelties. This is true. Far from eradicating socially induced suffering, however, the modern worldview merely changed the rules of what was accepted and expected—and upped the ante as technology enabled the imposition of increasingly devastating cruelties on an increasingly large scale.

Let us indeed remember with resolve and compassion the victims of premodern times: those who were mocked for being insufficiently pious, or ostracized from their medieval village, or required to live in circumscribed areas of medieval cities, or terrorized by threats of fire and brimstone, or stoned, or murdered.

But let us also memorialize the casualties of modernity—those who raised objections that were crushed by the arrogance of the new worldview with its absolute certainties:

To all the women who risked their lives in the American and French revolutions, only to discover the patriarchal character of the Enlightenment, which was never meant for them,

To all the country people whose love for the earth and its cycles made them objects of contempt in the modern urban mind,

To all the native people who resisted genocide and forced assimilation, modernity's fate for those considered "backward,"

To all the victims of mass murder by fascist regimes using modern bureaucratic efficiency and disengaged, instrumental reason,

To all the people brutalized and murdered by Marxist armies and police because they resisted the "scientific theory of history,"

To all who fought to save their communities and livelihood from the callous control of giant corporations and cartels,

To all the parents who pleaded with officials of the industrialized nation-state to recognize the connection between radiation, or toxic dumping, and their malformed or sickly children,

To all the people who persevered in cultivating a spiritual life even though they were mocked as "irrational," and

To all those children who tried valiantly to hold on to their early sense of the world as wondrously creative and vibrantly alive, even as they were jammed into the grid of modern schooling,

We here declare that YOU WERE RIGHT.

You were right, and your suffering was not in vain. Your tears have fertilized the earth, from which now grow more resistance efforts than can be counted, more resilience than can be known.

ENDNOTES

~

CHAPTER ONE: EPOCHAL RUMBLINGS IN THE 1990s

1. Matthew Budd, "Recovering the Wisdom of the Past," *Positive Personal Health*, published by The Shield Health Plans, vol. 3, no. 1, Winter 1995. Elsewhere in the newsletter, the following books were recommended to subscribers: *Wherever You Go There You Are* by Dr. Jon Kabat-Zinn, *Sound Mind, Sound Body* by Dr. Kenneth Pelletier, *Healing and the Mind* by Bill Moyers, and *The Relaxation Response* by Dr. Herbert Benson. Also see Barbara Whitaker, "Now in the H.M.O.: Yoga Teachers and Naturopaths," *New York Times*, November 24, 1996; the Health Policy Tracking Service of the National Conference of State Legislators predicts that more states will soon follow Washington State's lead and require healthcare insurers to provide coverage for an array of alternative medical procedures.

2. See "Health Maintenance Organizations Are Turning to Spiritual Healing," *New York Times*, December 26, 1995; "The Healing Power of Prayer Is Tested by Science," *Wall Street Journal*, December 20, 1995; and "Religion Can Be Good Medicine," Associated Press, *San Francisco Chronicle*, February 12, 1996.

3. See Herbert Benson, *Timeless Healing: The Power and Biology of Hope* (New York: Scribner, 1996); also see his earlier book, *The Relaxation Response* (New York: Avon Books, 1975).

4. Also see the following books by Larry Dossey: *Beyond Illness* (Boston: Shambhala, 1984), *Meaning and Medicine* (New York: Bantam, 1991), *Healing Words* (San Francisco: HarperCollins, 1993), and *Prayer Is Good Medicine* (San Francisco: HarperCollins, 1996). Also see the following books by Deepak Chopra: *Perfect Health* (New York: Harmony Books, 1990), *Creating Health* (Boston: Houghton Mifflin, 1991), *Journey into Healing* (New York: Harmony Books, 1994), and *Ageless Body, Timeless Mind* (New York: Harmony Books, 1993). Also see the following books by Jeanne Achterberg: *Imagery in Healing* (Boston: Shambhala, 1985), *Woman as Healer* (Boston: Shambhala, 1990), and *Rituals of Healing* (New York: Bantam, 1994).

5. David Eisenberg et al., "Unconventional Medicine in the United States—Prevalence, Cost, and Patterns of Use," *New England Journal of Medicine*. vol. 328, January 28, 1993, pp. 246–52.

6. See, for example, Gerald Weissmann, *Democracy and DNA: American Dreams and Medical Progress* (New York: Hill & Wang, 1996); also see the approving review of this book by Lance Morrow, "Irrational Medicine," *New York Times Book Review*, March 3, 1996. In contrast, see Oscar Janiger and Philip Goldberg, *A Different Kind of Healing: Doctors Speak Candidly about Their Successes with Alternative Medicine* (New York: G. P. Putnam's Sons, 1993). Also see Caryle Hirschberg and Mark Ian Barasch, *Remarkable Recovery* (New York: Riverhead/Putnam, 1995).

7. See *Acupuncture Needle Status Changed*, FDA Talk Paper T96-21, April 1, 1996; also see Rick Weiss, "FDA Removes Bar to Coverage of Acupuncture by Insurance," *Washington Post*, March 30, 1996.

8. "Surprisingly High Failure Rate for Tubal Ligation," *San Francisco Chronicle*, April 15, 1996.

9. Candice Pert, quoted in Kenneth R. Pelletier and Denise Herzing, "Psychoneuroimmunology: Toward a Mindbody Model," *Advances: Journal of the Institute for the Advancement of Health*, 1988, vol. 5, no. 1, p. 33. Also see Candace B. Pert, "The Wisdom of the Receptors: Neuropeptides, the Emotions, and the Bodymind," *Advances: Journal of the Institute for the Advancement of Health*, 1986, vol. 3, no. 3, pp. 8–16. Also see Leonard A. Wisneski, "Biopsychology: Overlapping Systems of Mind-Body-Environment," *Noetic Sciences Review*, no. 9, Winter 1988.

10. Laurie Garrett, *The Coming Plague: Newly Emerging Diseases in a World Out of Balance* (New York: Farrar, Straus and Giroux, 1994), p. 513.

11. "Greening the Building and the Bottom Line," Rocky Mountain Institute, Snowmass, CO, 1995.

12. See Steven Halpern, *Tuning the Human Instrument: An Owner's Manual* (Palo Alto, CA: Spectrum Research Institute, 1978).

13. Aaron Sachs, "Humboldt's Legacy and the Restoration of Science," *World Watch*, March/April 1995, p. 30.

14. See Fritjof Capra, *The Web of Life: A New Scientific Understanding of Living Systems* (New York:Anchor Books / Doubleday, 1996); also see Joanna Macy, *Mutual Causality in Buddhism and General Systems Theory* (Albany, NY: State University of New York Press, 1991).

15. Ilya Prigogine, "The Philosophy of Instability," *Futures*, August 1989, p. 399.

16. Cited by M. Mitchell Waldrop in *Complexity: The Emerging Science at the Edge of Order and Chaos* (New York: Simon & Schuster, 1992), p. 37. Also see Roger Lewin, *Complexity: Life at the Edge of Chaos* (New York: Macmillan, 1992). Also see Stuart Kauffman, *At Home in the Universe: The Search for the Laws of Self-Organization and Complexity* (New York: Oxford University Press, 1995).

17. In addition to Margaret Wheatley's book, other books on management that draw from complexity science include the following: William Berquist, *The Postmodern Organization: Mastering the Art of Irreversible Change* (San Francisco: Jossey-Bass, 1993); Peter M. Senge, *The Fifth Discipline: The Art and Practice of the Learning Organization* (New York: Doubleday/Currency, 1990); Jill Janov, *The Inventive Organization: Hope and Daring at Work* (San Francisco: Jossey-Bass, 1994); and Jeff McCallum, "Chaos, Complexity, and Servant-Leadership," in *Reflections on Leadership*, edited by Larry C. Spears (New York: Wiley, 1995).

18. An example is the critically acclaimed *Landscape and Memory* by Simon Schama (New York: Knopf, 1995). His study is quite an interesting compilation of the ways layers of human history and values have been projected onto

nature, but the other half of the exchange—the ways in which nature "speaks to" and evokes responses from humans—is missing, an oversight that went unnoticed by modern book reviewers.

19. See Bernard Nietschmann, "Third World War," *Cultural Survival Quarterly*, vol. 11, no. 3, 1987, 1-15. Also see *State of the Peoples: A Global Human Rights Report on Societies in Danger* by the Cultural Survival Center Staff (Boston: Beacon Press, 1993).

20. Jon Stewart, "Arms Merchants as Welfare Kings," *San Francisco Chronicle*, August 18, 1996. Cited data are from a recently released report by William Hartung of the World Policy Institute. A report written by Richard Gimmett of the Congressional Research Service in 1996 asserted that Russia had edged ahead of the United States in arms sales to *developing* nations in 1995; see "Russia Once Again Is Top Seller of Arms to Developing Nations," Associated Press, *San Francisco Chronicle*, August 21, 1996. This report notes that the U.S. accounted for 45.3 percent of arms sales to developing nations from 1992 to 1995.

21. John Naisbitt, *Global Paradox: The Bigger the World Economy, the More Powerful Its Smallest Players* (New York: Morrow, 1994), p. 74.

22. "A Survey of Multinationals: Everybody's Favourite Monsters," *The Economist*, London, March 27, 1993, p. 17; cited in David C. Korten, *When Corporations Rule the World* (West Hartford, CT and San Francisco: Kumarian Press and Berrett-Koehler, 1995), p. 223.

CHAPTER TWO: THE RISE AND FALL OF MODERN IDEOLOGIES OF DENIAL

1. See Marija Gimbutas, *The Language of the Goddess: Unearthing the Hidden Symbols of Western Civilization* (San Francisco: HarperCollins, 1989) and *The Civilization of the Goddess: The World of Old Europe* (San Francisco: HarperCollins, 1991).

2. See Luigi Luca Cavalli-Sforza, "A Geneticist Maps Ancient Migrations," interview conducted by Louise Levathes, *New York Times*, July 27, 1993. Also see his essay "Genetic Evidence Supporting Marija Gimbutas' Work on the Origins of Indo-European People," in *From the Realm of the Ancestors: An Anthology in Honor of Marija Gimbutas*, edited by Joan Marler (Manchester, NH: Knowledge, Ideas, and Trends, 1997).

3. Max Weber, *The Protestant Ethic and the Spirit of Capitalism* (London and New York: Routledge, 1992), originally published as a two-part article in 1904–05.

4. See Gary B. Deason, "Reformation Theology and the Mechanistic Conception of Nature," in *God and Nature: Historical Essays on the Encounter Between Christianity and Science*, edtied by David C. Lindberg and Ronald L. Numberg (Berkeley and Los Angeles: University of California Press, 1986).

5. For a fuller, and beautifully written, discussion of the Copernican Revolution and the entire emergence of the modern worldview, see Richard Tarnas, *The Passion of the Western Mind: Understanding the Ideas that Have Shaped Our World View* (New York: Harmony Books, 1991), Part V.

6. See, for instance, Antonio Damasio, *Descartes' Error: Emotion, Reason, and the Human Brain* (New York: G. P. Putnam, 1994). Damasio is a pioneering research scientist in the "biology of reason." Also see Benjamin Libet, "Conscious subjective experience vs. unconscious mental functions: A theory of the cerebral processes involved," in *Models of Brain Function*, edited by R.M.J. Cotterill (New York: Cambridge University Press, 1989). Also see Daniel Goleman, *Emotional Intelligence* (New York: Bantam, 1995).

7. See Anne Llewellyn Barstow, *Witchcraze: A New History of the European Witch Hunts* (San Francisco: Pandora/HarperSanFrancisco, 1994).

8. Particularly influential in planting this notion in modern German consciousness was Wilhelm Riehl's *Die Naturgeschichte des deutschen Volkes als Grundlage einer deutschen Sozialpolitik (The Natural History of the German People as the Basis of German Social Policy)*, published in four volumes between 1851 and 1869. I am grateful to Iain Boyd Whyte for bringing this work to my attention. Also see Michael Zimmerman's summary of Nazi manipulation of public concerns, in Heidegger's *Confrontation with Modernity* (Bloomington, IN: Indiana University Press, 1990).

9. See Zygmunt Bauman, *Modernity and the Holocaust* (Ithaca, NY: Cornell University Press, 1989), p. 17.

10. Ibid., p. 18. Also see Wolfgang Sofsky, *The Order of Terror: The Concentration Camp* (Princeton: Princeton University Press, 1996), which shows the concentration camp as a complex site of modern civilization.

11. Ashis Nandy, ed., *Science, Hegemony, and Violence: A Requiem for Modernity* (Delhi, India: Oxford University Press, 1988).

12. Ibid., p. 2.

13. Yvonne Dion-Buffalo and John Mohawk, "Thoughts from an Autochthonous Center: Postmodernism and Cultural Studies," *Cultural Survival Quarterly*, Winter 1993: 33–35.

14. See Frederique Apffel-Marglin, "Development or Decolonization in the Andes," *Daybreak*, vol. 4, no. 3, pp. 6–10.

15. Jane Flax, "Responsibility without Grounds," in *Rethinking Knowledge: Reflections Across the Disciplines*, edited by Robert F. Goodman and Walter R. Fisher (Albany, NY: State University of New York Press, 1995).

16. Since *States of Grace: The Recovery of Meaning in the Postmodern Age* (HarperCollins, 1991) addresses the meaninglessness inherent in modernity, I had to explore the "denial of meaning" asserted by the deconstructionists. About 10 percent of that book became a critical engagement with deconstructionist thought. It appears in various spots in the text and may be tracked down by using the index. See especially the appendices and the relevant sections in Chapters 1, 4, and 6.

17. Just kidding! I had a history professor in college whose family was from Spain. At the end of every historical period taught in the course on European history, he would draw himself up to his full, if modest, height and declaim: "Always remember, class: the French . . . are indefensible." Dear Professor Sanchez's words often surfaced in my mind while I was reading the deconstructionists' texts.

18. Marshall Berman, "Modernist Anti-Modernism," *New Politics Quarterly*, Spring 1991. Also see his "Why Modernism Still Matters," *Tikkun*, vol. 4, no. 1, Jan./Feb. 1989, pp. 11–14, 81–86.

19. Alan D. Sokal, "Transgressing the Boundaries: Toward a Transformative Hermeneutics of Quantum Gravity," *Social Text*, no. 46–47, Spring/Summer 1996, pp. 217–252. Also see his "A Physicist Experiments with Cultural Studies," *Lingua Franca*, May/ June 1996, pp. 62–64. Also see Steven Weinberg's, "Sokal's Hoax," *New York Review of Books*, August 8, 1996. Unfortunately, his engagement suffers from his knowing far less about deconstructionism than does Sokal. More importantly, Weinberg bemoans the contemporary misunderstandings about science without responding to the nondeconstructionist, nonextremist evidence presented by various philosophers of science that both the theorizing and practice of science are sometimes influenced by culture. Like most scientists, he insists that no such influences "taint" science but will not answer the hard questions, merely scoff at the ridiculous ones. Also see "Sokal's Hoax: An Exchange," *New York Review of Books*, October 3, 1996. See the discussion in Chapter 4 of *The Resurgence of the Real* on the conference sponsored by the New York Academy of Sciences on "The Flight from Science and Reason" in 1995.

20. Paul R. Gross and Norman Levitt, *Higher Superstition: The Academic Left and Its Quarrels with Science* (Baltimore: Johns Hopkins University Press, 1994).

21. Hence the memorable meeting I had in 1992 with a bright young woman who was about to graduate from a prestigious university with a degree in feminist studies: Her aim, she told me proudly, was to be accepted into a graduate program in (deconstructionist) "cultural studies" so that she could "subvert" feminist theory.

22. The current slogan "Women's Rights Are Human Rights!" is a relatively new approach that challenges the traditional separation of the two categories. Until the 1990s, ill treatment of women was still considered a private, domestic matter unrelated to the lofty, public concept of human rights. One of the attorneys who tried to dissolve that boundary is Riane Eisler; see her "Human Rights: Toward an Integrated Theory for Action," *Human Rights Quarterly*, 9 (1987), 287–308. Also see *Human Rights Are Women's Rights*, a report published by Amnesty International in 1995.

23. Max Weber, *The Protestant Ethic and the Spirit of Capitalism* (London and New York: Routledge, 1992), p. 182.

24. Charles Taylor, *Sources of the Self: The Making of the Modern Identity* (Cambridge, MA: Harvard University Press, 1989).

25. Ibid., p. 513.

26. Ibid., p. 512–513.

27. David Ray Griffin's "Series on Constructive Postmodern Thought" published by the State University of New York Press, includes the following anthologies that he has edited: *Spirituality and Society: Postmodern Visions* (1988); *The Reenchantment of Science: Postmodern Proposals* (1989); *Sacred Interconnections: Postmodern Spirituality, Political Economy, and Art* (1990); *Postmodern Politics for a Planet in Crisis*, co-edited with Richard Falk (1993); and *Jewish Theology and Process Thought*, co-edited with Sandra B. Lubarsky (1996). The series also includes the following books by David Ray Griffin: *God and Religion in the Postmodern World* (1989); *Varieties of Postmodern Theology*, with William A. Beardslee and Joe Holland (1989); *Primordial Truth and Postmodern Theology*, with Huston Smith (1989); *Founders of Constructive Postmodern Philosophy: Peirce, James, Bergson, Whitehead, and Hartshorne*, with John B. Cobb, Jr., Marcus P. Ford, Pete A. Y. Gunter, and Peter Ochs (1993); and *Parapsychology, Philosophy, and Spirituality: A Postmodern Exploration* (1997). Books in the series by other authors include Robert Inchausti, *The Ignorant Perfection of Ordinary People* (1991); David W. Orr, *Ecological Literacy: Education and the Transition to a Postmodern World* (1993); J. Baird Callicott and Fernando J. R. da Rocha, editors, *Earth Summit Ethics: Toward a Reconstructive Postmodern Philosophy of Environmental Education* (1996); Frederick Ferré, *Being and Value: Toward a Constructive Postmodern Metaphysics* (1996); Steve Odin, *The Social Self in Zen and American Pragmatism* (1996); and Jay Earley, *Transforming Human Culture: Social Evolution and the Planetary Crisis* (1997).

28. Richard Falk, *Explorations at the Edge of Time: The Prospects for World Order* (Philadelphia: Temple University Press, 1992) and *On Humane Governance: Toward a New Global Politics* (University Park, PA: Pennsylvania State Press, 1995).

29. Charles Jencks, *What is Postmodernism?* (London: Academy Editions, 1996). Also see his "The Postmodern Agenda" in an anthology he edited: *The Postmodern Reader* (London: Academy Editions, 1992).

30. Mark Johnson, *The Body in the Mind: The Bodily Basis of Meaning, Imagination, and Reason* (Chicago: University of Chicago Press, 1987), p. x.

31. Also see George Lakoff, *Women, Fire, and Dangerous Things: What Categories Reveal about the Mind* (Chicago: University of Chicago Press, 1987).

32. David Abram, *The Spell of the Sensuous: Perception and Language in a More-Than-Human World* (New York: Pantheon, 1996), p. 65.

33. Theodore Roszak, *The Voice of the Earth* (New York: Simon & Schuster, 1992), p. 321.

34. Sigmund Freud, *Civilization and Its Discontents*, translated by James Strachey (New York: Norton, 1961), p. 14.

35. Theodore Roszak, "Where Psyche Meets Gaia," *Ecopsychology: Restoring the Earth, Healing the Mind*, edited by Theodore Roszak, Mary E. Gomes, and Allen D. Kanner (San Francisco: Sierra Club Books, 1995), pp. 10–11.

36. See, for example, Maxine Sheets-Johnstone, *The Roots of Thinking* (Philadelphia: Temple University Press, 1990); *The Roots of Power: Animate Form and Gendered Bodies* (Chicago: Open Court, 1994); and *Giving the Body Its Due*, ed. (Albany, NY: State University of New York Press, 1992). Also see Carol Bigwood, *Earth Muse: Feminism, Nature, and Art* (Philadelphia: Temple University Press, 1993). Also see Luce Irigaray, *An Ethics of Sexual Difference* (Ithaca, NY: Cornell University Press, 1993); *Je, Tu, Nous: Toward a Culture of Difference* (New York and London: Routledge, 1993); and *Sexes and Genealogies* (New York: Columbia University Press, 1993). Also see Susan Bordo, *Unbearable Weight: Feminism, Western Culture, and the Body* (Berkeley and Los Angeles: University of California Press, 1993). Also see Linda Holler, "Thinking with the Weight of the Earth: Feminist Contributions to an Epistemology of Concreteness," *Hypatia: A Journal of Feminist Philosophy* (Bloomington: Indiana University Press), vol. 5, no. 1, Spring 1990, pp. 1–20. Also see Edward S. Casey, *Getting Back into Place: Toward a Renewed Understanding of the Place-World* (Bloomington: Indiana University Press, 1993). Also see the works mentioned in Chapter 2 by David Abram, George Lakoff, and Mark Johnson, as well as the forthcoming book by Lakoff and Johnson, *Philosophy in the Flesh.*

CHAPTER THREE: PROMETHEUS ON THE REBOUND

1. Malcolm W. Browne, "Scientists Deplore Flight from Reason," *New York Times,* June 6, 1995.

2. See Christina Hoff Sommers, "The Flight from Science and Reason," *Wall Street Journal*, op-ed page, July 10, 1995. No stranger to polemics, Sommers is the author of *Who Stole Feminism?* She approvingly cites a presentation at the conference by Rene Denfield, author of *The New Victorians: A Young Feminist's Challenge to the Old Feminist Order*, who ridiculed the pioneering archaeological work of the late Marija Gimbutas, apparently ignorant of such scientific validation of Gimbutas's conclusions about the migrations into southeastern Europe from the Pontic steppes, beginning around 4400 B.C.E. as the historical genetic mapping research being conducted by Luca Cavalli-Sforza at Stanford University has shown. Cavalli-Sforza's work is part of the Human Genome Project, which I would think the New York Academy of Sciences would consider to be more than chopped liver. In an interview in the *New York Times* (July 27, 1993) and elsewhere, Cavalli-Sforza has stated that the gene pool from the Eurasian steppes came into Europe where and when Gimbutas maintained. See Luca Cavalli-Sforza, "Genetic Evidence Supporting Marija Gimbutas' Work on the Origin of Indo-European People," in *From the Realm of the Ancestors: Essays in Honor of Marija Gimbutas,* edited by Joan Marler (Manchester, NH: Knowledge, Ideas, and Trends, 1997). For a related discussion, see Charlene Spretnak, "Beyond the Backlash: An Appreciation of the Work of Marija Gimbutas," *Journal of Feminist Studies of Religion*, Harvard School of Divinity, vol. 12, no. 2, Fall 1996.

This is merely one example of the ideological slant of Sommers's piece. It is actually a succinct example of the highly agonistic response to critics of science, which did indeed dominate the conference.

Another op-ed piece written in the wake of the conference was Robert L. Park's "The Danger of Voodoo Science," *New York Times,* July 9, 1995.

3. Paul R. Gross and Norman Levitt, *Higher Superstition: The Academic Left and Its Quarrels with Science* (Baltimore: Johns Hopkins University, 1994).

4. For an overview of the current state of the "science wars," see Langdon Winner, "The Gloves Come Off: Shattered Alliances in Science and Technology Studies," *Social Text,* special issue on the Science Wars, Spring/Summer 1996, nos. 46–47. Winner is the author of *The Whale and the Reactor* (Chicago: Chicago University Press, 1986) and *Democracy in a Technological Society* (Hingham, MA: Kluwer Academic, 1992).

    For a collection of responses from scientists to the deconstructionist view of science, see Michael Soulé and Gary Lease, editors, *Reinventing Nature? Responses to Postmodern Deconstruction* (Washington, DC: Island Press, 1995).

5. See, for example, Helen E. Longino, *Science as Social Knowledge: Values and Objectivity in Scientific Inquiry* (Princeton: Princeton University Press, 1990); Londa Schiebinger, *Nature's Body: Gender in the Making of Modern Science* (Boston: Beacon Press, 1993); Evelyn Fox Keller, *Reflections on Gender and Science* (New Haven, CT: Yale University Press, 1986); *Secrets of Life, Secrets of Death: Essays on Language, Gender, and Science* (New York: Routledge, 1992); Ruth Hubbard, *Genes and Gender: Pitfalls in Research on Sex and Gender* (Staten Island, NY: Gordian Press, 1979); *The Politics of Women's Biology* (New Brunswick, NJ: Rutgers University Press, 1991). Also see Evelyn Fox Keller and Helen Longino, editors, *Feminism and Science* (New York: Oxford University Press, 1996).

6. Gerald Holton, *Einstein, History, and Other Passions: The Rebellion against Science at the End of the Twentieth Century* (Reading, MA: Addison-Wesley, 1996).

7. C. J. S. Clarke, *Reality through the Looking-Glass: Science and Awareness in the Postmodern World* (London: Floris Books, 1995); David Ray Griffin, editor, *The Reenchantment of Science: Postmodern Proposals* (Albany, NY: State University of New York Press, 1989); and Willis Harman with Jane Clark, editors, *New Metaphysical Foundations of Modern Science* (Sausalito, CA: Institute of Noetic Sciences, 1994). Also see John Cornwell, ed., *Nature's Imagination: The Frontiers of Scientific Vision* (Oxford: Oxford University Press, 1995).

8. See David C. Korten, *When Corporations Rule the World* (West Hartford, CT, and San Francisco: Kumarian Press and Berrett-Koehler, 1995), p. 171. Also see the fact sheets about the results of World Bank projects and IMF policies available from the "Fifty Years Is Enough" Network (1025 Vermont Avenue NW, Suite 300, Washington, DC 20005). Also see publications from the Third World Network, Martin Khor, Director (87, Cantonment Road, 10250 Penang, Malaysia).

9. Sudarsan Raghavan, "Growing Plague Grips Africa—Child Sex," *San Francisco Chronicle*, August 31, 1996, an article related to the first World Congress Against the Commercial Exploitation of Children, which was held in Stockholm in late August 1996. Also see *Poverty Reduction and the World Bank* (1996), a report available from the World Bank (1818 H Street, NW, Washington, DC 20433).

10. See Vandana Shiva, "Biotechnological Development and the Conservation of Biodiversity," in *Biopolitics: A Feminist and Ecological Reader on Biotechnology*, ed. by Vandana Shiva and Ingunn Moser (London: Zed Books, 1995), pp. 199–201.

11. See Jeremy Rifkin, "New Technology and the End of Jobs," in *The Case against the Global Economy*, edited by Jerry Mander and Edward Goldsmith (San Francisco: Sierra Club Books, 1996), pp. 117–118.

12. Ibid.

13. See Vandana Shiva, "Piracy by Patent: The Case of the Neem Tree," in *The Case against the Global Economy*, edited by Jerry Mander and Edward Goldsmith (San Francisco: Sierra Club Books, 1996), pp. 154–155.

14. Subcomandante Marcos, "La Larga Travesia del Delor a la Esperanza: Un Texto del Subcomandante Marcos," *La Jornada*, 22 de Septiembre de 1994.

15. See, for example, Sarah Kerr, "The Mess in Mexico," *New York Times Book Review*, July 14, 1996. In this review of *Bordering on Chaos: Guerillas, Stockbrokers, Politicians, and Mexico's Road to Prosperity* by Andres Oppenheimer, both the author and the reviewer agree that Subcomandante Marcos's labelling of the Zapatistas as "postmodern" is impossible because they hear his anti-corporate analysis as mere "stale, intransigent Marxist dogma." Someone is unclear on the concept. Marxist governments have run roughshod over native peoples for decades, and they favor a centralized state in which the government owns the economy. The Zapatistas, no doubt aided by non-Indian activists, as this review emphasizes, specifically challenge the hyper-modern "free market" world order of " neoliberalism, " which threatens all small-scale, subsistence indigenous societies.

16. See Jason Bennetto, "N. Y. Bank Memo May Have Led to Mexico Crackdown," *London Independent*, reprinted in the *San Francisco Examiner* on March 5, 1995. For a photo essay and article on the "violent realities of free trade" in Mexico, see Charles Bowden, "While You Were Sleeping," *Harper's Magazine*, December 1996, pp. 44–52.

17. Molly Ivens, "Bob Dole's Voodoo Economics II," *San Francisco Chronicle*, August 15, 1996. Also see William Greider, *Who Will Tell the People* (New York: Simon & Schuster, 1992). Also see the 1996 study cited in Endnote 18: The United States is slipping into a category of countries— among them Brazil, Britain, and Guatemala—in which economic stratification is the most pronounced, with the national per capita income four or more times higher than the average income of the poor. The ratio of the top 20 percent of American incomes to the poorest 20 percent is now 9 to 1.

18. "Rich and Poor Further Apart Around the World, U.N. Says," *San Francisco Chronicle* (reprinted from the *New York Times*), July 15, 1996, reporting on the Human Development Report 1996, compiled by the UN Development Programme.

19. David C. Korten, *When Corporations Rule the World*, op. cit., p. 261.

20. See Walter W. Haines, professor emeritus of economics, New York University, "The Bankruptcy of Classical Economics," *Human Economy Newsletter* (P.O. Box 28, West Swanzey, NH 03469-0028), vol. 14, no. 3, Fall 1994. Also see Herman Daly and John B. Cobb, Jr., *For the Common Good: Redirecting the Economy toward Community, the Environment, and a Sustainable Future* (Boston: Beacon Press, 1994). Also see all books by Hazel Henderson (see Bibliography in this book).

21. The Human Development Index is available from the UN Development Programme. The System of National Accounts is available from the World Bank. Hazel Henderson's Country Futures Indicators is described in her book titled *Building a Win-Win World: Life beyond Global Economic Warfare* (San Francisco: Berrett-Koehler, 1996). Herman Daly's and John B. Cobb's Index of Sustainable Economic Welfare is described in the expanded, paperback edition of their book titled *For the Common Good: Redirecting the Economy toward Community, the Environment, and a Sustainable Future* (Boston: Beacon Press, 1994). Clifford Cobb's and Ted Halstead's Genuine Progress Indicator was featured in a cover article in *The Atlantic* (Oct. 1995) titled "If the GDP Is Up, Why Is America Down?"; a fuller description of the GPI is available from Redefining Progress, 1 Kearny Street, 4th Floor, San Francisco, CA 94108.

For a spirited critique of the assumptions and tendencies of such expanded versions of quantification, see Marilyn Waring, "Ecological Economics," in *Close to Home: Women Reconnect Ecology, Health and Development Worldwide*, edited by Vandana Shiva (Philadelphia: New Society Publishers, 1994).

22. Paul Glover, "Ithaca HOURS," in *Invested in the Common Good* by Susan Meeker-Lowry (Philadelphia: New Society Publishers, 1995), pp. 155–156; figures were updated in a telephone conversation on August 8, 1996. A "Hometown Money Starter Kit" is available for $25 from Ithaca Money, P.O. Box 6578, Ithaca, NY 14851; a video is available from them for $15. A newsletter, *Local Currency News*, is available from the E. F. Schumacher Society, 140 Jug End Road, Great Barrington, MA 01230.

23. See, for example, Susan Meeker-Lowry, *Invested in the Common Good* (Philadelphia: New Society Publishers, 1995). Several excellent publications on community-based economics are available from the following institutes and think-tanks: the Economic Renewal Program at the Rocky Mountain Institute, Amory and Hunter Lovins, Directors (1739 Snowmass Creek Road, Snowmass, CO 81654-9199); the Institute for Local Self-Reliance, Neil Seldman and David Morris, Founders, (2425 18th Street NW, Washington, DC 20009); the E. F. Schumacher Society, Robert Swann and Susan Witt, Directors (140 Jug End Road, Great Barrington, MA 01230); the Center for

Neighborhood Technology, Scott Bernstein, Director (2125 W. North Avenue, Chicago, IL 60647); the Center for Economic Conversion , Michael Closson, Director (222 View Street, Suite C, Mountain View, CA 94041-1344); the Appalachian Center for Economic Networks (ACEnet), June Holley, Director, (94 N. Columbus Road, Athens, OH 45701): the *Grassroots Economic Organizing Newsletter* (P.O. Box 5065, New Haven, CT 06525); and the Ontario Worker Co-op Federation (83 Grove Street, Guelph, Ontario N1E 2W6, Canada). Also see the newsletter *Human Economy: Economics as if People Mattered* (P.O. Box 28, West Swanzey, NH 03469-0028).

For publications regarding community-based economics in the Three-Quarters World, contact the following institutes: Center of Concern, Maria Riley and Mary Jo Griesgraber, project directors (address in the following footnote); Global Education Associates, Patricia Mische, Director (475 Riverside Drive, Suite 1848, New York, NY 10115); and The People-Centered Development Forum, David C. Korten, Director (14 E. 17th Street, Suite 5, New York, NY 10003). Also see the organizations that extend microloans to the Three-Quarters World, some of which are listed in Endnote 32. Also see Benjamin A. Gilman (U.S.), Wakako Hironaka (Japan), Jim Lester (U.K.), and Winifried Pinger (Germany), "Microcredit: A Plan to Help Millions," *International Herald Tribune*, September 27, 1996; a "Microcredit Summit" is planned for February 1997.

24. Sir James Goldsmith, *London Times*, cited in Jerry Mander and Edward Goldsmith, editors, *The Case against the Global Economy — and for a Turn to the Local* (San Francisco: Sierra Club Books, 1996). Also see William Greider, *One World, Ready or Not* (New York: Simon & Schuster, 1997). Also see publications on GATT, NAFTA, and "free trade" ideology versus reality from the following institutes: International Forum on Globalization (P.O. Box 12218, San Francisco, CA 94112-0218); Global Trade Watch (c/o Public Citizen, 1600 20th Street NW, Washington, DC 20009); Center of Concern (3700 13th Street NE, Washington, DC 20017); Alternative Women-in-Development (c/o Center of Concern); Institute for Policy Studies (1601 Connecticut Avenue NW, Suite 500, Washington, DC 20009); and Global Exchange (2017 Mission Street, Rm. 303, San Francisco, CA 94110). Also see Robert W. Benson, "Free Trade as an Extremist Ideology: The Case of NAFTA," *University of Puget Sound Law Review*, vol. 17, no. 3, Spring 1994, pp. 555–585.

25. For an example of using chaos science to serve laissez-faire economics, see David Parker and Ralph Stacey, *Chaos, Management, and Economics: The Implications of Non-Linear Thinking* (London: Institute of Economic Affairs, 1994). For a rebuttal, see the following works by Peter Allen of the International Ecotechnology Research Centre at Cranfield University in England: "Chaotic Motion," *System Dynamics Review*, vol. 4, nos. 1–2, 1988, p. 119; "Policy in a World of Evolution, Learning and Ignorance," in *A Systems-Based Approach to Policy Making*, edited by Kenyon De Greene (Lancaster, England: Kluwer, 1993); and his chapter in *Evolutionary Economics and Chaos Theory*, edited by Loet Leydesdorff and P. Van den Besselaar (London: Pinter Publishers, 1994).

26. Richard Falk, "False Universalism and the Geopolitics of Exclusion: The Case of Islam," paper presented at the conference "Universalizing from Particulars: Islamic Views of the Human and the UN Declaration of Human Rights in Comparative Perspective," Center of International Studies, Princeton University, May 24–26, 1996.

27. One of the publications in which Falk has begun to develop his sense of the reconstituted state is *On Humane Governance: Toward a New Global Politics* (University Park, PA: Pennsylvania State University Press, 1995).

28. Molly Moore, "Toxic Cleanup Along Border a Huge Flop, GAO Study Says," *Washington Post*, reprinted in the *San Francisco Examiner*, August 4, 1996.

29. See *Home! A Bioregional Reader*, edited by Van Andruss, Christopher Plant, Judith Plant, and Eleanor Wright (Philadelphia: New Society Publishers, 1990). Also see Kirkpatrick Sale, *Dwellers in the Land: The Bioregional Vision* (San Francisco: Sierra Club Books, 1985); Peter Berg, Beryl Magilavy, and Seth Zuckerman, *A Green Cities Program for San Francisco Bay Area Cities and Towns* (San Francisco: Planet Drum Foundation, P.O. Box 31251, San Francisco, CA 94131; 1989); Stephanie Mills, *In Service of the Wild: Restoring and Reinhabiting Damaged Land* (Boston: Beacon Press, 1995); and Beatrice B. Briggs, *Kiss the Ground: Collected Essays, 1982–1993* (available from the author, 3432 N. Bosworth, Chicago, IL 60657). Also see publications from the Bioregional Association of the North Americas (BANA), P.O. Box 31251, San Francisco, CA 94131.

30. See publications from the Alliance for Responsible Trade, (100 Maryland Avenue, NE, Box 74, Washington, DC 20002). Also see David C. Korten, *When Corporations Rule the World* (West Hartford, CT and San Francisco: Kumarian Press and Berrett-Koehler, 1995), especially the chapters on "An Awakened Civil Society" and "Agenda for Change." Also see Jerry Mander and Edward Goldsmith, editors, *The Case against the Global Economy* (San Francisco: Sierra Club Books, 1996), especially "Shifting Direction from Global Dependence to Local Interdependence" by Helena Norberg-Hodge and "In Favor of a New Protectionism" by Colin Hines and Tim Lang.

31. There are several proposals in the air for restructuring the United Nations. An ecological-postmodern source of thought on this matter and related topics is *Breakthrough News*, edited by Patricia Mische and published by her institute, Global Education Associates (475 Riverside Drive, Suite 1848, New York, NY 10115).

32. Some of the major providers of micro-loans are CARE (New York), the Foundation for International Community Assistance (Tucson, AZ), Accion International (Cambridge, MA), Freedom from Hunger Foundation (Davis, CA), The Institute for International Development (Oak Brook, IL), Save the Children Federation (Westport, CT), the World Women's Bank (New York), Working Women's Forum (Madras, India), Self-Employed Women's Association (Ahmadabad, India), and The Grameen Bank (Dhaka, Bangladesh). See Hal Kane, "Micro-Enterprise," *World-Watch*, vol. 9, no. 2 March/April 1996, pp. 10-19.

33. The best overview of the struggles of captive nations can be found in the publications of the Unrepresented Nations and Peoples Organization (UNPO), Javastraat 40a, 2585 AP The Hague, The Netherlands. The Americas Coordination Office is located at 444 North Capitol Street, Suite 846, Washington, DC 20001-1570.

34. See publications available from the Women's Environment and Development Organization (WEDO) (845 Third Avenue, 15th Floor, New York, NY 10022).

35. For a fuller critique, see "What Went Unsaid at UNCED," Real WORLD, England, Summer 1992.

36. The connection between political and environmental security, which had been preached by Green and environmental activists for some twenty-five years, caught the attention of the Washington, DC, establishment only when Robert Kaplan successfully retailed the link as a journalistic discovery in a cover story, "The Coming Anarchy," in *The Atlantic*, February 1994. Suddenly study groups were formed in governmental circles, and satellites were redeployed to track environmental breakdown.

37. Alex Barnum, "Weaving Environment into Foreign Policy," *San Francisco Chronicle*, April 9, 1996. The article covers a speech Warren Christopher made at Stanford University announcing the policy direction he had initiated in February within the U.S. State Department. The various measures include the placing of environmental issues on the agenda of foreign visits by U.S. officials, assembling "environmental teams" at U.S. embassies to address problems, creating a new Deputy Assistant Secretary of State position to work with the Department's seven regional bureaus, and hosting an international conference in two years on compliance with international treaties concerning environmental issues.

38. See Mark Hertsgaard, "The Cost of Climate Change," *Greenpeace Quarterly*, Summer 1996, pp. 28-31.

39. Interview with Fred Smith, Jr. on "The MacNeil-Lehrer News Hour" (June 15, 1992).

40. See *The Politics of the Real World: Meeting the New Century*, written and edited for the Real World Coalition by Michael Jacobs (London: Earthscan, 1996). For the *Real World Action Programme for Government* and other publications, contact the Real World Coalition (227a City Road, London EC1V 1JT). The umbrella organization that includes the Real World Coalition and other programs is Forum for the Future (same address), directed by Paul Ekins, Sara Parkin, and Jonathon Porritt.

41. William Greider, *Who Will Tell the People?* (New York: Simon & Schuster, 1992), p. 54.

42. Robert Putnam, *Making Democracy Work* (Princeton, NJ: Princeton University Press, 1994).

43. Francis Fukuyama, *Trust: The Social Virtures and the Creation of Prosperity* (New York: Free Press, 1996). His earlier book is *The End of History and the Last Man* (New York: Free Press, 1992).

44. Amitai Etzioni, *Rights and the Common Good: The Communitarian Perspective* (New York: St. Martin's Press, 1995).

45. See, for example, the inspiring and innovative newsletter *Doing Democracy*, which bears the slogan "Democracy is not what we have. It's what we do." It is published by Frances Moore Lappé and her colleagues at the Center for Living Democracy (RR #1, Black Fox Road, Brattleboro, VT 05301).

46. Harper's Index, *Harper's*, August 1990. Also see "Adults Who Can't Read" (sidebar), *San Francisco Chronicle*, July 14, 1996: 80 percent of juveniles who appear in U.S. courts are functionally illiterate.

47. "Adults Who Can't Read" (sidebar), *San Francisco Chronicle*, July 14, 1996.

48. Sven Birkerts, *The Gutenberg Elegies: The Fate of Reading in an Electronic Age* (New York: Fawcett Columbine, 1995), pp. 19 and 27.

49. See the many studies described by Joseph Chilton Pearce in *Evolution's End: Claiming the Potential of Our Intelligence* (San Francisco: HarperSanFrancisco, 1992). Also see the discussion on child development in Madeline Levine, *Viewing Violence* (New York: Doubleday, 1996).

50. Laurie Hays, "PC May Be Teaching Kids the Wrong Lessons," *Wall Street Journal*, April 24, 1995. Marie Winn, author of *The Plug-in Drug* on the effects of television, states in this article that computer play is "a debased form of play."

51. Chet Bowers, *The Culture of Denial: Why the Environmental Movement Needs a Strategy for Education in Public Schools and Colleges* (Albany, NY: State University of New York Press, 1997), Chapter 1. Also, see all books by Chet Bowers listed in the bibliography. Also see Theodore Roszak, *The Cult of Information: The Folklore of Computers and the True Art of Thinking* (New York: Pantheon, 1986).

52. Chet Bowers, "Ideology, Educational Computing, and the Moral Poverty of the Information Age," *Critical Essays on Education, Modernity, and the Recovery of the Ecological Imperative* (New York: Teachers College Press, 1993), p. 98.

53. Nanette Asimov, "Closing the Book on Classics," *San Francisco Chronicle*, February 14, 1996.

54. See Torin M. Finfer, *School as a Journey* (Hudson, NY: Anthrosophic Press, 1994). Also see Maria Montessori, *To Educate the Human Potential* (Oxford, England: Clio Press, 1993).

55. See publications from the Center for Ecoliteracy, founded by Fritjof Capra (2522 San Pablo Avenue, Berkeley, CA 94702).

56. See the interview with David Orr in Derrick Jensen's *Listening to the Land: Conversations about Nature, Culture, and Eros* (San Francisco: Sierra Club Books, 1995). Also see Frank Traina and Susan Darley-Hill, *Perspectives in Bioregional Education* (P.O. Box 400, Troy, OH 45373: North American Association of Environmental Education, 1996). Also see Peter Berg, *Discovering Your Life-Place: A First Bioregional Workbook* (San Francisco: Planet Drum Foundation, 1996). Also see *Gardens for Growing People: Resources for Garden-based Education* (available from Gardens for Growing People, P.O. Box 630, Point Reyes, CA 94956).

57. See, for example, Peter Reason, editor, *Participation in Human Inquiry* (London and Thousand Oaks, CA: Sage Publications, 1994). Also see Robert F. Goodman and Walter R. Fisher, editors, *Rethinking Knowledge: Reflections Across the Disciplines* (Albany, NY: State University of New York Press, 1995). Also see Willis Harman with Jane Clark, editors, *New Metaphysical Foundations of Modern Science* (Sausalito, CA: Institute of Noetic Sciences, 1994).

58. Steve Connor, "World's Languages Dying at Alarming Rate," *San Francisco Examiner/Chronicle* (reprinted from the London *Independent*), February 19, 1995.

59. Jerry Mander, "Television: Audiovisual Training for the Modern World," in *In the Absence of the Sacred: The Failure of Technology and the Survival of the Indian Nations* (San Francisco: Sierra Club Books, 1991), p. 96. Also see Jerry Mander, *Four Arguments for the Elimination of Television* (New York: Morrow, 1978). Both of these books also address advertizing as a delivery system of modern values. For a creative and highly irreverent rebuttal of those values and the ads that bear them, see the magazine *Adbusters* (published in Vancouver but available in the United States via Adbusters Media Foundation, P.O. Box 8110, Blaine, WA 98231-9834).

60. See Andrew Kimbrell, *The Human Body Shop: The Engineering and Marketing of Life* (San Francisco: HarperSanFrancisco, 1993), p. 191. Also see publications from the institute founded by Kimbrell: the International Center for Technology Assessment, (310 D Street NE, Washington, DC 20002). Also see books by Jeremy Rifkin listed in the bibliography as well as publications from his institute, the Foundation for Economic Trends (1130 17th Street NW, Suite 630, Washington, DC 20036).

61. Ibid., p. 288

62. "With Pesticides, 1 Plus 1 Sometimes Equals 1,000," *San Francisco Chronicle*, June 7, 1996.

63. "CBS Evening News with Dan Rather", April 18, 1996.

64. See Richard E. Sclove, "Democratizing Technology," *Chronicle of Higher Education*, vol. XL, no. 19, January 12, 1994. Also see publications from his Loka Institute (P.O. Box 355, Amherst, MA 01004-0355). Also see Harold Glasser, *Towards a Descriptive, Participatory Theory of Environmental Policy Analysis and Project Evaluation* (forthcoming).

65. See Kirkpatrick Sale, *Rebels against the Future: The Luddites and Their War on the Industrial Revolution* (Reading, MA: Addison-Wesley, 1995).

66. For a thoughtful rebuttal, see William Grassie, "The Nine Laws of God: Kevin Kelley's *Out of Control* Techno-Utopic Program for a *WIRED* World," paper presented at the American Academy of Religion, New Orleans, November 24 1996. Available from Prof. Grassie, Intellectual Heritage Program, Temple University, Philadelphia, PA, 19122.

67. Jerry Carroll and Laura Evenson, "The Sage of Cyberspace: Paul Saffo, Mapper of Uncertainty, Seems to Know Everything in the Whole Wired World," *San Francisco Chronicle*, June 9, 1996.

CHAPTER FOUR: DON'T CALL IT ROMANTICISM!

1. Keay Davidson, "A Rage against Science," *San Francisco Examiner*, April 30, 1995.

2. Cited by H.G. Schenk in *The Mind of the European Romantics* (New York: Frederick Ungar Publishing, 1996,) p. 7.

3. See Paula Feldman, editor, *Female Romantic Poets* (Baltimore: Johns Hopkins University Press, 1997); Ann Mellor and Richard Mattak, editors *British Literature, 1780–1830* (New York: Harcourt Brace, 1996); and Roger Lonsdale, editor, *Eighteenth Century Women Poets* (Oxford: Oxford University Press, 1990).

4. See, for example, Patrick Hodgkinson, review of Fiona MacCarthy's *William Morris: A Life for Our Time,* in *Building Design*, England, June 16, 1995, p. 22. A review/essay of the American edition of that biography in the *New York Review of Books* (Nov. 30, 1995) was philosophically barren with regard to comprehending Morris's sensibilities.

5. The best defense of Morris I saw during that public debate was put forth by Simon Jenkins, "The Man Who Never Stopped," *London Times*, May 18, 1996.

6. Gropius used the phrase "a cathedral of the future" in an untitled essay in *Exhibition of Unknown Architects* in 1919. He elaborated on the concept in his brochure describing the Bauhaus, which is included in *The Bauhaus*, edited by Hans M. Winger (Cambridge, MA: MIT Press, 1969), p. 31. Both are cited in Rose-Carol Washton Long's essay "Expressionism, Abstraction, and the Search for Utopia in Germany," in *The Spiritual in Art: Abstract Painting, 1890-1985*, ed. by Maurice Tuchman (New York: Abbeville Press, 1986).

7. Cited in Will Grohmann, *Wassily Kandinsky: Life and Work*, translated by Norbert Guterman (New York: Harry Abrams, 1958), p. 54.

8. Wassily Kandinsky, *Concerning the Spiritual in Art* (New York: Dover Publications, 1977), pp. 1–2.

9. Jean Arp, quoted by Herbert Read in *A Concise History of Modern Sculpture* (New York: Praeger, 1964), p. 148.

10. Cited from lectures delivered by T. S. Eliot in 1931, in *Twentieth-Century Culture: Modernism to Deconstructionism*, by Norman F. Cantor (New York: Peter Lang Publishing, 1988), p. 48.

11. D. H. Lawrence, "A Propos of Lady Chatterley's Lover," in *Phoenix II: More Uncollected Writings by D.H. Lawrence*, edited by Warren Roberts and Harry T. Moore (New York: Viking Press, 1968), p. 504.

12. T. J. Jackson Lears, *No Place of Grace: Antimodernism and the Transformation of American Culture, 1880–1920* (Chicago: University of Chicago Press, 1994), p. 181.

13. Lewis Mumford, *The Myth of the Machine* (Volume 2 of *The Pentagon of Power*) (New York and San Diego: Harcourt Brace Jovanovich, 1970), p. 386.

CHAPTER FIVE: EMBRACING THE REAL

1. Vincent Busch, *Hope for the Seeds* (Quexon City, Phillipines: Claretian Publications, 1989). The story of the mango tree is one told by the late Bishop Benny Tudtud, who told many such stories during his radio program and who worked for peace and understanding among the Christian, Muslim, and native perspectives on Mindanao. The publisher's address is U.P. Box 4, Quezon City, 1101 Phillipines. I am grateful to Fr. Thomas Berry, who has taught and learned on the island of Mindanao, for bringing this book to my attention.

2. See Helena Norberg-Hodge, *Ancient Futures: Learning from Ladakh*. (San Francisco: Sierra Club Books, 1991.) The Ladakh Project can be contacted in the United States through the International Society for Ecology and Culture, P. O. Box 9475, Berkeley, CA 94709.

BIBLIOGRAPHY

~

CHAPTER ONE: EPOCHAL RUMBLINGS IN THE 1990s

Abraham, Ralph, Terence McKenna, and Rupert Sheldrake. *Trialogues at the Edge of the West: Chaos, Creativity, and the Resacralization of the World.* Santa Fe, NM: Bear & Co., 1992.

Bohm, David and Basil J. Hiley. *The Undivided Universe: An Ontological Interpretation.* London and New York: Routledge, 1993.

Briggs, John. *Fractals: The Patterns of Chaos—Discovering a New Aesthetic of Art, Science, and Nature.* New York: Simon & Schuster, 1992.

Briggs, John and F. David Peat. *The Turbulent Mirror: An Illustrated Guide to Chaos Theory and the Science of Wholeness.* New York: Harper & Row, 1989.

Bunyard, Peter and Edward Goldsmith, editors. *Gaia and Evolution: Proceedings of the Second Annual Camelford Conference on the Implications of the Gaia Thesis.* Camelford, Cornwall, England: Wadebridge Ecological Centre, 1989.

Capra, Fritjof. *The Web of Life: A New Scientific Understanding of Living Systems.* New York: Anchor Books/Doubleday, 1996.

Cultural Survival Center. *State of the Peoples: A Global Human Rights Report on Societies in Danger.* Boston: Beacon Press, 1993.

Dossey, Larry. *Prayer Is Good Medicine.* San Francisco: HarperSanFrancisco, 1996.

Evernden, Neil. *The Natural Alien.* Toronto: University of Toronto Press, 1993.

Garrett, Laurie. *The Coming Plague: Newly Emerging Diseases in a World Out of Balance.* New York: Farrar, Straus and Giroux, 1994.

Goodwin, Brian. *How the Leopard Changed Its Spots: The Evolution of Complexity.* New York: Charles Scribner's Sons, 1994.

Gordon, James S. *Manifesto for a New Medicine.* Reading, MA: Addison-Wesley, 1996.

Halpern, Steven. *Tuning the Human Instrument: An Owner's Manual.* Palo Alto, CA: Spectrum Research Institute, 1978.

Hayles, N. Katherine. *Chaos Bound: Orderly Disorder in Contemporary Literature and Science.* Ithaca, NY: Cornell University Press, 1990.

———. *The Cosmic Web: Scientific Field Models and Literary Strategies in the Twentieth Century.* Ithaca, NY: Cornell University Press, 1984.

Hayles, N. Katherine, editor. *Chaos and Order: Complex Dynamics in Literature and Science.* Chicago: University of Chicago Press, 1991.

Ho, Mae-Wan. *The Rainbow and the Worm: The Physics of Organisms.* London: World Scientific, 1993.

Jantsch, Erich. *The Self-Organizing Universe: Scientific and Human Implications of the Emerging Paradigm of Evolution.* Oxford, England: Pergamon, 1980.

Jencks, Charles. *The Architecture of the Jumping Universe: How Complexity Science Is Changing Architecture and Culture.* London: Academy Editions, 1997.

Kauffman, Stuart. *At Home in the Universe: The Search for the Laws of Self-Organization and Complexity.* New York: Oxford University Press, 1995.

Keller, Evelyn Fox. *Refiguring Life: Metaphors of Twentieth-Century Biology.* New York: Columbia University Press, 1996.

Krieger, Dolores. *Therapeutic Touch Inner Workbook.* Santa Fe, NM: Bear & Company, 1996.

Lewin, Roger. *Complexity: Life at the Edge of Chaos.* New York: Macmillen, 1992.

Macy, Joanna. *Mutual Causality in Buddhism and General Systems Theory: The Dharma of Natural Systems.* Albany, NY: State University of New York Press, 1991.

Nader, Ralph et al. *The Case against "Free Trade": GATT, NAFTA, and the Globalization of Corporate Power.* San Francisco: Earth Island Press, 1993.

Northrup, Christiane. *Women's Bodies, Women's Wisdom.* New York: Bantam, 1994.

Peat, F. David. *Einstein's Moon: Bell's Theorem and the Curious Quest for Quantum Reality.* Chicago: Contemporary Books, 1990.

Roszak, Theodore. *The Voice of the Earth.* New York: Simon & Schuster, 1992.

Sheldrake, Rupert. *The Rebirth of Nature: The Greening of Science and God.* New York: Bantam Books, 1991.

Siegel, Bernie. *Love, Medicine, and Miracles.* New York: HarperCollins, 1990.

Swimme, Brian. *The Universe Is a Green Dragon: A Cosmic Creation Story.* Santa Fe, NM: Bear & Co., 1985.

_____. *The Hidden Heart of the Cosmos: Humanity and the New Story.* Maryknoll, NY: Orbis Books, 1996.

Swimme, Brian and Thomas Berry. *The Universe Story—from the Primordial Flaring Forth to the Ecozoic Era: A Celebration of the Unfolding of the Cosmos.* San Francisco: HarperCollins, 1992.

Waldrop, M. Mitchell. *Complexity: The Emerging Science at the Edge of Order and Chaos.* New York: Simon & Schuster, 1992.

Weil, Andrew. *Spontaneous Healing.* New York: Knopf, 1995.

Wheatley, Margaret J. *Leadership and the New Science: Learning about Organization from an Orderly Universe.* San Francisco: Barrett-Koehler, 1992.

Worwood, Valerie Ann. *The Fragrant Mind.* Novato, CA: New World Library, 1996.

Zohar, Donah. *The Quantum Self: Human Nature and Consciousness Defined by the New Physics.* New York: Morrow, 1990.

Zohar, Donah and Ian Marshall. *The Quantum Society: Mind, Physics, and a New Social Vision.* New York: Morrow, 1994.

CHAPTER TWO: THE RISE AND FALL OF MODERN
IDEOLOGIES OF DENIAL AND
APPENDIX: MODERNITY IS TO US AS WATER TO A FISH

Abram, David. *The Spell of the Sensuous: Language and Perception in a More-than-Human World.* New York: Pantheon Books, 1996.

Apffel-Marglin, Frederique and Stephen Marglin, editors. *Decolonizing Knowledge: From Development to Dialogue.* Oxford and New York: Clarendon Press, 1996.

Alexander, Jeffrey C. *Fin de Siècle Social Theory: Relativism, Reduction, and the Problem of Reason.* London and New York: Verso, 1995.

Armstrong, Karen. *The Gospel According to Woman: Christianity's Creation of the Sex War in the West.* New York: Doubleday/Anchor Books, 1991.

Barbato, Joseph and Barry Lopez, editors. *Heart of the Land: Essays on the Last Great Places.* New York: Vintage, 1996.

Barstow, Anne Llewellyn. *Witchcraft: A New History of the European Witch Hunts.* San Francisco: Pandora/HarperCollins, 1994.

Bauman, Zygmunt. *Modernity and Ambivalence.* Cambridge, England: Polity Press, 1991.

———. *Modernity and the Holocaust.* Ithaca, NY: Cornell University Press, 1989.

Berger, Peter, Brigitte Berger, and Hansfried Kellner. *The Homeless Mind: Modernization and Consciousness.* New York: Random House, 1973.

Berman, Morris. *Coming to Our Senses: Body and Spirit in the Hidden History of the West.* New York: Simon & Schuster, 1989.

———. *The Reenchantment of the World.* Ithaca, NY: Cornell University Press, 1981.

Berry, Thomas. *The Dream of the Earth.* San Francisco: Sierra Club Books, 1988.

Bertens, Hans. *The Idea of the Postmodern: A History.* London and New York: Routledge, 1995.

Bigwood, Carol. *Earth Muse: Feminism, Nature, and Art.* Philadelphia: Temple University Press, 1993.

Bordo, Susan. *Unbearable Weight: Feminism, Western Culture, and the Body.* Berkeley and Los Angeles: University of California Press, 1993.

Brodribb, Somer. *Nothing Mat(t)ers: A Feminist Critique of Postmodernism.* Melbourne, Australia: Spiniflex Press, 1992.

Casey, Edward S. *Getting Back into Place: Toward a Renewed Understanding of the Place-World.* Bloomington, IN: Indiana University Press, 1993.

Clinebell, Howard. *Ecotherapy: Healing Ourselves, Healing the Earth.* Binghamton, NY: Haworth Press, 1996.

Connolly, William E. *Political Theory and Modernity.* Ithaca, NY: Cornell University Press, 1993.

Damasio, Antonio R. *Descartes' Error: Emotion, Reason, and the Human Brain.* New York: G. P. Putnam, 1994.

Dupré, Louis. *Passage to Modernity: An Essay in the Hermeneutics of Nature and Culture*. New Haven, CT: Yale University Press, 1993.

Dussel, Enrique. *The Invention of the Americas: Eclipse of "the Other" and the Myth of Modernity*. New York: Continuum, 1995.

Ferguson, Harvie. *Melancholy and the Critique of Modernity: Søren Kierkegaard's Religious Psychology*. London and New York: Routledge, 1995.

Ferré, Frederick. *Being and Value: Toward a Constructive Postmodern Metaphysics*. Albany, NY: State University of New York, 1996.

Gablik, Suzi. *Has Modernism Failed?* New York: W.W. Norton, 1985

_____. *The Reenchantment of Art*. London and New York: Thames and Hudson, 1991.

Giddens, Anthony. *The Consequences of Modernity*. Stanford, CA: Stanford University Press, 1990.

_____. *Modernity and Self-Identity: Self and Society in the Late Modern Age*. Stanford, CA: Stanford University Press, 1991.

Goleman, Daniel. *Emotional Intelligence*. New York: Bantam Books, 1995.

Goodman, Robert F. and Walter R. Fisher, editors. *Rethinking Knowledge: Thinking Across the Disciplines*. Albany, NY: State University of New York Press, 1995.

Griffin, David Ray. *God and Religion in the Postmodern World*. Albany, NY: State University of New York Press, 1989.

_____. *Parapsychology, Philosophy, and Spirituality: A Postmodern Exploration*. Albany, NY: State University of New York Press, 1997.

_____, editor. *The Reenchantment of Science: Postmodern Proposals*. Albany, NY: State University of New York Press, 1989.

_____, editor. *Sacred Interconnections: Postmodern Spirituality*. Albany, NY: State University of New York Press, 1990.

_____, editor. *Spirituality and Society*. Albany, NY: State University of New York Press, 1988.

Griffin, David Ray, William A. Beardslee, and Joe Holland. *Varieties of Postmodern Theology*. Albany, NY: State University of New York Press, 1989.

Griffin, David Ray, John B. Cobb, Jr., Marcus P. Ford, Pete A. Y. Gunter, and Peter Ochs. *Founders of Constructive Postmodern Philosophy: Peirce, James, Bergson, Whitehead, and Hartshorne*. Albany, NY: State University of New York Press, 1993.

Griffin, David Ray and Huston Smith. *Primordial Truth and Postmodern Theology*. Albany, NY: State University of New York Press, 1989.

Griffin, David Ray and Richard Falk, editors. *Postmodern Politics for a Planet in Crisis*. Albany, NY: State University of New York Press, 1993.

Griffin, Susan. *Woman and Nature: The Roaring Inside Her*. New York: Harper & Row, 1978.

Heilbroner, Robert L. *The Wordly Philosophers: The Lives, Times and Ideas of the Great Economic Thinkers*, Third Edition. New York: Simon & Schuster, 1967.

Hill, Christopher. *The World Turned Upside Down: Radical Ideas during the English Revolution*. New York: Viking Press, 1972.

Huyssen, Andreas. *After the Great Divide: Modernism, Mass Culture, Postmodernism*. Bloomington, IN: Indiana University Press, 1986.

_____. *Twilight Memories: Marking Time in a Culture of Amnesia*. New York: Routledge, 1995.

Irigaray, Luce. *An Ethics of Sexual Difference*. Ithaca, NY: Cornell University Press, 1993.

_____. *Je, Tu, Nous: Toward a Culture of Difference*. London and New York: Routledge, 1993.

_____. *Sexes and Genealogies*. New York: Columbia University Press, 1993.

Jencks, Charles. *What Is Postmodernism?* Fourth Edition. London: Academy Editions, 1996.

_____. editor. *The Postmodern Reader*. London: Academy Editons, 1992.

Johnson, Mark. *The Body in the Mind: The Bodily Basis of Meaning, Imagination, and Reason*. Chicago: University of Chicago Press, 1987.

Jones, Prudence and Nigel Pennick. *A History of Pagan Europe*. London and New York: Routledge, 1995.

Kaufmann, Thomas DaCosta. *The Mastery of Nature: Aspects of Art, Science, and Humanism in the Renaissance*. Princeton, NJ: Princeton University Press, 1993.

Krieger, Murray. *A Reopening of Closure: Organicism against Itself*. New York: Columbia University Press, 1989.

Lakoff, George. *Women, Fire, and Dangerous Things: What Categories Reveal about Us*. Chicago: University of Chicago Press, 1987.

Lakoff, George and Mark Johnson. *Metaphors We Live By*. Chicago: University of Chicago Press, 1980.

Lash, Scott and Jonathan Friedman, editors. *Modernity and Identity*. Oxford, England: Basil Blackwell, 1992.

Merchant, Carolyn. *The Death of Nature: Women, Ecology, and the Scientific Revolution*. San Francisco: Harper & Row, 1980.

Midgley, Mary. *Science as Salvation: A Modern Myth and Its Meaning*. London and New York: Routledge, 1992

Porter, Bruce D. *War and the Rise of the State: The Military Foundations of Modern Politics*. New York: Free Press, 1994.

Reason, Peter, editor. *Participation in Human Inquiry*. London and Thousand Oaks, CA: Sage Publications, 1994.

Reed, Edward S. *The Necessity of Experience*. New Haven: Yale University Press, 1996.

Rockmore, Tom and Beth J. Singer, editors. *Anti-Foundationalism Old and New*. Philadelphia: Temple University Press, 1992.

Rose, Margaret. *The Post-Modern and the Post-Industrial: A Critical Analysis*. Cambridge, England: Cambridge University Press, 1991.

Roszak, Theodore. *The Voice of the Earth.* New York: Simon & Schuster, 1992.

Roszak, Theodore, Mary E. Gomes, and Allen D. Kanner, editors. *Ecopsychology: Restoring the Earth, Healing the Mind.* San Francisco: Sierra Club Books, 1995.

Sale, Kirkpatrick. *The Conquest of Paradise: Christopher Columbus and the Columbian Legacy.* New York: Knopf, 1990.

Schiebinger, Londa. *Nature's Body: Gender in the Making of Modern Science.* Boston: Beacon Press, 1993.

Sheets-Johnstone, Maxine. *The Roots of Power: Animate Form and Gendered Bodies.* Chicago: Open Court, 1994.

_____. *The Roots of Thinking.* Philadelphia: Temple University Press, 1990.

_____, editor. *Giving the Body Its Due.* Albany, NY: SUNY Press, 1992.

Spretnak, Charlene. *Lost Goddesses of Early Greece: A Collection of Pre-Hellenic Myths.* Boston: Beacon Press, 1981 (1978).

_____. *States of Grace: The Recovery of Meaning in the Postmodern Age.* San Francisco: HarperCollins, 1991.

Squires, Judith, editor. *Principled Positions: Postmodernism and the Rediscovery of Value.* London: Lawrence & Wishart, 1993.

Tarnas, Richard. *The Passion of the Western Mind: Understanding the Ideas that Have Shaped Our World View.* New York: Harmony Books, 1991.

Taylor, Charles. *Sources of the Self: The Making of the Modern Identity.* Cambridge, MA: Harvard University Press, 1989.

Toulmin, Stephen. *Cosmopolis: The Hidden Agenda of Modernity.* Chicago: University of Chicago Press, 1990.

_____. *The Return of Cosmology: Postmodern Science and the Theology of Nature.* Berkeley and Los Angeles: University of California Press, 1982.

Weber, Max. *The Protestant Ethic and the Spirit of Capitalism.* London and New York: Routledge, 1992.

Wildiers, N. Max. *The Theologian and His Universe: Theology and Cosmology from the Middle Ages to the Present.* New York: Seabury Press, 1982.

CHAPTER THREE: PROMETHEUS ON THE REBOUND

Ahmed, Akbar S. *Postmodernism and Islam: Predicament and Promise.* London and New York: Routledge, 1992.

Ahmed, Akbar S. and Hastings Donnan, editors. *Islam, Globalization and Postmodernity.* London and New York: Routledge, 1994.

Ahmed, Leila. *Women and Gender in Islam: Historical Roots of a Modern Debate.* New Haven, CT: Yale University Press, 1992.

Bandarage, Asoka. *Women, Population and Global Crisis: A Political Economic Analysis.* London: Zed Books, 1997.

Basu, Amrita, editor. *The Challenge of Local Feminisms: Women's Movements in Global Perspective.* Boulder, CO: Westview Press, 1995.

Berry, Wendell. *Another Turn of the Crank.* Washington, DC: Counterpoint Press, 1995.

———. *Sex, Economy, Freedom, and Community.* New York: Pantheon, 1993.

———. *The Unsettling of America: Culture and Agriculture.* San Francisco: Sierra Club Books, 1996 (1982).

Birkerts, Sven. *The Gutenberg Elegies: The Fate of Reading in an Electronic Age.* New York: Fawcett Columbine, 1994.

Bowers, C. A. *Critical Essays on Education, Modernity, and the Recovery of the Ecological Imperative.* New York: Teachers College Press, 1993.

———. *The Culture of Denial: Why the Environmental Movement Needs a Strategy for Reforming Universities and Public Schools.* Albany, NY: State University of New York Press, 1997.

———. *Educating for an Ecologically Sustainable Culture: Rethinking Moral Education, Creativity, Intelligence, and Other Modern Orthodoxies.* Albany, NY: State University of New York Press, 1995.

———. *Education, Cultural Myths, and the Ecological Crisis: Toward Deep Changes.* Albany, NY: State University of New York Press, 1993.

Brandt, Barbara. *Whole Life Economics: Revaluing Daily Life.* Philadelphia: New Society Publishers, 1995.

Brown, Lester et al. *State of the World: 1996.* New York: Norton, 1996.

Buchmann, Stephen L. and Gary Paul Nabhan. *The Forgotten Pollinators.* Washington, D.C.: Island Press, 1996.

Callicott, J. Baird and Fernando J. R. da Rocha, editors. *Earth Summit Ethics: Toward a Reconstructive Postmodern Philosophy of Environmental Education.* Albany, NY: State University of New York, 1996.

Clark, Mary. *Ariadne's Thread: In Search of a Greener Future.* New York: St. Martin's Press, 1989.

Clarke, C. J. S. *Reality through the Looking-Glass: Science and Awareness in the Postmodern World.* London: Floris Books, 1996.

Cobb, Edith. *The Ecology of Imagination in Childhood.* Dallas: Spring Publications, 1993 (1977).

Cobb, John B., Jr. *Sustainability: Economics, Ecology, and Justice.* Maryknoll, NY: Orbis Books, 1992.

Colborn, Theo, Dianne Dumanoski, and John Peterson Myers. *Our Stolen Future: Are We Threatening Our Fertility, Intelligence and Survival? A Scientific Detective Story.* New York: NAL/Dutton, 1996.

Cornwell, John, editor. *Nature's Imagination: The Frontiers of Scientific Vision.* Oxford: Oxford University Press, 1995.

Costanza, Robert, editor. *Ecological Economics: The Science and Management of Sustainability.* New York: Columbia University Press, 1991.

Daly, Herman. *Beyond Growth: The Economics of Sustainable Development.* Boston: Beacon Press, 1996.

Daly, Herman and John B. Cobb, Jr. *For the Common Good: Redirecting the Economy toward Community, the Environment, and a Sustainable Future.* Second Edition. Boston: Beacon Press, 1994.

Diamond, Irene. *Fertile Ground: Women, Earth, and the Limits of Control.* Boston: Beacon Press, 1994.

Dobson, Andrew. *Green Political Thought.* London: HarperCollins, 1990.

Dobson, Andrew, editor. *The Green Reader: Essays toward a Sustainable Society.* San Francisco: Mercury House, 1991.

Drengson, Alan. *The Practice of Technology: Exploring Technology, Ecophilosophy, and Spiritual Disciplines for Vital Links.* Albany, NY: State University of New York Press, 1995.

Ekins, Paul. *The Gaia Atlas of Green Economics.* New York: Anchor Books/Doubleday, 1992.

_____. *A New World Order: Grassroots Movements for Global Change.* New York and London: Routledge, 1992.

Ekins, Paul, editor. *The Living Economy: A New Economics in the Making.* London and New York: Routledge & Kegan Paul, 1986.

Ellul, Jacques. *The Technological Society.* New York: Vintage, 1964.

Falk, Richard. *Explorations at the Edge of Time: The Prospects for World Order.* Philadelphia: Temple University Press, 1992.

_____. *On Humane Governance: Toward a New Global Politics.* University Park, PA: Pennsylvania State University Press, 1995.

Finfer, Torin M. *School as a Journey.* Hudson, NY: Anthroposophic Press, 1994.

Fourth World Conference on Women. *Platform for Action and the Beijing Declaration.* New York: United Nations Department of Public Information, 1996.

Glendinning, Chellis. *My Name is Chellis, and I'm in Recovery from Western Civilization.* Boston: Shambhala, 1994.

_____. *When Technology Wounds: The Human Consequences of Progress.* New York: Morrow, 1990.

Goldsmith, Edward. *The Way: An Ecological World-view.* Boston: Shambhala, 1993.

Goldsmith, Edward and Nicholas Hilyard. *The Social and Environmental Effects of Large Dams.* San Francisco: Sierra Club Books, 1984.

Goldsmith, James. *The Trap.* New York: Carroll & Graf, 1994.

Grahn, Judy. *Blood, Bread, and Roses: How Menstruation Created the World.* Boston: Beacon Press, 1993.

Gran, Guy. *Development by People: Citizen Construction of a Just World.* New York: Praeger, 1983.

Greider, William. *One World, Ready or Not: The Manic Logic of Global Capitalism* New York: Simon & Schuster, 1997.

_____. *Who Will Tell the People?* New York: Simon & Schuster, 1992.

Gussow, Joan Dye. *Chicken Little, Tomato Sauce, and Agriculture: Who Will Grow Tomorrow's Food?* New York: Bootstrap Press, 1991.

Hannum, Hildegarde, editor. *People, Land, and Community: Collected E. F. Schumacher Society Lectures.* New Haven, CT: Yale University Press, 1997.

Harman, Willis with Jane Clark, editors. *New Metaphysical Foundations of Modern Science.* Sausalito, CA: Institute of Noetic Sciences, 1994.

Henderson, Hazel. *Building a Win-Win World: Life beyond Global Economic Warfare.* San Francisco: Berrett-Koehler, 1996.

_____. *Creating Alternative Futures: The End of Economics.* New York: Perigee Books/Putnam, 1978.

_____. *Paradigms in Progress: Life beyond Economics.* Indianapolis: Knowledge Systems, 1991.

_____. *The Politics of the Solar Age: Alternatives to Economics.* New York: Anchor Books/Doubleday, 1981.

Horgan, John. *The End of Science: Facing the Limits of Knowledge in the Twilight of the Scientific Age.* Reading, MA: Addison-Wesley, 1996.

Huckle, John and Stephen Sterling, editors. *Editing for Sustainability.* London: Earthscan, 1996.

Jencks, Charles. *Heteropolis: Los Angeles, the Riots, and the Strange Beauty of Hetero-Architecture.* London: Academy Editions, 1993.

Jensen, Derrick. *Listening to the Land: Conversations about Nature, Culture, and Eros.* San Francisco: Sierra Club Books, 1995.

Johnson, Huey D. *Green Plans: Greenprints for Sustainability.* Lincoln, NB: University of Nebraska, 1995.

Jones, Dorothy V. *A Code of Peace.* Chicago: University of Chicago Press, 1992.

Kassiola, Joel Jay. *The Death of Industrial Civilization: The Limits to Economic Growth and the Repoliticization of Advanced Industrial Society.* Albany, NY: State University of New York Press, 1990.

Kellert, Stephen R. *The Value of Life: Biological Diversity and Human Society.* Washington, DC: Island Press, 1996.

Kelly, Kevin. *Out of Control: The Rise of Neo-Biological Civilization.* Reading, MA: Addison-Wesley, 1994.

Kelly, Petra. *Thinking Green!: Essays on Environmentalism, Feminism, and Nonviolence.* Berkeley, CA: Parallax Press, 1994.

Kimbrell, Andrew. *The Human Body Shop: The Engineering and Marketing of Life.* San Francisco: HarperSanFrancisco, 1993.

Kinsley, Michael J. *Economic Renewal Guide: A Collaborative Process for Sustainable Community Development.* Old Snowmass, CO: Rocky Mountain Institute, 1997.

Korten, David C. *When Corporations Rule the World*. West Hartford, CT and San Francisco: Kumarian Press and Berrett-Koehler, 1995.

Kunstler, James Howard. T*he Geography of Nowhere: The Rise and Decline of America's Man-made Landscape*. New York. Simon & Schuster, 1993.

Lakoff, George. *Moral Politics: What Conservatives Know that Liberals Don't*. Chicago: University of Chicago Press, 1996.

Levine, Madeline. *Viewing Violence*. New York: Doubleday, 1996.

Longino, Helen E. *Science as Social Knowledge: Values and Objectivity in Scientific Inquiry*. Princeton, NJ: Princeton University Press, 1990.

Mander, Jerry. *Four Arguments for the Elimination of Television*. New York: Morrow, 1977.

_____. *In the Absence of the Sacred: The Failure of Technology and the Survival of the Indian Nations*. San Francisco: Sierra Club Books, 1991.

Mander, Jerry and Edward Goldsmith, editors. *The Case against the Global Economy—And For a Turn to the Local*. San Francisco: Sierra Club Books, 1996.

Marchand, Roland. *Advertising the American Dream: Making Way for Modernity, 1920–1940*. Berkeley and Los Angeles: University of California Press, 1985.

McKibben, Bill. *The End of Nature*. New York: Random House, 1989.

McLaughlin, Andrew. *Regarding Nature: Industrialism and Deep Ecology*. Albany, NY: State University of New York Press, 1993.

Meeker-Lowry, Susan. *Invested in the Common Good*. Philadelphia: New Society Publishers, 1995.

Milbrath, Lester W. *Envisioning a Sustainable Society: Learning Our Way Out*. Albany, NY: State University of New York Press, 1989.

Miller, Alan S. *Gaia Connections: An Introduction to Ecology, Ecoethics, and Economics*. Savage, MD: Rowman & Littlefield, 1991.

Montessori, Maria. *To Educate the Human Potential*. Oxford, England: Clio Press, 1993.

Mumford, Lewis. *The Myth of the Machine. Volume One: Technics and Human Development. Volume Two: The Pentagon of Power*. San Diego and New York: Harcourt Brace Jovanovich: 1967 and 1970.

Nabhan, Gary Paul and Stephen Trimble. *The Geography of Childhood: Why Children Need Wild Places*. Boston: Beacon Press, 1994.

Norberg-Hodge, Helena. *Ancient Futures: Learning from Ladakh*. San Francisco: Sierra Club Books, 1991.

_____. *Monoculture*. Forthcoming.

Norwood, Ken and Kathleen Smith. *Rebuilding Community in America: Housing for Ecological Living, Personal Empowerment, and the New Extended Family*. Berkeley: Shared Living Resource Center, 1995.

Oelschlaeger, Max, editor. *Postmodern Environmental Ethics*. Albany, NY: State University of New York Press, 1995.

Orr, David W.. *Ecological Literacy: Education and the Transition to a Postmodern World*. Albany, NY: State University of New York Press, 1992.

Parkin, Sara. *Green Parties: An International Guide*. London: Heretic Books, 1989.

_____. *Green Futures*. London: HarperCollins, 1990.

Parkin, Sara, editor. *Green Light on Europe*. London: Heretic Books, 1991.

Pearce, Joseph Chilton. *Evolution's End: Claiming the Potential of Our Intelligence*. San Francisco: HarperSanFrancisco, 1992.

Ponting, Clive. *A Green History of the World: The Environment and the Collapse of Great Civilizations*. New York: St. Martin's Press, 1991.

Porritt, Jonathon. *Seeing Green: The Politics of Ecology Explained*. London and New York: Blackwell, 1984.

Porritt, Jonathon and David Winner. *The Coming of the Greens*. London: Fontana, 1988.

Postman, Neil. *Amusing Ourselves to Death:Public Discourse in the Age of Show Business*. New York: Viking Press, 1985.

_____. *Technopoly: The Surrender of Culture to Technology*. New York: Knopf, 1992.

Real World Coalition (Michael Jacobs, editor). *The Politics of the Real World*. London: Earthscan, 1996.

Rensenbrink, John. *The Greens and the Politics of Transformation*. San Pedro, CA: R. & E. Miles, 1992.

Rifkin, Jeremy. *Biosphere Politics: A New Consciousness for a New Century*. New York: Crown, 1991.

_____. *The End of Work: The Decline of the Global Labor Force and the Dawn of the Post-Market Era*. New York: Tarcher/Putnam, 1995.

Roszak, Theodore. *Bugs*. Garden City, NY: Doubleday, 1981.

_____. *The Cult of Information: The Folklore of Computers and the True Art of Thinking*. New York: Pantheon, 1986.

_____. *The Memoirs of Elizabeth Frankenstein*. New York: Random House, 1995.

_____. *Person/Planet: The Creative Disintegration of Industrial Society*. New York: Anchor Books/Doubleday, 1979.

Sachs, Wolfgang, editor. *The Development Dictionary: A Guide to Knowledge as Power*. London: Zed Books, 1992.

Sale, Kirkpatrick. *Dwellers in the Land: The Bioregional Vision*. San Francisco: Sierra Club Books, 1985.

_____. *Human Scale*. New York: Coward, McCann & Geoghegan, 1980.

_____. *Rebels against the Future: The Luddites and their War on the Industrial Revolution*. Reading, MA: Addison-Wesley, 1995.

Sampson, Anthony. *Company Man: The Rise and Fall of Corporate Life*. New York: Times Books/Random House, 1995.

Schmitt, Richard. *Beyond Separateness: The Social Nature of Human Beings—Their Autonomy, Knowledge, and Power*. Boulder, CO: Westview Press, 1995.

Schmookler, Andrew Bard. *Fool's Gold: The Fate of Values in a World of Goods*. New York: HarperCollins, 1993.

____. *The Illusion of Choice: How the Market Economy Shapes Our Destiny*. Albany, NY: State University of New York Press, 1993.

Shepard, Paul. *The Others: How Animals Made Us Human*. Washington, DC: Island Press, 1996.

Shiva, Vandana. *Staying Alive: Women, Ecology, and Development*. London: Zed Books, 1988.

Shiva, Vandana, editor. *Close to Home: Women Reconnect Ecology, Health and Development Worldwide*. Philadelphia: New Society Publishers, 1994.

Shiva, Vandana and Ingunn Moser, editors. *Biopolitics: A Feminist and Ecological Reader*. London: Zed Books, 1995.

Slater, Philip. *A Dream Deferred: America's Discontent and the Search for a New Democratic Ideal*. Boston: Beacon Press, 1992.

Soulé, Michael and Gary Lease, editors. *Reinventing Nature: Responses to Postmodern Deconstruction*. Washington, DC: Island Press, 1995.

Spretnak, Charlene and Fritjof Capra. *Green Politics: The Global Promise*. New York: Dutton, 1984; Santa Fe, NM: Bear & Co., 1986.

Steingraber, Sandra. *Living Downstream: An Ecologist Looks at Cancer and the Enviroment*. Reading, MA: Addison-Wesley, 1997.

Stock, Gregory. *Metaman: The Merging of Humans and Machines into a Global Superorganism*. New York: Doubleday, 1993.

Stoll, Clifford. *Silicon Snake Oil: Second Thoughts on the Information Highway*. New York: Doubleday, 1995.

Taylor, Bron Raymond, editor. *Ecological Resistance Movements: The Global Emergence of Radical and Popular Environmentalism*. Albany, NY: State University of New York Press, 1995.

Taylor, Michael. *Not Angels but Agencies: The Ecumenical Response to Poverty— A Primer*. London and Geneva: SCM Press and the World Council of Churches, 1995.

Tickner, Ann. *Self-Reliance vs. Power Politics*. New York: Columbia University Press, 1987.

Tucker, Mary Evelyn and John A. Grim, editors. *Worldviews and Ecology: Religion, Philosophy, and the Environment*. Maryknoll, NY: Orbis Books, 1994.

Van Drimmelen, Rob, editor. *Development Assessed: Ecumenical Reflections and Actions on Development*. Geneva: World Council of Churches, 1995.

Wapner, Paul. *Environmental Activism and World Civic Politics*. Albany, NY: New York State University Press, 1996.

Wargo, John. *Our Children's Toxic Legacy: How Science and Law Fail to Protect Us from Pesticides*. New Haven, CT: Yale University Press, 1996.

Weizenbaum, Joseph. *Computer Power and Human Reason: From Judgment to Calculation*. San Francisco: W. H. Freeman, 1976.

Winn, Marie. *The Plug-In Drug: Television, Children and the Family*. New York: Penguin Books, 1985.

Winner, Langdon. *Democracy in a Technological Society*. Hingham, MA: Kluwer Academic Publications, 1992.

_____. *The Whale and the Reactor*. Chicago: University of Chicago Press, 1986.

Zimmerman, Michael. *Contesting Earth's Future: Radical Ecology and Postmodernity*. Berkeley and Los Angeles: University of California Press, 1994.

CHAPTER FOUR: DON'T CALL IT ROMANTICISM!

Abrams, M. H. *The Correspondent Breeze: Essays on English Romanticism*. New York: Norton, 1984.

_____. *The Mirror and the Lamp: Romantic Theory and the Critical Tradition*. London and New York: Oxford University Press, 1953.

_____. *Natural Supernaturalism: Tradition and Revolution in Romantic Literature*. New York: Norton, 1971.

Anscombe, Isabelle. *Arts and Crafts Style*. Oxford: Phaidon, 1991.

Boris, Eileen. *Art and Labor: Ruskin, Morris, and the Craftsman Ideal in America*. Philadelphia: Temple University Press, 1986.

Bortoft, Henri. *The Wholeness of Nature: Goethe's Way toward a Science of Conscious Participation in Nature*. Hudson, NY: Lindisfarne Press, 1996.

Burkhauser, Jude, editor. *Glasgow Girls: Women in Art and Design, 1880–1920*. Edinburgh: Canongate, 1990.

Chadwick, Whitney. *Women Artists and the Surrealist Movement*. New York: Thames and Hudson, 1985.

Cumming, Elizabeth and Wendy Kaplan. *The Arts and Crafts Movement*. London: Thames and Hudson, 1991.

Fidler, Patricia, editor. *Art with a Mission: Objects of the Arts and Crafts Movement*. Lawrence, KN: Spencer Museum of Art, 1991.

Fuller, Peter. *Theoria: Art, and the Absence of Grace*. London: Chatto & Windus, 1988.

Grohmann, Will. *Wassily Kandinsky: Life and Work*. New York: Harry Abrams, 1958.

Harries, John. *Pugin*. Princes Risborough, Buckinghamshire, England: Shire Publications, 1994.

Hartley, Keith et al., editors. *The Romantic Spirit in German Art, 1790-1990*. Edinburgh: Scottish National Gallery; London: Hayward Gallery, 1994.

Harvey, Charles and Jon Press. *William Morris: Design and Enterprise in Victorian Britain*. Manchester: Manchester University Press, 1991.

Hoffmann, Donald. *Frank Lloyd Wright: Architecture and Nature*. New York: Dover, 1986.

_____. *Understanding Frank Lloyd Wright's Architecture*. New York: Dover, 1995.

Jencks, Charles. *Modern Movements in Architecture*. London and New York: Penguin Books, 1973, 1985.

Kallir, Jane. *Viennese Design and the Weiner Werkstatte*. New York: Gallerie St. Etienne/George Braziller, 1986.

Kandinsky, Wassily. *Concerning the Spiritual in Art*. New York: Dover, 1977 (1913).

Kuspit, Donald and Lynn Gamwell. *Health and Happiness in Twentieth-Century Avant-Garde Art*. Ithaca, NY: Cornell University Press, 1996.

Lears, T. J. Jackson. *No Place of Grace: Antimodernism and the Transformation of American Culture, 1880–1920*. Chicago: University of Chicago Press, 1981.

Lipsey, Roger. *An Art of Our Own: The Spiritual in Twentieth-Century Art*. Boston: Shambhala, 1989.

MacCarthy, Fiona. *William Morris: A Life for Our Times*. London: Faber and Faber, 1994.

Makinson, Randell L. *Greene & Greene: Architecture as a Fine Art*. Salt Lake City: Peregrine Smith Books, 1977.

_____. *Greene & Greene: Furniture and Related Designs*. Salt Lake City: Peregrine Smith Books, 1979.

Morris, William. *The Political Writings of William Morris*. London: Lawrence Wishart, 1979.

_____. *Three Works by William Morris: News from Nowhere, The Pilgrims of Hope, and A Dream of John Ball*. London: Lawrence Wishart, 1986.

_____. *The Wood Beyond the World*. Fascimile of the Kelmscott Press Edition *(1894)*. New York: Dover, 1972.

Onslow Ford, Gordon. *Creation*. Basel: Galerie Schreiner, 1978.

_____. *Insight*. Inverness, CA: Lapis Press, 1991.

_____. *The Quest of the Inner-Worlds: Paintings by Gordon Onslow Ford*. Berkeley, CA: John F. Kennedy University, 1996.

Peterson, William S. *The Kelmscott Press: A History of William Morris' Typographical Adventure*. Oxford: Oxford University Press, 1991.

Read, Herbert. *A Concise History of Modern Sculpture*. New York: Praeger, 1964.

Roszak, Theodore. *The Making of a Counterculture: Reflections on the Technocratic Society and Its Youthful Opposition*. Garden City, NY: Doubleday, 1969.

_____. *Where the Wasteland Ends: Politics and Transcendence in Postindustrial Society*. Garden City, NY: Doubleday, 1972.

Rubin, William S. *Dada, Surrealism, and Their Heritage*. New York: The Museum of Modern Art, 1968.

Rubin, William, editor. *"Primitivism" in Twentieth-Century Art: Affinity of the Tribal and the Modern*, 2 vols. New York: Museum of Modern Art, 1984.

Ruskin, John. *Unto this Last and Other Writings*. London and New York: Penguin Books, 1985.

Sale, Kirkpatrick. *Rebels against the Future: The Luddites and Their War on the Industrial Revolution*. New York and Reading, MA: Addison-Wesley, 1995.

Tames, Richard. *William Morris*. Princes Risborough, Buckinghamshire, England: Shire Publications, 1972.

Trapp, Kenneth R., editor. *Living the Good Life: The Arts and Crafts Movement in California*. Oakland, CA: The Oakland Museum; New York: Abbeville Press, 1993.

Tuchman, Maurice, editor. *The Spiritual in Art: Abstract Painting, 1880–1985*. Los Angeles: Los Angeles County Museum of Art; New York: Abbeville Press, 1986.

Tucker, Michael. *Dreaming with Open Eyes: The Shamanic Spirit in Twentieth-Century Art and Culture*. San Francisco: HarperSanFrancisco, 1992.

Watkinson, Ray. *William Morris as Designer*. London: Trefoil Publications, 1990.

Wilson, Richard Guy, Dianne H. Pilgrim, and Dickran Tashjian. *The Machine Age in America, 1918-1941*. New York: The Brooklyn Museum and Harry N. Abrams, Inc., Publishers, 1986.

CHAPTER FIVE: EMBRACING THE REAL

Adams, Carol J., editor. *Ecofeminism and the Sacred*. New York: Continuum, 1993.

Andruss, Van, Christopher Plant, Judith Plant, and Eleanor Wright, editors. *Home! A Bioregional Reader*. Philadelphia: New Society Publishers, 1990.

Berg, Peter, Beryl Magilavy, and Seth Zuckerman. *A Green City Program: For San Francisco Bay Area Cities and Towns*. San Francisco: Planet Drum Foundation, 1989.

Bodner, Joan, editor. *Taking Charge of Our Lives: Living Responsibly in the World*. San Francisco: Harper & Row, 1984.

Griffin, Susan. *The Eros of Everyday Life*. New York: Anchor Books/Doubleday, 1995.

Hogan, Linda. *Dwellings: A Spiritual History of the Living World*. New York: W.W. Norton, 1995.

Johnson, Don Hanlon. *Body: Recovering Our Sensual Wisdom*. Berkeley: North Atlantic Books, 1992.

Kunstler, James Howard. *Home from Nowhere: Remaking Our Everyday World for the Twenty-First Century*. New York: Simon & Schuster, 1996.

Lippard, Lucy R. *Overlay: Contemporary Art and the Art of Prehistory*. New York: Pantheon, 1983.

Lopez, Barry. *Crossing Open Ground*. New York: Scribner, 1988.

_____. *Crow and Weasel*. New York: Harper Perennial, 1993.

Macy, Joanna. *World as Lover, World as Self.* Berkeley: Parallax Press, 1991.

McLuhan, T. C. *The Way of the Earth: Encounters with Nature in Ancient and Contemporary Thought.* New York: Simon and Schuster, 1994.

Mendieta, Ana. *The "Silueta" Series, 1973-1980.* New York: Galerie Lelong, 1991.

Mills, Stephanie. *In Service of the Wild: Restoring and Reinhabiting Damaged Land.* Boston: Beacon Press, 1995.

Olsen, W. Scott and Scott Cairns, editors. *The Sacred Place: Witnessing the Holy in the Physical World.* Salt Lake City, : University of Utah Press, 1996.

Register, Richard. *Ecocity Berkeley: Building Cities for a Healthy Future.* Berkeley: North Atlantic Press, 1987.

Robbins, John. *Diet for a New America: How Your Food Choices Affect Your Health, Happiness, and the Future of Life on Earth.* Walpole, NH: Stillpoint Publishing,1987.

Roth, Gabrielle. *Maps to Ecstasy.* Mill Valley, CA: Nataraj, 1989.

Seamon, David, editor. *Dwelling, Seeing, and Designing: Toward A Phenomenological Ecology.* Albany, NY: State University of New York Press, 1993.

Snyder, Gary. *Good, Wild, Sacred.* Madley, Hereford, England: Five Seasons Press, 1984.

———. *No Nature.* New York: Pantheon, 1992.

———. *A Place in Space: Ethics, Aesthetics, and Watersheds.* Washington, DC: Counterpoint Press, 1995.

———. *The Practice of the Wild.* San Francisco: North Point Press, 1990.

Stine, Annie, editor. *The Earth at Our Doorstep: Contemporary Writers Celebrate the Landscapes of Home.* San Francisco: Sierra Club Books, 1996.

Todd, Nancy Jack and John Todd. *Bioshelters, Ocean Arks, City Farming: Ecology as the Basis of Design.* San Francisco: Sierra Club Books, 1984.

Troy-Smith, Jean. *Called to Healing: Reflections on the Power of Earth's Stories in Women's Lives.* Albany, NY: State University of New York Press, 1996.

Van der Ryn, Sim and Stuart Cowan. *Ecological Design.* Washington, DC: Island Press, 1996.

Williams, Terry Tempest. *Refuge: An Unnatural History of Family and Place.* New York: Pantheon, 1991.

———. *An Unspoken Hunger: Stories from the Field.* New York: Pantheon, 1994.

———. *Desert Quartet.* New York: Pantheon, 1995.

Willis, Delta. *The Sand Dollar and the Slide Rule: Drawing Blueprints from Nature.* Reading, MA: Addison-Wesley, 1995.

ACKNOWLEDGMENTS

~

FOREMOST, BOUNTEOUS GRATITUDE once again to my husband, Daniel Moses, a witty prince of the Bronx who keeps me laughing and loving through too much research and too many deadlines.

The Portrack Conferences on reconstructive (or "restructive") postmodernism, convened by Charles Jencks and the late Maggie Keswick Jencks in London, Santa Monica, and Dumfries, Scotland, were enormously helpful in the creation of this book. They provided me an opportunity to present and discuss my ideas in both the formal presentations and informal conversations. For instance, I devised the table on ecological postmodernism, in Chapter 2, for one of my Portrack presentations. When it caused three rather deconstructionist participants to become apoplectic, I concluded that it was indeed effective and have used it ever since in my teaching. As eight of these small conferences were held, between July 1992 and May 1996—usually composed of about six invited participants in addition to the ongoing, five-person planning group—the list of names is too long to include here, but their pioneering work in various fields is cited throughout this book and has enriched my own understanding of numerous subjects.

I am particularly appreciative of the collegial engagement, friendship, and support within the Portrack planning group, composed of Charles Jencks, Richard Falk, David Ray Griffin, myself, and, until her vibrant life was cut short by breast cancer in 1995, Maggie Keswick Jencks. Our differing emphases within the reconstructive orientation are argued with good-natured verve. In that light, let me take this opportunity to document for the record a declaration made by Professor Jencks, albeit jokingly, following the conference in May 1996: *"Je suis plus Spretnakian que Spretnak!"*

Another group of colleagues I wish to thank are the faculty of the Philosophy, Cosmology, and Consciousness program at the California Institute for Integral Studies in San Francisco, to whom I presented some of the material in this book: Mara Keller, Robert McDermott, Larry Spiro, Brian Swimme, Richard Tarnas, David Ulansey, and, for a time, William

Irwin Thompson. I was also able to develop three courses from the research I conducted in recent years to write this book, thanks to the flexibility of the director of this graduate program, Richard Tarnas.

I wish to thank the following people for reading and commenting on the manuscript: Tyrone Cashman, Richard Falk, David Ray Griffin, Linda Holler, Charles Jencks, Mara Keller, Andrew Kimbrell, Daniel Moses, Brian Swimme, and Richard Tarnas.

I thank the following people for research or other assistance: James Adams, Peter Allen, Yu M. Chen, Pamela Crawford, Christian de Quincey, Pamela Eakins, William Grassie, Sue Grim, Inge Hildebrand, Ann Jacqua, Judith Kenney, Michael Koetting, Lubica Lacinová, Fiona MacCarthy, Ellen McDermott, Chris Ann Moore, Nicholas Ottavio, David Shiang, Mario and Blaženeka Škugor, Kris and Doug Tomkins, Lori Wallach, Pamela Westfall-Bohte, and Iain Boyd Whyte.

My passion for the Arts and Crafts movement was kindly indulged by Charles and Maggie Jencks, who took me around to the Charles Rennie Macintosh sites in Glasgow and to several of the William Morris sites in or near London. Their secretary, Val Zakian, also was most helpful on many occasions. Donah Zohar drove me from her home in Oxford to Morris's Kelmscott Manor for a memorable afternoon. Concerning the dialogue for the Morris character in "News Clips from Sciotopia" in Chapter 5, much of it is taken from his speeches or letters, but a few spots in the parts I invented were fine-tuned during a trip I made to Britain in September 1996, by Seonaid Robertson and by the participants at a conference convened by Peter Reason and Judi Marshall of the University of Bath. Of that group, I especially thank David Hicks.

I am grateful to Terry Tempest Williams for bringing to my attention Edith Cobb's book, *The Ecology of Imagination in Childhood*, which is mentioned in Chapter 3.

I thank my daughter, Lissa Merkel, for her support and wonderful sense of humor, as well as my mother, Donna Spretnak, and sister, Nikki Spretnak.

For their support and enthusiasm for this book, I thank my editor at Addison-Wesley, Henning Gutmann, and his assistant, Albert DePetrillo; my literary agent, Frances Goldin, and her associate, Sydelle Kramer; and my British literary agent, David Grossman. Thanks also to the copyeditor, Kathy O'Brien, and the project manager, Julie Stillman.

INDEX

~

ABOUT THE AUTHOR

CHARLENE SPRETNAK was born in Pittsburgh and raised in Columbus, Ohio. She holds degrees from St. Louis University and the University of California at Berkeley. She has written several books on social issues, ecology, and spiritual concerns, including *Green Politics* and *States of Grace: The Recovery of Meaning in the Postmodern Age.*